am.BITCH.ous

(def.) a woman who: 1. makes more money 2. has more power 3. gets the recognition she deserves 4. has the determination to go after her dreams and can do it with integrity

Let's reclaim ambition as a virtue.

am·BITCH·ous

Learn to Be Her Now

Debra Condren, Ph.D.

MORGAN ROAD BOOKS
New York

MORGAN ROAD BOOKS

Published in the United States by Morgan Road Books,
an imprint of The Doubleday Broadway Publishing Group,
a division of Random House, Inc., New York.
www.morganroadbooks.com

MORGAN ROAD BOOKS and the M colophon are trademarks of
Random House, Inc.

Grateful acknowledgment is made to the following:

Lilith Fair: A Celebration of Women in Music DVD copyright © 2000,
used with the permission of Mr. Terry McBride, a principle and director
in Lilith Fair and owner of the copyright.

Searching for Debra Winger DVD copyright © 2001, used with the
permission of Ms. Rosanna Arquette, Mr. Happy Walters, Mr. Mark
Cuban, and Mr. Todd Wagner, owners of the copyright, film's content.

Book design by Nicola Ferguson

LIBRARY OF CONGRESS CATALOGING-IN-PUBLICATION DATA

Condren, Debra, 1961–
AmBITCHous : (def.) a woman who: 1. makes more money
2. has more power 3. gets the recognition she deserves
4. has the determination to go after her dreams and can do it with
integrity / Debra Condren.
    p. cm.
Includes bibliographical references.
  1. Women executives—Handbooks, manuals, etc.   I. Title.
HD6054.3.C682 2006
658.4'09082—dc22   2006048229

ISBN: 978-0-7679-2313-2

PRINTED IN THE UNITED STATES OF AMERICA

10 9 8 7 6 5 4 3 2 1

FIRST EDITION

For Devin, Stephen, and Jake,
my parents, Marjorie and Tommy Condren,
Ella Martin Boyes Daily
and The Girlfriends

Let's reclaim ambition as a virtue:

am•BITCH•ous: (def.) a woman who:

1. makes more money

2. has more power

3. gets the recognition she deserves

4. has the determination to go after her dreams and can do it with integrity

Contents

Author's Note

A number of women shared with me their personal stories and thoughts about ambition, which are incorporated in this book. Some stories represent composites of many women. In order to disguise the individuals involved, certain names and some of the identifying characteristics of women depicted have been significantly changed to such an extensive degree that any resemblance to any person, living or dead, is purely coincidental. For those who are not composites, the woman is identified by first and last name. The ideas, techniques, and advice in this book are not intended as a substitute for consultation with a qualified professional.

Part I

Ambition
Is a Virtue

one

Wouldn't It Be Great?

She's a staple of movies, novels, and TV: the hard-charging female executive in her Armani power suit and Manolo heels. She's smart, aggressive, successful—and most people can't wait to see her get her well-deserved comeuppance. When her fall from grace over her latest business failure or scandal lands her above the fold in the newspaper, it seems only right that she gets knocked to her knees.

Let's face it, there's just one word that our culture bestows on that supremely ambitious woman who unrepentantly values a career: *bitch*. It's our prevailing cultural paradigm: ambitious men are go-getters, but ambitious women are bitches.

It's been open season on ambitious women for a long time. It's been almost twenty years since Madonna made her then-outrageous claim that she wanted to rule the world. Despite her largely making good on her promise with an astonishingly successful multimedia empire, the media stories trumpeting her alleged foibles (trendily embracing Kabbalah, creating new personas, kissing women to grab headlines, being the unconventional mom) outnumber tenfold the stories broadcasting her entrepreneurial triumphs. Jennifer Lopez, her contemporary doppelgänger, gets the same treatment, with far more ink spilled on her marital merry-go-round than on her business savvy with a successful line of clothes and perfume on top of her acting and recording successes.

When Carly Fiorina was ousted as chairman and CEO of Hewlett-Packard, how many people, women and men alike, felt that she got what she deserved, either because she'd lost sight of the fact that she was a woman and had overshot her ambitious mark, or because she was being punished for forgetting her female roots and sisterly loyalties in her climb to the top? Oh—and Carly's crowning deficiency? She chose not to be a mother.

On the other hand, each time the media reports an interview with yet another professional woman who has seen the light and taken time out for motherhood, everyone breathes a collective sigh of relief—finally, this woman has figured out what's *really* important.

No wonder so many women simultaneously crave and fear their ambitious goals.

Wouldn't it be great if women could ignore what our culture thinks about high-achieving women and eliminate the fear part of our ambition equation? Just imagine how that would change our perspective.

Can You Imagine?

Wouldn't it be great if you could reclaim and redefine ambition in its most gloriously positive sense? Wouldn't it be great if you could look yourself in the eye in the mirror and, with pride and without ambivalence, say, "I am ambitious." Wouldn't it be great if you could say that—and feel it—without cringing ever so slightly? Wouldn't it be inspiring if you could acknowledge straight up, to yourself and to others, that you have big, wild, and precious professional goals? That you crave excellence? Wouldn't it feel great to challenge yourself fiercely? To unapologetically derive a big part of your self-worth from your professional identity? And wouldn't it be great if you could experience all that as a virtue, not a vice?

Wouldn't it be great if you believed that you could be audaciously ambitious and happy at the same time? Wouldn't it feel great to trust that you could be determined to achieve your career goals without compromising your personal life, but rather enhancing it? Wouldn't it be so freeing to acknowledge, in your core, that your ambitious goals were sacrosanct, just as inviolable as other nonnegotiable priorities in your life?

Wouldn't it be such a relief to know deep down that you are *great* at what you do? Wouldn't you love to learn to shut up—and shut out—that nagging inner critic that sometimes warns, "Watch out . . . who do you think you are? Aren't you getting too big for your breeches? You're just an impostor heading for a searing humiliation!" Wouldn't you feel fabulous if you could bitch-slap that doubting voice in your head that accuses you of not having earned your spot at the grown-ups' table, of not deserving your share of the power, the recognition, the credit—and the money? And wouldn't it be thrilling if you could then pull up to that power table with a relaxed sense of professional entitlement and an inner voice that says, "I've worked hard for this place. I'm worthy. This is my time to shine"?

Wouldn't it be great if you felt comfortable making sure that you get recognition for your contributions without apology and without fear? Wouldn't it feel great if you could walk into a meeting and know how to take credit for your work without feeling guilty about it, and also how to reclaim stolen credit that is rightfully yours? What if you had the know-how, confidence, and guts to confront someone who was shamelessly trying to steal your thunder? What if you could do that with grace and aplomb that earned you self-respect *and* the admiration of your coworkers? Wouldn't it feel great to walk into your boss's or client's office and demand in a disarming but utterly firm way to be paid what you're worth? Without worrying that you might not be giving them their money's worth? Without being afraid that you'll be fired or lose an offer, a promotion, or some other opportunity? And without always feeling that one way or the other you will ultimately have to back down, oh so submissively?

Wouldn't it be great to set free your aspiring, bold voice? To say, "I'm ambitious," with pride, not reticence? Without worrying about what others will think of you because *you* know that you're a decent, ethical woman who acts with integrity? Without believing that you're a self-absorbed, aggressive, flat-out bitch who blows through the workplace leaving countless enemies in her wake? Wouldn't it feel fabulous if you could finally reach for the moon, shouting your deepest-held ambitions from the rooftops without feeling guilty or believing that you're neglecting a husband, a child, family, or friends? Wouldn't it feel amazing to regard your determination to go after your career dreams as an attribute—as a tribute, really—to the *greatest* part of who you are as a woman?

Wouldn't it be great to be amBITCHous?

Well, you can, and you should be. If you don't, you're letting the best part of you, the part that the world deserves to have you contribute, rot in a basement. Let's get her out. This book will show you why you ought to be an ambitchous woman—and how to be her now.

Be More, Not Less, Ambitchous. Go for Harmony, Not Balance

This is most emphatically not a book about how to be unapologetically bitchy to get what you want. This is a book about redefining your ambition in the face of social sanctions and unapologetically going after your dreams. I wrote it to encourage you to be more, not less, ambitchous. I'm here to tell you that you don't have to sacrifice—or "balance"—your ambition to have a great life; in fact, just the opposite is true. This book will reveal to you that the real way to have a great life is to see your ambition as a virtue—as a part of your value system that you must give equal attention to, along with other priorities you hold dear, including your spouse, children, and friends. Our culture encourages women to derive our sense of self from being selfless, by giving to everyone else first and foremost. Could there be a more confusing, contradictory recipe for self-satisfaction? No wonder we drop-kick our dreams! This book will show you how being the best woman you can possibly be comes from always staying true to your most ambitious self rather than feeling pressured, under social duress, to put your ambition last, after every other priority in your life.

I know you may not believe me that working harder to fulfill your ambitions will make your very busy and complicated life of juggling family, career, and social life easier, but it will. There's another way of seeing things that will make you happier, more fulfilled at work, and more content in the rest of your life. There's another way to think about achieving your big, inspiring career dreams and whatever else you cherish in your personal life. There's another, more rewarding, and less stressful way of framing the big picture.

I'm here to tell you that all of your priorities—personal and ambitious career goals alike—can fit together harmoniously. I'll show you how, like thousands of women I've worked with over the years, you can make more money, earn the credit and recognition you deserve, have more power, and be as ambitious as you want to be. I'll show you how you can be ambitious without compromising your ethics and integrity. I'll show you that you can feel worthy and entitled to all of this without fear that you risk sacrificing your desire to have a full, happy personal life and without being afraid that you'll be less of a woman. It's worked for me. It's worked for countless ambitious women I've advised. It will work for you.

Why Should You Trust Me?

"Who is this ambitchous woman?" you may be asking. "Why should I trust her?"

I'm a business psychologist, executive coach, and career adviser who has spent more than fifteen years helping women embrace their ambition and achieve their career goals. As the founder and president of Manhattan Business Coaching, a professional development firm based in New York City and San Francisco, I've worked with thousands of clients throughout the United States and the world. I served as an advisory member to an American Psychological Association Presidential Task Force for empowering adolescent girls. I lead dozens of workshops every year and lecture frequently on women's need to embrace their ambition.

In 1995, I founded—and currently am the executive director of—the Women's Business Alliance, an organization that has served as a motivational think tank for more than twenty-five hundred women over twelve years. I founded the WBA specifically to help women overcome the barriers that keep them from reaching the top in their chosen fields. The U.S. Small Business Administration recognized my work with a "Women in Business Advocate of the Year 2000" award.

I've worked with women of every stripe, from students and recent graduates embarking on their brand-new career paths, to successful women in the corporate, nonprofit, and government sectors. I've met with small business owners, heads of fast-growing start-ups, consultants, physicians, attorneys, investment bankers, architects, and executives and professionals in a wide array of fields. I've advised women as young as sixteen and women in their early sixties. Wherever they've been on their professional paths, my mission has been to increase women's business acumen by teaching them strategies for identifying meaningful, challenging work; increasing profitability; building and keeping wealth; competing with power and confidence in traditional and male-dominated corporate sectors; establishing themselves as experts; and tapping their competitive advantage.

As I spoke to and coached thousands of women, however, I began to detect a striking pattern: even self-professed successful women were hitting walls, unable to achieve the next level in their professional lives—and they didn't know why. Certainly they were well aware of the external barriers to their success—the famed glass ceiling, lack of support for those who choose to juggle work and family. However, they had no idea that the greatest factor holding them back was a barrier they themselves had created and internalized.

Based on my conversations with so many women, I suspected I knew exactly what mistaken belief was holding them back. Seven years ago, I began a systematic investigation of professional women's attitudes toward ambition. I interviewed more than five hundred women from every corner of the country and between the ages of nineteen and sixty-five.

These were all women who regarded themselves as high-achieving. Many were rookies with brand-new, promising careers in front of them. Many were already quite successful. Many had established impressive track records of in-the-trenches professional experience, had broken through at least some gender barriers to become established in their fields, made comfortable to sizable incomes, and either had the title and position they wanted or were drawing a bead on the prize. I asked these women their definitions of success and ambition, how they saw themselves, how they visualized an ambitious woman, and what held them back from achieving even greater success and fulfillment.

I made a fascinating discovery. High-achieving women all harbor the same dirty little secret, no matter what our backgrounds: we all struggle with socially sanctioned failure to embrace our ambition. We all have the same pernicious audio loop playing between our ears:

> Will being as ambitchous as I dream of being make me less of a woman? Can I? Should I? Dare I? Have I gone too far? Will it cost me my personal life? Will I make enemies? Will it make those I care about suffer? Is it impossible to be ambitchous and happy? Am I charging too much? Am I giving my employer or my clients their money's worth? Will I lose an opportunity if I ask for more money? Who do I think I am, calling myself an expert? Do I really know what I'm doing, or am I in over my head? Does sticking up for myself and taking credit mean I'm greedy, arrogant, and being unfair to people I work with? Am I deserving of recognition and power? Am I worthy of going after my biggest, most precious career dreams?

Ambition isn't a dirty word, but as far as many women are concerned, it might as well be. It doesn't matter where we grew up, went to school, or go to work. It's the same whether we're in our twenties and new to our careers, or in our fifties and sixties and among the most highly regarded professionals in our industries. Today, the greatest barrier to earning more money, getting the power and recognition we deserve, and feeling entitled to stay the course comes from inside of ourselves. We agonize over whether or not we deserve to be ambitious—and about what it will cost us.

I looked for books to recommend to supplement my own findings and recommendations. I found that most proposed to teach women how to succeed on their own terms, with a huge emphasis on mastering the life-in-balance issue. None of them challenged the notion that the accepted definition of success might actually be holding women back because it is couched in such a positive way: "You don't have to be unabashedly ambitious. You're above all that. You are sophisticated enough to realize that ambition isn't as important as getting the life-balance equation right." Or: "You don't have to be ambitious the way a man is. You've come around to realize that success is a different—and better—goal than ambition. You can win with empathy, cooperation, and being generous. You don't have to give up being a woman to get ahead."

I count it as a Pyrrhic victory that our modern, progressive culture is no longer pushing the idea that women cannot have it all. The message these books and popular media are transmitting is: We *can* have it all—so long as we're willing to redefine what "it" is. Now it's not the killer job and the great home life; it's balancing the two, which, practically speaking, means less of each: women should be just thrilled to have a not-ideal job and a not-ideal life as long as they feel the two are balanced.

How can we take seriously the necessary soul-searching required to discover what we were meant to do professionally when our pure, unadulterated ambition is never discussed explicitly—only game plays and hardball techniques, softened for the female player?

I decided to write this book to address the great hunger on the part of high-aiming women for advice that speaks to our discontent—and to our ambition to be purely and freely ambitious.

It Takes an Ambitchous Woman to Know and Encourage One

People always ask me why I founded the Women's Business Alliance. Like you, I have had to struggle to stay true to my ambitchous dreams. I got to where I am today because a group of ambitchous women supported and taught me early in my career. I was raised in Arkansas, where, in the seventies, the pinnacle of success for a teen girl was to be a cheerleader (in the days before it was a varsity sport). The public high school I attended held an annual Southern Belle Beauty Pageant. Even in grade school, I was never inspired by those socially sanctioned goals for females. It just wasn't in my DNA. My best friend, Tam, and I survived adolescence by keeping an optimistic eye on our futures as smart young women who had more important contributions to make than shaking a pom-pom or kicking up our tanned legs in formation. We made up a mantra: "We will escape the South." Surely moving to a different part of the country was the answer.

When I attended college in the Midwest, I realized that geography wasn't the obstacle. Discouraged by a lack of mentoring that left me drawing a blank about inspiring real-world career options, I dropped out after my freshman year. Without an ambition target, I worked various odd jobs, from selling used cars to eventually becoming a residential real estate property manager. Three years later, I returned to college and was lucky enough to find a professor who encouraged me to get my ambitchous self back on track. I earned my bachelor of science degree with a double major in sociology and psychology and a minor in computer science.

I married at twenty-three. A few years later, my husband and I packed up our house to move cross-country so that I could begin a Ph.D. program in clinical psychology and the psychological study of social issues and he could pursue his own professional goals. We were just about to hit the road when I found out that birth control didn't always work; I was pregnant. In shock, I called my mom, who was elated and asked, "Are you still going to California?" I snapped, "Of course!"

My beloved mother's traditional upbringing unquestioningly put motherhood before work, but I wasn't prepared to sacrifice my career ambitions on the altar of parenthood. I figured that Berkeley had to be a far more supportive environment for an ambitchous woman than where I'd come from. Nevertheless, I followed my instincts and didn't reveal to professors or peers that I was going to have a baby. Even in that progressive setting, there were red flags that I wouldn't be taken seriously as a doctoral candidate if people knew I was pregnant. I wore loose clothing and divided my time between classes and studying, waiting until the moment seemed right to make my announcement.

As it turned out, I didn't have the luxury of breaking the news on my own terms. Pre-term labor complications forced me into bed rest for the last three months of my pregnancy, and I had to take a leave of absence after only a single semester of graduate school. I gave birth to my son, Devin (now eighteen years old), and immediately went back to graduate school and training as an intern, plus working as a bookkeeper to pay the bills.

My marriage faltered, then failed. Suddenly I found myself in the inauspicious position of being a divorced single mother struggling to raise a small child, complete a graduate degree, and pay the rent and tuition. I had very little support and no road map. My life was a patchwork quilt of working whatever job I could grab, self-employment, scrambling for child care, and cramming in coursework and research for my doctoral dissertation whenever I had a spare moment.

I finished my thesis and Ph.D. in record time; I was both inspired to move forward with my career goals and scared about survival issues. I had a fire lit inside as well as under my butt; my progress in those early career years was often slowed because of the compromises I had to make for the practical concerns of supporting myself and my son. I plugged away, with my ambition target always on the horizon.

When I was thirty-two years old, my professional life finally took on some semblance of stability. I had a coveted academic-track research position in San Francisco. Devin was about to enter grade school, which meant fewer child care woes. I'd finally gotten my license and was a bona fide psychologist. Even though I was struggling financially, there was light at the end of the tunnel.

Except that I found myself yearning to sunbathe in a different kind of light. Inspired by a business article profiling what struck me as an intriguing up-and-coming field, I decided I wanted to start my own career-advising firm. On the face of it, this made no sense. I was trained as a licensed clinical psychologist with a background in neuropsychological testing and forensic evaluations. I hadn't gone to business school and I had no real training in launching this kind of venture. And unlike today, at that time career and executive coaching were barely on the radar; this was a brand-new, emerging specialty. My psychologist colleagues said, "You're crazy to do this. It's career suicide."

But this was an ambition I yearned to fulfill. I knew that I loved researching and thinking about what was going on in the business world. I knew that I was smart, creative, and tenacious. I craved the independence, opportunity, and challenge of running my own professional organization. Pursuing my career destiny felt as vital and organic as mothering Devin, maintaining my friendships, and other equally precious pursuits. I knew that I had something meaningful to contribute.

And so I jumped right in.

I'd been in business for a little over a year when I discovered a mentoring program for women in San Francisco. Once a month for a year, I would travel into the city with my business plan, strategies, and a raftload of problems in hand, and be mentored by a board of advisers on everything from setting up my accounting and books, sales, marketing, and public relations to the emotional highs and lows of being self-employed. In these two-hour meetings I, along with three other protégées, discussed our business goals and all the related obstacles and challenges with a group of fifteen to twenty seasoned, powerful professional women. We received frank, direct, nuts-and-bolts business tactics and real-time feedback and advice from CEOs, attorneys, CPAs, marketing gurus, bankers, and senior executives in sales, public relations, and finance. Having my career aspirations ratified in the face of so much personal upheaval was profoundly transformative. Listening to the experiences and varied perspectives of so many successful businesswomen left me feeling confident and unabashed about pursuing my own big ambitions. It also taught me how to avoid naive mistakes, how to recognize talent, how to work collaboratively, and how to ask for and make great use of expert advice.

Yet it also made me begin to recognize common ways ambitious women hold themselves back. For example, one of the protégées in my group routinely closed her mind to advice given to her by our advisory team. At every meeting, she would get extraordinary advice and feedback on her business plan. Without fail, she would counter with what I named the "Yeah, But Rebuttal." As in: "Yeah, but here's why that won't work in my case . . ." Finally a mentor came down hard on her in one of the meetings: "Why are you here if you want to dismiss every piece of great advice we give you?" I saw this "yeah, but" theme repeat itself with countless other women over the years, along with other common self-sabotaging behaviors I identified. It became apparent to me that all of us—even women who are manifestly talented and experienced—struggle with confidence, don't feel entitled to get paid what we're worth, feel reluctant to go after the power and recognition we've earned, and don't pursue careers with wholehearted passion. I began spotting and thinking about these common socially sanctioned self-sabotage traps into which ambitchous women fall.

I completed the mentoring program and continued running my business just north of San Francisco. I helped scores of motivated, interesting women (and men) discover or refine what they were meant to do and find their professional calling. But for all the success stories I midwifed, I also continued to see women who were consistently struggling with going after their ambitchous goals. I knew we needed a sophisticated support organization for women in business to help us identify and navigate these issues. When I looked around Marin County, where I lived and worked, for organizations that provided ongoing, hard-hitting business information and support for ambitchous women, there were none.

That was the genesis of the Women's Business Alliance. We needed something besides those dreary networking groups where men and women fall over one another passing out business cards and trying to generate leads. I wanted to offer cutting-edge professional guidance for ambitchous women like myself, and I wanted to surround women with role models to help them envision achieving their career dreams.

I cold-called and lined up six months' worth of top-notch guest speakers and laid out a meeting schedule. Then I phoned women I'd read about in the local newspapers and invited them to participate. By the end of the first week, I had fifty women on board, and the Women's Business Alliance was launched.

For the next six years, the Women's Business Alliance hosted one-and-a-half-hour working lunch meetings that were attended by between thirty and one hundred fifty women. Once a month I brought in heavy-hitting experts to talk and answer questions about a diverse array of business and professional topics. I held a second monthly meeting called Open Forum Roundtable to serve as a think tank for women to throw business dilemmas, questions, and professional plans on the table and get a wealth of feedback, advice, and support from other successful, ambitchous women.

After analyzing the results of my research into women's views of ambition, I began making the subject a centerpiece topic in my biweekly Women's Business Alliance conferences. In every meeting ideas would fly across the room; women were starving for this type of gold-standard information and peer advice and support. At the same time, each and every one of these women did battle within themselves with the same self-sabotaging traps I'd first spotted years earlier.

In my work in the Women's Business Alliance and in my career- and executive-advising practice, I challenged my clients to confront their fear of embracing their ambition. I helped thousands of women make dramatic course corrections by showing them how to break through those internal barriers and to wholeheartedly embrace their ambition.

In 2000, I met my husband Stephen. We figured out a bicoastal *Brady Bunch* setup that would work for his son, Jake, and my son, Devin, and that would also allow the two of us to continue focusing on our individual ambition goals. I expanded the Women's Business Alliance and my professional advising firm to New York City. I guessed for sure that the same socially sanctioned self-sabotaging ambition issues I'd helped ambitchous women in the San Francisco Bay Area spot and conquer wouldn't be an issue for professional women in the world's capital. Boy, was I wrong. Same pressures, opposite coast. Each and every ambitchous woman I've worked with and interviewed in New York City— and there have now been hundreds—is just like the rest of us. No matter where we live, no matter if we have an Ivy League pedigree and a professional track record to die for, we all struggle, under social duress, to stay true to our big career dreams without feeling like freaks.

I'm convinced, personally and professionally, that we can and must do better.

Shine the Light on Your Ambition

My guess is that if you're reading this, you too are a woman who struggles with these issues. You too are dying for advice and encouragement on how to stay true to your ambitchous career dreams. Perhaps you're barely twenty and are already feeling stymied from the get-go. Perhaps you're relatively new to the business world but are already experiencing Sisyphean battles in keeping your professional goals at the forefront of your life. Perhaps you've been momentarily derailed—by deciding to relocate with a boyfriend so that he can do his ambition dream first, before it's your turn? or marriage? kids? an ailing loved one? your own illness? burned out and biding your time?—and you're finding that that *moment* is stretching into infinity. You need help getting back on track. Or perhaps you've been in the game for a long time, but you're not advancing the way you'd like to—or feel you deserve.

No matter where you are in your career, to say that you've worked hard is a major understatement. This is undoubtedly true whether you're a student or recent graduate, or a professional who has established a solid professional track record, or a professional who is well on the way to doing so. You've paid your dues. You're willing to pay plenty more. You've had some serious chunks taken from your hide. You've had the s____t kicked out of you. You've hung in there and pored over your mistakes to figure out how to do it better next time. You've built up substantive knowledge and business acumen. You've gotten tougher when it comes to taking and learning from criticism. You've become more skilled at using your instincts in the marketplace. You've gotten into the tough game of business, and you fight every day to keep yourself in.

Yet somehow, for some reason, something's not quite right. You're not satisfied. Sometimes you feel that you're settling for less in your career when what you really want is more. Sometimes your gut tells you that you're holding yourself back, if ever so slightly, from wholeheartedly going for it where your *most* ambitious career goals are concerned. Something inside of you wants to be less tame. Something inside of you wants to be free to be as bold as you want to be. Yet it's as if you're pulling back on your own reins.

Here's what I know to be true.

First, you give a woman support for being ambitchous. You encourage her to see that she can have a great, happy life—at home and at work. And you show her that, counterintuitive though our culture makes it seem, the *real* life course for becoming the happiest woman, the best friend, lover, spouse, mother, and community member she can possibly be is *always* to honor her ambition as a virtue. You support her to see that the *real* way to make the contribution she was born to make is to place her inspiring career dreams at the top of her priorities list, not at the bottom of the pile. Next you give her gold-standard business information and strategies that are easy to use in her day-to-day work and personal life. You show her simple, effective, potent tactics that build on one another and that empower her to hit her career targets.

Then a lightbulb goes on in her consciousness. And she never looks back.

She takes charge of her career destiny. She learns to insist firmly on getting paid what she's worth. She feels powerful in a new way—and owning it feels comfortable to her. She learns to feel great about being recognized for her professional accomplishments. She learns to set boundaries with colleagues and people in her personal life so that her needs get met, not trampled on. She learns that she can act with integrity and treat others like human beings, but that she feels just fine about the fact that not everyone is going to like her when she stands up to those who would steal her thunder.

She becomes ambitchous.

I've seen this transformation occur with thousands of women I've worked with. I'm here to support that same shift in you. I'm going to show you how to be your most ambitchous self—and how to be her right now.

In this book, I'll work with you to help you get a handle on the overt messages we have been taught about being ambitious women, the covert messages that have filtered in unconsciously, and the self-sabotaging behaviors they cause. I'll provide self-assessment quizzes, checklists, and exercises so you can quickly and easily figure out whether you're prone to selling yourself short where your ambitchous goals are concerned. Then I'll offer proven, fresh solutions—the same ones I use with my career-advising and executive-coaching clients—to help you overcome these internalized barriers. By the way, none of these strategies will ask you simply to think more like a man. My solutions will help you draw effective boundaries around your positive qualities so they won't work against you. Once you learn to do this, you'll be free. You can dare to be truly great on your own terms. You'll be able to redefine the meaning of ambition and embrace the value of unleashing your sacrosanct career dreams.

Your Ambition Journal

As you begin reading and working through this book, you are going to have your brain cells firing with career insights and questions. I want you to start an Ambition Journal to record what you discover during this process. Date each entry so that you can track your progress. Words are powerful, and writing down your ideas is a great way to power up your most ambitchous self.

An Ambition Journal is a must. It will keep you from losing all the little bits of career information you pick up along the way. You know what I mean: you jot down a note or name or idea—but the one day you need it, and fast, it's nowhere to be found. Your Ambition Journal will be a place to compile all of your notes, contacts, articles, and resources. This isn't a diary for your personal life; it is strictly a career tool.

Also use your Ambition Journal to record your responses to the exercises, quizzes, and questionnaires that appear throughout the book. This will provide you with a confidential record of what you discover as you dig out your most ambitchous self. If you prefer, you can also print out the quizzes and questionnaires from my Web site, www.amBITCHous.com, and then fill them out and put them into your Ambition Journal. You can also order an amBITCHous Ambition Journal from the amBITCHous.com Web site.

Your Ambition Journal will serve you throughout your entire career. It will be a fresh, solid professional foundation you have built and a template you can refer back to and use as a lifelong guide.

Now get ready to unleash your most ambitchous self.

■ ■ ■ ■ ■ ■ ■ ■ ■ ■ ■ ■ ■ ■ ■ ■ ■ ■ ■ ■

two

What a Difference a Word Makes

■ ■ ■ ■ ■ ■ ■ ■ ■ ■ ■ ■ ■ ■ ■ ■ ■ ■ ■

Why do women have such a hard time acknowledging the importance of loving our work?

—Gail Evans

Today, in the year 2007, what's our cause? That's what the women I know are asking. The answer is—it's almost like making it your right to have passion for your work.

—Lindsay Edgecombe, twenty-three, Barnard College graduate, former editor of the *Columbia Review*, poet, editorial assistant, New York City literary agency

IF YOU are a woman for whom career greatness and passion for your work matter, then your professional goals ought to be sacrosanct. Actualizing the talents you were born with must always hold equal importance with any other nonnegotiable priority in your life, including family, romantic relationships, children, and community. The world deserves to hear from you.

Does this sound odd to you? Is it the first time anyone has said this to you? Take a minute and count how many times in your adult life you have been counseled to be more ambitious. Now count how many times you have been advised to value and protect your ambition as you would any other virtue. You can probably count all of this on one hand.

And yet if you were to put your ambition first, it would make you a better person in every other aspect of your life. You would be not only more fulfilled and productive in your work, but also a happier individual, a better partner, a more present parent, a more compassionate friend, and and a more engaged community member. You would, in fact, be more alive and grounded in every realm of your life.

The cornerstone of your capacity to live a life with few regrets is laid when you truly understand, on a visceral level, the importance of loving your work, no matter where you are in your life and career, and no matter what competing obligations and pressures challenge your resolve to be true to your ambition. Living fully and authentically hinges on your ability to stay connected to the experience of lifelong passion for your work, to remain continually inspired, to stretch, to be open to fresh opportunities, and ultimately to be the best you can be at what you do. Simply put, your ambition should be nonnegotiable. It fuels the core of your being.

Yet all too often, for women of all ages, ambition is negotiable.

Ambition Is Not a Dirty Word—Is It?

I want to change the world. True, I couldn't live without my work, without being inspired every day. I'm successful—things have just sort of fallen into place in my career. But no, I'm not ambitious—I want to effect positive change in the world, yet my family is very important to me.

—Vera, fifty-seven. Longtime high-seven-figure earner, famously referred to as a rock star and legend in her corporate industry

Why do women have so much trouble acknowledging the importance of loving their work with a grand passion? They can admit to liking their work. But what if they say that they love their work? What if they say they're ambitious?

Read the following two stories carefully and see if you notice any thoughts and feelings coming up about these two women. First, meet Meredith:

> I value success. I am a thirty-four-year-old senior creative director with a large, award-winning advertising firm in San Francisco, earning in the upper seventy-fifth percentile of comparable salaries in my industry. I have an M.B.A. To me, being successful means loving my work, having challenging opportunities in my job, with ample downtime to have dinner with friends once or twice a month, go sailing on Saturdays, and spend quality time with my fiancé.

Now, meet Jane:

> I am ambitious. I'm a thirty-four-year-old woman with an M.B.A. To me, being ambitious means loving my work as a senior managing director with a large, award-winning public relations firm in New York City, earning in the upper seventy-fifth percentile of comparable salaries in my industry. It also means having challenging opportunities in my job, with ample downtime to have dinner with friends once or twice a month, play racquetball on Saturdays, and spend quality time with my fiancé.

How did your attitude change reading about Jane as compared with how you felt about Meredith?

Did you see Meredith as having admirable goals and as a woman who keeps her priorities straight? Did you get the sense that her life is well-balanced between home and work? As embodying a so-called positive, feminine definition of success that allows for other personal priorities?

When you read Jane's profile, and the fact that she values ambition, did you get the sense that she might just be a little bit of a bitch (is there any other word?) whose priorities are out of whack? Were you quite sure she is heading for a fall somewhere down the line? Did the fact that she sees her friends only once, maybe twice a month, and that she gets to the gym only once a week (so she's probably out of shape to boot!), indicate to you that she places too much emphasis on work? Did it seem obvious to you that her characterization of spending quality time with her fiancé is actually an indictment that she isn't spending *enough* time with him?

Now go back and reread the two profiles. Notice that other than different geographical locations, job descriptions, and hobbies, the two were identical, with the exception that only one word changed: Meredith values *success*; Jane values *ambition*.

If you had these reactions to these two women, you're not alone. In business workshops and conferences where I present this exercise, the majority of women respond positively to the woman who values success. But something just doesn't sit right with them when they read the description of the woman who values ambition. What a difference a word makes.

Why does that word drive women so crazy? You'd think it means admitting we've got genital warts.

This is emphatically not a game of semantics. The women I've surveyed don't simply prefer the word *successful* to *ambitious*. They don't mind being regarded as successful, but they're afraid of being called ambitious. If they do get as far as attempting to say, "I am ambitious," it makes them cringe, even if they can't quite put their finger on why that is.

It's no accident that we are allergic to this word. There is, in fact, a primary driving force behind women's reluctance to see their ambition as a virtue.

I still think that girls are encouraged to be nice and to be liked, and to be about the team and everybody else. To say you're ambitious means you want to rise above everybody else or be different. I don't think that we cheer on ambition enough among women, and certainly not among young women. . . . I don't know how many people cheered Carly Fiorina's ambition. Or Andrea Jung's . . . It's almost like the word is "am-bitchin'."

—*Mary Lou Quinlan, founder and CEO of*
Just Ask a Woman, author of Just Ask a Woman
and Time Off for Good Behavior

I think we should throw out the word *ambition,* because I don't like that word. I like the word *aspiration,* which means "a desire with focus." I like that. Desire with focus equals happiness. Or the word *passion.* I prefer synonyms rather than the word *ambition.* For me, *ambition* is not a dirty word. But it could be that for many women the word has subliminal, negative connotations.

—*Catherine, forty-one, M.D., researcher,*
and associate clinical professor,
major New York City university teaching hospital

What makes us feel we have to deny that part of who we are, that part of ourselves that is aching, on some level, to recognize our ambition as a worthy part of our makeup?

How do you really feel about acknowledging your own ambition? Is it tough for you to freely define yourself as an ambitious woman? If so, what gets in the way? What prevents you from feeling comfortable identifying yourself as a woman who loves her work with a grand passion and who is determined to achieve her loftiest career dreams? If the desire to be successful is easier to acknowledge than being ambitious—if you can look yourself in the eye in your mirror and feel comfortable saying you value success, but not ambition, why is that? What makes the word *success* more palatable than *ambition*? Write the answer in your Ambition Journal.

Consider the following *Webster's* definitions of the word *ambition*:

am•bi•tion } *n.* (def.)

1. an earnest desire for some type of achievement or distinction, as power, honor, fame, or wealth, usually in a chosen field, and the willingness to strive for its attainment
2. the object, state, or result desired or sought after
3. desire for work or activity; energy, interest, passion in professional activity

. . . and now consider these definitions of the word *ambitious*:

am•bi•tious } *adj.* (def.)

1. having ambition; eagerly desirous of achieving or obtaining success, power, wealth, or a specific goal
2. requiring exceptional effort, ability, etc.
3. aspiring, enterprising; wishing to rise (mentally or spiritually) to a higher level or plane, or to attain some end above ordinary expectations
4. aggressive; self-centered

Which of these seven definitions do you suppose the vast majority of women I've interviewed and advised—from age sixteen to sixty-something—zero in on to describe a high-aiming woman who refuses to compromise her career goals? You guessed it:

am•bi•tious } *adj.* (def.)

4. aggressive; self-centered (it's a woman thing)

No big surprise, then, that many a professional woman feels free to say she enjoys work and wants to become a *success,* but she chooses her words carefully, being certain to qualify her meaning—and, of course, not to use that dirty, unspeakable word *ambitious.*

Let's reclaim ambition as a virtue and make it ours:

am•BITCH•ous} *adj.* (def.) a woman who:

1. makes more money
2. has more power
3. gets the recognition she deserves
4. has the determination to go after her dreams and can do it with integrity

Now I'd like you to dig deeper into your thoughts about ambition and do a reality check. Encouraging reality checks is something women are great at—if we're asking a close girlfriend to do it. We do it for other women in our lives all of the time, whether it be about work or relationships or children. Think about it—a woman in your life who trusts you asks, "Am I crazy for wanting to get my M.B.A. before my husband has finished medical school?" "Am I imagining it, or are the nurses less responsive to my orders because I'm the only female surgeon in our department?" "Am I really a bad person because there's only one other mother in my daughter's kindergarten class who works full-time?" "Did I overstep my bounds by asking for a raise, or did I do the right thing?" And I am certain that you are excellent at reassuring her, very effective at debunking her self-punishing ideas, and great at giving her some inspiring words about how to view her situation with fresh eyes.

It's just that we're not so good about doing the same thing for ourselves; we're typically reluctant to support ourselves to do a fair-minded, but gentle, reality check. Of course not! Because no one is harder on a woman than she, herself, is. And I'm betting no one is harder on you than you, yourself, are. That's okay. That's what I'm here for—to support you to be less hard on yourself as you do some serious soul-searching about what it means, to you, to be ambitchous.

REALITY CHECK
Why Can't I See My Ambition as a Virtue?
Ambition Journal Exercise

- Does calling myself ambitious make me feel kind of dirty, selfish, or greedy?
- Do I feel foolish, like an interloper in the business world?
- Does it make me feel just a little bit less feminine?
- Does a twinge of guilt come up?
- Do I feel ashamed?
- Do I feel arrogant, entitled, and conceited? That I might as well be saying I'm better than everyone else?
- Am I afraid people won't like me as much, or won't respect me in the same way?
- Do I fear that I'll repel the kind of mate I want to attract? That I won't be a good enough wife or mom?

If you really think about it, does calling yourself ambitious make you feel pretty much everything a woman is not supposed to feel about herself?

Think about what just came up for you as you worked through the questions above. Now let's go deeper to see if any of this is based in reality. As you ask yourself the following questions, try to be as objective as you would be in a frank, supportive discussion with a close female friend.

- Does being ambitious actually make me a selfish, conceited person?

  Probably not _____ (Why not?)

  Probably _____ (Why do I think so?)

  I'm not sure _____ (What keeps me from answering definitively?)

- If I am ambitious, am I greedy? Dirty? Are my morals and values askew?

  Doubtful _____ (Why not?)

  Probably _____ (How so? What makes me feel that way?)

  I'm not sure _____ (What clouds my thinking on this issue?)

- Does acknowledging and tending to that ambitious fire in the belly really take away from my relationships?

  Unlikely _____ (Because . . . ?)

  Yes, probably _____ (How so? In what specific ways?)

  I'm not sure _____ (Why am I uncertain about answering this?)

- If I admit to being ambitious, do I fear that I am going to be punished?

  No, I don't _____ (Because . . . ?)

  Yes, it's likely to bite me in the butt _____ (What are my worst fears?)

  I'm not sure _____ (What prevents me from saying yes or no?)

Success versus ambition: one word makes all the difference in our comfort level.

But what about different types of ambition? There is a certain category of ambition that is socially acceptable for women to lay claim to. I call it honorable ambition. I for one am not satisfied buying into that paradigm. Once I expose it for what it really is, I suspect the same will be true for you.

three

Honorable Ambition?

What would happen if one woman told the truth about her life?
The world would split open.

—Muriel Rukeyser

WHAT if your ambition is to be a great mother? Or a loyal friend? What if your primary ambition is to be an easygoing, fair-minded coworker who refuses on moral grounds to educate herself about office politics? Or a great partner or wife? That kind of ambition doesn't bother you, does it? No, because that's socially sanctioned ambition. For example, read the following women's stories and I'm guessing you'll regard them each as having chosen honorable ambition.

Amy was a high-profile thirty-six-year-old Chicago-based pediatric cardiologist. She loved her career. She found working with her patients and colleagues challenging and fulfilling. She earned a seven-figure income. She and her husband, a neurosurgeon, had three boys. Their oldest, now thirteen, is severely autistic. Their middle child, now ten, is mildly autistic. Their youngest, who is seven, has no health problems. Amy and her husband had trouble finding good schools for their autistic children. She eventually decided to scale down her practice to where she was working only about 10 percent of the time. She lost most of her patients. She did this so that she could help start a charter school for autistic children. Her husband also commanded a high salary. They agreed that money was not an issue and that he would support her and their boys.

Nan, twenty-seven, was a single, hardworking midlevel marketing director in a Seattle-based Fortune 500 company. She prided herself on "not doing company politics." Everyone in her division liked her; she was careful not to step on colleagues' toes or cross over into other people's turf. She found strategizing and paying attention to shifting power hierarchies and competitive plays made by her peers "distasteful" and figured that her Ivy League degree, hard work, and team loyalty would get her the recognition and advancement opportunities she deserved.

Rusti, twenty-six, won a place in Stanford University's M.B.A. program, plus a free ride on tuition and a fast-track-to-success internship opportunity to boot. Around the same time, her fiancé, a promising young lawyer who was "clearly my soul mate," was offered an associate position at a leading New York law firm and wanted Rusti to move with him rather than struggle with a long-distance relationship for three years. Rusti ultimately decided to give up her place at Stanford and try the following year for acceptance into a top-tier New York City business school. She reasoned, "He'll line up his dream first; then it will be my turn next fall."

Julie, forty-seven, has been happily married for twenty-four years and is the mother of two daughters, now in college. Before she had kids, Julie completed the three thousand postdoctoral hours required to sit for the state boards and become a licensed clinical psychologist. She made the decision—"sort of consciously, sort of not, but I did let the ten-year deadline for getting licensed expire"—to forgo putting in the hours required to study for and pass the exams. She did this in favor of continuing her role as an anchor for many friends and community members in the greater Boston area. She spent the next eighteen years feeling very fulfilled in that role. "My home is a place where many people have gathered frequently over the years for community events, holidays, and special occasions. Our door has always been open. It's been a blessing for me, my husband, and our girls to have so many people we feel deeply connected to."

When I met Kathy, she was a forty-three-year-old mother of six-year-old identical-twin girls. She told me her story of falling in love with "a caring, loving man who supported my ambition, and I his." She married "my best friend and the love of my life" in her mid-thirties. They both worked in New York City, he as an investment banker and she as a tax attorney. The couple's daughters were born. Though they were "passionate urbanites," they decided that they would move to "the more young-child-friendly" suburb of Westchester just until their girls were old enough to start private elementary school in New York City. The two-hour daily commute got to be too much for Cathy, so she decided to make a lateral move to a small firm closer to her new home. "I knew the work would be uninspiring, but figured I could live with it for three or four years until we moved back to the city."

Sher, thirty-two, was thriving in her role as a senior program developer and product design manager for a high-tech company in San Jose, California. She loved her work and was inspired daily by her colleagues. When she'd been with her company for five years, she and her husband jointly agreed that he would leave his depressing corporate job to launch his own small architectural design firm. With her solid six-figure income and hefty incentive bonuses, she was already the higher earner. They both felt comfortable taking the risk of having him sacrifice his income and benefits to make his entrepreneurial move.

Amy drastically scaled back her ambition to support her autistic boys' educations. Nan took the high road with her ambition and refused to get her hands dirty with company politics. Rusti put her ambition on hold to keep her love relationship strong and healthy. Julie put her ambition into being a community leader. Kathy substituted her full-throttle ambition for a short-term solution for making her career commute and parenting easier. Sher ramped up her ambition and happily invested in her husband's dream of being his own boss by signing on as sole family breadwinner.

Many would say these women did the right thing, that they made noble decisions and sacrifices that any woman should make. Many would point out that these women freely chose to do what they did for their own well-thought-out reasons.

But is it really honorable to dilute your ambition or channel it into your lover, family, or community? Is it really honorable ambition to play softball at work in favor of being piously apolitical? Is it really honorable to invest in someone else's dream ahead of your own? We often think that this version of ambition is good and right and virtuous. But we never think about what it costs us. What if it hurts you in ways you may not be aware of or haven't bargained for? And in ways that no one encouraged you to think about before making your honorable ambition decision? Is it then truly an informed choice? What if it doesn't turn out the way you planned and your turn never comes? Then what?

Acting on Your Ambition, or Not, Is Your Choice— But How Do You Weigh the Costs of Choosing?

We are all born with some level of ambition. The need to move ahead, to compete, to achieve and accomplish and leave a legacy is within the human soul. How much ambition is in an individual person's genes is not really his or her choice, but acting on it is a choice.

Sometimes we make conscious choices—and we then deliberately act, or not, based on that measured decision. For example, I decide that I've had enough of being undervalued in my current company role; I've exhausted all reasonable efforts and patience and nothing has improved. So one day, I leap into the abyss and start putting my résumé out there; I start contacting people in my network; I choose to act in order to find a better outlet for my ambition. Other times we make choices simply by *not* taking action; the act of doing nothing, or of doing things the same way we've always done them, are, themselves, choices. For example, I'm miserable with my current career situation, I'm feeling unfulfilled, and I feel this way day in and day out for a year, but I do nothing. So by taking no action, I've chosen to settle for my current level of discontent.

Every choice has consequences—pros and cons. But, as ambitchous women, just how do we go about weighing our choices in a mindful, conscious way—particularly in light of the fact that we are given very little support for doing so? How do we choose correctly when we aren't encouraged to think today about our futures? How do we avoid setting ourselves up for pain and suffering when we aren't taught to try to calculate very specific if/then scenarios: If I make this choice now, and things go as planned, how will my life be affected? If this or that unexpected thing happens, then where would that leave me? What would my options be then? And if I thoroughly consider and analyze real potential future outcomes, do I still feel comfortable right now making this choice?

As ambitchous women, we need to tell one another our stories. We need to tell the truth about our lives. We need to talk openly rather than feeling alone, ashamed, guilty, and like we are the only ones who have faced tough decisions and made career and life choices. Opening up to one another will help clarify what we ought to consider when weighing alternatives and making judgment calls about our own ambition. For example, notice whether reading the outcomes of the six stories below changes what you originally thought about the choices these women made. Then use their stories to jump-start talking openly with your ambitchous women friends and colleagues about your experiences.

At first Amy, the esteemed pediatric cardiologist, had been reluctant to give up her thriving medical practice and the ability to support herself financially. But honorable ambition triumphed. For a long time it seemed to be working out:

> For nine years I wasn't working much as a physician in order to devote myself to the school and our kids. My husband was supporting us. I was thrilled when he got involved. At one point he and I were both on the fund-raising committee. We had several meetings at our house with other parents who were on that task force. The fund-raiser was a big success. It was all so heartwarming and community focused. It was all about the children.

But Amy's plan didn't play out the way she'd envisioned it:

> Then I found my husband in bed with a woman who had been on the committee. Long story short, we went through a horrific divorce. In the midst of all that pain and suffering, I had to go back, at forty-five, and try to revive my practice. I did it: at forty-nine, my patient load and professional reputation are finally starting to take off again. But at my age, and with everything I had to deal with, getting back into the game was f____g hard, let me tell you.

When I asked Amy if she would have made different choices about her career had she known then what she knows now, she said, "Absolutely," and explained why:

> You go into marriage and you make these agreements. I was in my late thirties when it really hit me that our oldest autistic son was never going to improve. The decision was: "I'm going to basically put my career on hold while we raise our kids, and you need to support us while *we* do this." And we agree on this. Then he goes and has an affair. I had faith in him. I believed in him. And at the end of the day, he didn't give a damn about what I'd sacrificed for him and our family.

I asked Amy to calculate all the ways in which her decision had cost her.

> I paid big-time. It's unknowable how much it cost me. I'd sent out letters to all of my patients saying they were going to have to find another doctor. And when I went back, by that time, all of my former patients had other doctors. So think of all the business I lost over those nine years, not to mention all of the lost referrals that would have accrued.

I pressed, echoing a question many people would ask: What could she have done differently? For God's sake, she had two autistic children, one who was severely impaired, both of whom required care and attention. Did she really have a choice?

> I didn't have to get so involved in building up the school that it required me to give up my practice. We had money. You have to learn how to integrate your life with this sick child's life *and* keep a life of your own, or you're going to go crazy. You make enough money so that you hire people to help. You cannot stop living

your own life because of the circumstances that are going on around you. You're still a person. Just because you have a disabled child doesn't mean that you no longer have needs.

I asked Amy for more specifics about what she now thinks she should have done differently:

I should never have shut down my practice, never. I loved my work; I loved it all. I should have figured out a way to keep it going and take care of my kids. The school was going to get started whether I was involved or not. My thirteen-year-old, whom I love dearly, is at the same place developmentally as he would have been, regardless of what I did. It hasn't made a difference in his life to have me so involved with his school behind the scenes. He's always going to be severely disabled. Had I kept working and had him in a great school, it would have played out just the same for him. But his mom would have been a hell of a lot less stressed, financially and emotionally. And I would have kept my intellectual stimulation and professional traction, which would have been better for me and for my kids.

Nan, the twenty-seven-year-old apolitical manager, is like countless ambitchous women I've worked with who express contemptuous disdain for company politics. Often when they dig deeper they discover it is because they are afraid. They don't know how to influence others, take credit, stand up to bullies, and get the power and recognition they deserve. And like many women who avoid politics in favor of a more honorable ambition outlook, Nan ended up getting backstabbed by peers who were gunning for plum opportunities that she had stars in her eyes for. She was passed over for countless promotions before she finally decided to get savvy about how to play the game in the workplace. What would Nan have done differently?

I wouldn't have been so willingly naive, hiding behind the guise of taking the moral high road. I would have educated myself and learned a thing or two about how to navigate office politics in a way that advanced my career goals rather than letting people trod on me and leave me in their wake.

Rusti and her lawyer fiancé didn't end up getting married. Because she'd spent much of her savings relocating twice, first to New York City with him, and then back to the San Francisco Bay Area, she hasn't yet been able to get herself back on track to go after the top-tier M.B.A. degree she dreams of earning. What would she have done differently? "I should have entered the Stanford program and insisted that my fiancé be willing for us to simultaneously pursue our ambition dreams, even if it meant having a long-distance relationship. Who knows? Maybe we even would have made it had we gone that route. Maybe I would have been less resentful had I stuck to my guns about my own dreams. Maybe my career disappointment wouldn't have had such a corrosive effect on our relationship."

Now that Julie's daughters are both in college, she is longing to get back into the workforce. She regrets not having pursued professional licensure so that she could have had the option of working as a psychologist in a higher-paying job than those that are now available to her. She has decided to go back to school in accounting and has long-term plans to pursue a Chartered Financial Analyst certification. She says it is hard because of her age and energy level, and also given that she will have to put in five to six years before she can even begin to work in her new career.

Kathy's husband worked in one of the World Trade Center towers and perished on 9/11. Though she is longing to leave the suburbs and "move back home to Manhattan," she is reluctant, for now, to put her young twins through additional difficult transitions. She says that she has nothing in common with any of the parents in her community, and that only one other mother in her children's school works. She told me how her daughters came home from school one day and said, "Mommy, why do we have to be the only kids in our class who don't have a daddy *and* the only kids whose mommy works?" What would she have done differently? She told me that a big part of her wishes that she and her husband had remained in New York City, where they felt so at home. And that in any case, she wishes she had stuck it out with her difficult commute, looking for excellent child care, trying to tag-team more with her husband on parenting and scheduling responsibilities rather than quitting the job she loved just because it seemed easier. She says that while they made what they thought was the right decision, she obviously could not possibly have foreseen what a tragic turn their lives would take.

Sher's company was acquired in a merger in 2000. Her boss got the boot, most of her team got laid off, and she found herself working for an emotionally abusive supervisor while carrying a workload that had previously been shared by three people. When this unexpected development hit, Sher's husband's business was at least two years away from profitability. Then the high-tech bubble burst and the Silicon Valley economy took a nosedive; Sher's ability to make a job move was suddenly nonexistent. She refused her husband's offers to go back to a steady-paying corporate job, which he had the option of doing. She believed that she'd made this commitment and she was going to see it through, no matter what it took out of her hide. She showed up at my office seeking career advice after having stuck it out for two years feeling so depressed that she could barely drag herself out of bed each day to face her ogre boss. She'd had enough of being handcuffed to a toxic job and unable to leave because of her role as sole supporter of herself and her husband. Still, she didn't want to ask her spouse to give up his now almost-profitable business. It took her two more years of toughing it out in her demoralizing job while going back to school for advanced certificate degree training at night and on weekends before she found a new career opportunity that restored her happiness and peace of mind.

What would Sher have done differently? She told me that she had no regrets about having supported her husband, whose business was thriving the last time we spoke. But she said that she would have planned differently for unexpected contingencies by not taking her job security and income for granted, doing far less discretionary spending in favor of saving money, and preserving six months minimum to a year or more in emergency reserve. She also said she would have paid much closer attention to news in the marketplace so that she might have gotten a whiff of her company's upcoming merger. And that she would have kept more on top of her networking to stay apprised of other career opportunities before her back was against the wall in an imploding job market.

We Can't Blame the Guys

Sometimes, like Amy's and Nan's stories above, there is a marriage or engagement or partnership that unravels. Sometimes we get involved with partners who betray us. Sometimes it just doesn't work out; it was a bad match. In any case, we have to take responsibility for allowing ourselves to get into such a vulnerable ambition position to begin with. Leaving our ambition behind or making it a lesser priority was *our* choice. Those guys we loved who ended up not caring about us didn't put a gun to our heads and say, "Leave your ambition behind for me." And even if there was coercion involved that swayed our decision, we could have said no. We could have stood our ground where our ambition dreams were concerned.

And there's not always a bad guy involved in a woman's decision to go for honorable ambition at the expense of her own big career dreams. Frequently I see professional women who say, "You go do your career dream first; then I'll do mine later. That's what I want. It's fine." And her partner or spouse says, "Okay." Wouldn't you do the same if someone were offering it up to you on a silver platter? Then sometimes the relationship ends up being wonderful and she stays with her man, but life gets in the way of her plans and her turn never comes. She has kids, so she puts her ambition on hold for a few more years. Or they rack up debt buying a house, putting their kids into private school, driving SUVs—and suddenly it no longer seems feasible to her, or maybe to her partner, for her to go after that M.B.A. or law degree. Or it no longer seems realistic for her to leave her steady-income job with benefits to launch her own company, or to make a move to a riskier but more rewarding opportunity. Whose fault is that? It's not always a guy who derailed our ambition. And if there is a bad guy involved, it's never completely his fault. We have to take responsibility for our complicity in allowing our own ambition to get waylaid.

Now that you've read these women's stories, work through the following Reality Check. Ask yourself if you, too, struggle with feeling that you must at times sacrifice your ambitchous career goals to be a good woman. And ask yourself what honorable ambition does to your life.

REALITY CHECK
Is Sacrificing My Needs at the Expense of My Ambition Honorable?
Ambition Journal Exercise

- How do I give to others at the expense of my own needs and ambition dreams? How does this leave me feeling? Fulfilled and energized? Or am I exhausted?

- Has it been more than a month since I've had time for myself? Am I sometimes so frustrated that I cry alone?
- Do I find that some days I just don't want to get out of bed because I'm utterly uninspired?
- Do I still think it's the right thing to do?

Let's think about what it could cost you to give up or compromise your ambition:

- Are you earning far less than your peers because you passed up opportunities that initially required long hours and you felt pressure to wait until your kids were more self-sufficient? Are you bored with the job you've settled for, stuck because you need the paycheck and haven't built a competitive track record to land more rewarding work? Has your dream of earning an advanced degree been on hold so long that it now seems pointless or impossible?
- How could it affect your financial security? Even if you're in a great relationship, life holds no guarantees and anything could happen. What if you were left to support yourself and your kids? Would you lose your home because your income wouldn't cover the mortgage payments? Would you be sweating each month to pay bills? Would you ever be able to retire? Would you be able to support yourself as you moved into your senior years and health problems hit?
- Recall a time you knowingly ignored your ambition. What did that feel like? List five emotions.
- Will you feel inferior, disappointed in yourself around friends and family who've succeeded? Will you see yourself as a weak role model for your kids as they're ready to launch their own education and careers?
- How could it affect your confidence in meeting and engag-

ing with new people? If someone says to you in conversation, "You turned that amazing job down? Why?," how might your self-image be compromised?

Now reconsider all of those things that you do for others, all the time, day in and day out, at the expense of your ambitchous dreams, because you think putting yourself last makes you a good woman. And ask yourself again—and be truthful—does this really make you a virtuous person? Are you still confident that this value system, this setup you've bought into under social duress, makes you the best person you could possibly be?

Maybe, just maybe, in order to do the things you think you must do to be your best self, you are, paradoxically, sacrificing a core part of who you are, an essential part of your being—your ambitchous, big-dreaming self. And in doing so, you may actually be shortchanging yourself—in a big way. You may be sabotaging your efforts to be your best self.

four

Embracing Your Ambition
Makes You the Best You Can Be

The cost of giving up your ambition is . . . death.
> —Abbey Dehnert, twenty-eight, lead singer/dancer
> of BomberGirl—a New York City–based
> theatrical music group—and self-employed
> personal trainer

Squandering one's talents and ambition is having a dead life. Why be alive if you're essentially dead?
> —Elizabeth Conn, president of ECONN Design

Women who are driven by a passion for what they do cannot be expected to give that up. Without acknowledgment of your ambition, a core part of you goes missing—the part of you that can only be fulfilled by pursuing your career ambition. Think about just what this means in your own unique, complicated, and precious life.

If you are the kind of person who has ever dreamed big or

thrived on challenging yourself creatively and intellectually in your profession, if you've ever loved the thrill of setting impressive goals, then you've got to be ambitchous to be happy. When ambition is in your blood, you will never find the same satisfaction in the home sphere or in the I'm-just-in-it-for-the-paycheck mentality. Abbey Dehnert described to me her take on this distinction: "To be successful, all you have to do is accomplish the kind of things you're supposed to do at work. Whereas when you are ambitious, you're being a bit more extraordinary."

REALITY CHECK
What Can I Get *Only* from Career Ambition?
Ambition Journal Exercise

Think back to a time when you were engrossed in a compelling, fascinating work project—a time when you felt yourself craving passion, drive, or a certain craziness, where you fell asleep thinking about your inspiring goals and then you woke up the next morning and couldn't wait to get back to your work. How did it feel? Be as specific as possible. Take your time and recall and savor the details. What were the circumstances that made you feel so fired up? How did you feel during the process? Try to specifically recall the kaleidoscope of thoughts and feelings—the fears, excitement, self-doubt, and redemption you experienced. How did you feel hitting obstacles and failures and having to come up with plan B, or plan C, or plan Z until you got it right?

How did you feel in that moment in which you realized you'd finally, miraculously, achieved your goal? What recognition, compliments, bonuses, and raises came with your win to make it an even sweeter victory? How did you feel being singled out as someone who had done a great job and had been ambitious enough to make something difficult happen? What did people say to you? How did you respond? How did you feel being the center of attention because you'd achieved an ambitious goal? Did you allow yourself even a moment to feel inspired by your own accomplishment? Something along the lines of, "Hey! I really did this! *I* made the thing happen! It was me! Wow. Who would've thunk it?" In what ways did this accomplishment make you want to set the bar higher for yourself? Did you follow through?

How Do I Get Back on Track?

Now that you realize your ambition is a great thing, and costly to give up, let me ask you to think about these questions: Are you being as ambitious as you really want to be? Is it possible that you are settling for less when what you truly want is more?

If you've gotten off course with your ambition, you may be like so many women who have compromised their most ambitchous goals because they've bought into a false dichotomy—that we can be ambitchous or we can lead healthy, balanced lives, but we must not attempt to do both. So if you want to be a woman who makes more money, has more power, gets the recognition she deserves, and has the determination to go after her dreams while respecting herself and others, you must first get rid of any I-Must Mandates that knock you off of your ambitchous career course.

I have never heard a cultural message that outright encourages women to be more ambitious, that declares, "Go down just as hard for your ambition as you do for any other primary priority in your life, be it lover, friend, child, community; do not sacrifice your ambition for any reason." This is going to be our new way of thinking about how valuable and precious our ambitchous goals and the contributions we were born to make are.

I-Must Mandates I Must Ignore

- Rising in my career and being as ambitchous as I really want to be **must** take a backseat to love relationships, family, friendships, and community priorities when push comes to shove.
- Wanting more out of my professional life **must** mean that I'm less of a woman.
- I **must** settle for a subpar job with no immediate upward prospects because I'm so focused on life outside the office.
- I **must** not be too ambitchous when, in fact, my career is far more important to me than I'm admitting.
- I **must** be satisfied with where I am professionally even if I am aching to unleash my most ambitchous self.

I-Must Mandates I must not ignore:

I MUST BELIEVE THAT MY AMBITION
IS A VIRTUE, NOT A VICE
and
I MUST BELIEVE THAT THE WORLD
DESERVES TO HEAR FROM ME

You Win, Your Way

I believe opportunity is limitless. I am very ambitious. I am incredibly passionate about my work. But I'm equally passionate about my family and friends. If you are a woman who is ambitious, a woman with a vital contribution to make, you needn't choose between a meaningful career and a happy, fulfilling life outside of work. You just have to manage your life so that you can be a full recipient of all of it. Is this goal a virtue, and is it attainable? Absolutely.

—Deborah Saweuyer-Parks, President and
CEO of Homestead Capital

Consider this virtuous definition of winning as an ambitchous woman competing in and contributing to the marketplace:

1. You must love your work. You must be willing to aggressively pursue the professional work you were meant to do and to strive for any career opportunities that inspire you.

2. You must regard your deepest career aspirations as unconditionally sacrosanct. Your career ambitions are just as important as any other nonnegotiable priorities in your life, including your boyfriend, your spouse, your babies, your grade-schoolers, your middle school kids, your teens, your friends, your parents, and your community responsibilities. To become your very best self—and to live a life you will look back on with few regrets—you must believe this with all your heart.

3. You must feel entitled to earn your worth. You must be able to charge your full marketplace value without self-reproach, without leaving money on the table, and without feeling like an impostor because you make as much as—or more than—a man.

A New Mind-set: Go Down Hard for Your Ambition

We women are willing to bleed ourselves dry for so many things. To be clear, I consider this a strength, not a weakness—as long as we allow for continual self-rejuvenation and renewal. I value my own resiliency, strength, and courage. Just as those attributes define who I am and how I see myself, those traits are undoubtedly a big part of how you see yourself, a part of your own self-image as a woman. But we should feel just as free to value our ambition without apology and without punishing ourselves for doing so.

My vision is that we make a collective shift in thinking where we all understand that our right career path, our true professional calling—our ambitchous desire to love our work—is as much a part of the who-I-am equation as feeling that we are good mothers, loyal wives, worthy colleagues, trusted friends. And that we do so with an uncompromising, unyielding belief in our right and ability and obligation to do so.

We've redefined what it means to be an ambitchous woman and what we must value to learn to be her. Now we're ready for a brand-new set of rules custom-tailored for the determined, ambitchous woman who wants to make more money, have more power, get the recognition she deserves, and do it with integrity. Then we'll add lifetime maintenance strategies for tending to our ambitchous dreams throughout the entire span of our careers.

Part II

am·BITCH·ous Rules

five

Stop Ambition Sabotage

You're chomping at the bit to learn powerful strategies and techniques that will allow you to make more money and get the power, the credit, the recognition, and the fulfillment you deserve. Now I'm going to show you precisely how to do just that. I'm going to show you how you've come to embrace watered-down ambition compromises in the first place. This will keep you from falling into common self-imposed traps that cause ambitchous women to unwittingly sell themselves short.

Socially Sanctioned Self-Sabotage: The Wolf in Sheep's Clothing

It has been said that "the surest way to keep a man in prison is not to let him know he's there." And the surest way to keep a woman from embracing her pure career ambition is to make her believe she's already done it.

Why do so many of us self-sabotage without noticing that we're doing it? Everywhere, there are disempowering ideas about women disguised in positive, and even sometimes flattering, terms. The ideas translate into seemingly desirable traits women should cultivate, and we buy into them and internalize them. But these views and attributes are not desirable—they are wolves in sheep's clothing, and they lead to self-sabotaging beliefs and behavior. By accepting them, and acting on them, we women compromise our ambition—but we don't see what we are doing to ourselves. Think about it. You don't see how something you like about yourself—a characteristic you've been encouraged to develop and made to feel is a very pleasing part of your nature—is holding you back because it's a supposedly good quality. Why would you want to change something so excellent about yourself? This is what I call **socially sanctioned self-sabotage**, and it's causing us to tie our hands behind our own backs.

To be clear, a wolf in sheep's clothing is a harmful thing masquerading as something beneficial. The overt messages—the sheep's clothing—are the seemingly positive attributes we have been trained to embrace. For example, women are natural team players, or women are born to be moral compasses. The covert messages—the wolves—are the subtle, sometimes unconscious beliefs we metabolize from those overt messages. For example, because women are natural team players, it's wrong to toot our own horns and grab for the credit; or as moral role models, it is a duplicitous violation of personal and social ethics to acknowledge and master workplace politics. Believing these messages makes us behave in ways that sabotage us over and over. Here are examples of self-sabotaging behaviors:

- Giving away credit in favor of always sharing with the team
- Being afraid to jump into the ring and compete as a serious contender
- Not asking for professional help and advice because it makes us look weak
- Avoiding confrontation and allowing jerks and fools to steal our thunder

- Not getting paid what we're worth
- Not knowing how to spot power thieves and those who might see us as easy targets
- Not trusting our gut and fighting off saboteurs and naysayers
- Being too responsible to others—and irresponsible to our own needs
- Not speaking up and being visible because we secretly fear we are interlopers

There's nothing wrong with being unselfish, fair, agreeable, and responsible, but there's a lot wrong with denying or ignoring the fact that, where your ambitchous passions are concerned, all of these tendencies can backfire and work against you if you aren't paying attention. As I'll demonstrate, they can keep you from going for your share of the opportunity pie, from taking risks that can have huge payoffs, from standing up to people when you need to, from being tough even if it brings on disapproval from others, from taking the credit you deserve. Any good quality, taken too far, is going to bite you on the backside. Women are praised for and expected to embody these qualities—so much so that we go nuts with them. In the following amBITCHous Rules, I'll help you locate these blindspots and behaviors in yourself, change them, and stop self-sabotage.

six

Am•BITCH•ous Rule 1
Be a Contender

We are bred in my company to say "we." Saying "I did this" would get me up a creek. So how do I take credit I'm not getting without violating my company's mandate of "no me"s?

—Anita, thirty-seven, senior VP, international
PR firm, Los Angeles

A huge project opportunity came in. All candidates had to submit comprehensive pitch materials to the prospective client, including fee estimates, on short notice. My boss was away on a family emergency, so I was in charge of the pitch process. I had to gather pieces from sales, marketing, publicity, financial, and new media, but I was the architect of the whole thing, and I reworked marketing as well as creating a big chunk of the new media section myself. I was responsible for making all of the creative and judgment calls. When I got the call telling me we'd won the assignment, the new client singled me out as a crucial factor in awarding the deal to our firm. When my boss came back, he said, "I don't know who wrote this pitch, but it's perfectly positioned. It's a great job." I told him that we all worked on it, it was a team effort, the usual "girl" stuff. But when I got back to my desk, I felt like crap for not taking credit.

—Adrianne, thirty-two, investment banker,
New York

Many women don't experience themselves as serious contenders. They tell themselves that they have no business being in the ring. Or they decide that maybe they could be a contender, but then overprepare and miss the deadline. Or they tell themselves they're too busy to bother. Whatever the rationale, they blow their chance. And even when they do take that chance, they don't ensure that they get the credit they deserve, which is an absolute prerequisite for earning leadership opportunities, recognition, promotions, and a salary commensurate with expertise and contributions. Why is it so hard for women to lay claim to their accomplishments? Why don't we grab more opportunities to compete as team leaders, as power brokers, as hungry and effective movers and shakers? Why are we reluctant to showcase our strengths? Why can't we say, "Yes, *I* [not *we*] made the thing happen"?

We're socialized to believe that being consummate team players is our natural strength, and that competition—going after individual credit—is antithetical to that value. There is a reason ambitchous women fall into this trap.

Sheep's Clothing (overt message): Women are polite, ladylike collaborators who are naturally team-oriented and look for the win-win solution. It's nice to share. Women can and should use these advantages in the marketplace.

Wolf (covert message): Taking credit is selfish and wrong. Competition means someone wins and someone loses, which is unacceptable. *Competition* is a dirty word. Strategically, aggressively, and proactively jumping in to be a visible part of the group is impolite. Interrupting, even in a fast-paced brainstorming session, standing out, or standing up to someone more senior compromises their femininity, makes women seem aggressive, rude, and ballbusting and might even put their job at risk.

Socially Sanctioned Self-Sabotage: You don't speak up, stand up, or stand out. You don't throw your ideas out there unless you are absolutely certain those ideas are correct and will be well received. You wait for others to finish and end up running out of time and missing your turn. You sit on the sidelines for fear of offending someone with your natural competitiveness. You lose out to rivals. You cut yourself off from advancement because you don't allow yourself to shine. And if you do decide to put yourself in the running, you don't do enough to make certain your accomplishments are noted.

If you are unwilling to jump into the ring and get your ideas out there, if you don't take seriously the need to feel and to act like a serious competitor in the marketplace, then your career recognition will blow right by you. The true-or-false Reality Check below will help you determine whether you are comfortable accepting the credit you've earned, whether you unambivalently believe in your right to do so—and whether you project creditworthiness in the workplace.

REALITY CHECK
Do I Get What I Deserve?
Ambition Journal Exercise

- I am crystal-clear that, in the business world, if I don't jump into the ring, I'm going to be left behind.
- When I see an opportunity to showcase my talents, I take it.
- I think strategically about keeping my accomplishments visible.
- I understand that there are elegant, strategic ways to get my due credit without coming across as a bitch.

- I am not afraid to toot my own horn when a project has gone well.
- When I achieve a goal or someone recognizes me, I never say, "Oh, I just got lucky."
- I never downplay my talents or accomplishments.
- If nominated for an award, I would accept without hesitation.

If you answered true to all of the above, you are in very good shape. If, however, you answered false to one or more of the questions, you have some work to do. Not to worry! We're going to change that now. Read on.

Taking Credit

One day, I opened a major national business magazine and discovered that a journalist who had phoned me for a comment on a story had used, verbatim, two paragraphs of quotes I'd e-mailed to her without crediting me as the contributing expert. Yes, I did call her and confront her unethical behavior, and yes, I did get some sort of concrete resolution in terms of an interview in a subsequent piece. Of course, there was nothing I could do about it after the theft of my intellectual property, but I could stand up and speak out and know that at least I'd done right by myself.

I am continually astonished by the number of ambitious, successful women I work with who choose to remain silent—or put themselves through a self-punishing, mighty internal battle to justify speaking up or taking action—when someone else spends, or threatens to steal, their intellectual capital. How many times in your own life can you look back on (with your teeth gritted, no doubt) when you didn't stick up for yourself when someone took credit for work you'd put your heart and soul into? Or when you were passed over for someone less talented and who'd made a far less significant contribution than you had, because they were a better boaster?

During my research for this book, I e-mailed queries to thousands of women and always received a flood of responses that generated a flurry of debate, discussion, ideas, and stories from the trenches. But after sending this one—"What advice do you have for other women, and what works for you when it comes to the art of taking credit at work?"—my in-box remained conspicuously empty. I might as well have asked, "Who has a vibrator in her bedroom nightstand, and for those of you who do, do you mind if I use your real name in this book and include a photo of you holding your special friend?" Do any of the following examples sound all too familiar?

- You did more than half the research and wrote 90 percent of the report. So why are you listed as an equal with four other contributors, or not listed at all?

- Your boss compliments you on an outstanding third-quarter result; instead of acknowledging the recognition you deserve, you immediately list other people who work for you, none of whom played an instrumental role in the outcome. Then, during your next performance review, you're shocked when you get a cost-of-living adjustment and nothing more.

- You build a new division from the ground up. You assume that your boss, who oversees many other divisions, supports your efforts and will acknowledge your role to others, so you're caught completely off guard when he, without telling you, jumps up and appoints himself spokesperson for your baby (and doesn't credit you as the driving force) at the quarterly company-wide meeting attended by the CEO and other company power brokers. You sit there in stunned silence.

Without a doubt, deciding how and when to take credit, when to share it with other parties, and when to negotiate for it in both explicit and subtle ways is a tough balance to strike. We often resort to two extreme and costly behaviors.

Credit Extreme #1: I'll Just Keep My Head Down and Work Quietly

On the one end of the spectrum, if we believe that "keeping quiet and working our little heads off" will attract the credit we deserve, or that being a consummate team player is more important than making sure our individual accomplishments are rewarded, then we lose. We'll remain the nice, competent worker whom no one ever notices. There are extreme and real consequences to this churchmouse approach.

You share or give away credit all the time, like a good girl is supposed to do. You're stunned when you get a raise that doesn't reflect your contribution to the company's bottom line. You keep your mouth shut, and it costs you tens of thousands of dollars just this year alone in terms of your yearly salary and the bonus you deserve. It costs you potentially hundreds of thousands of dollars over the course of your career. It costs you promotions, raises, and industry recognition that could lead to bigger and better and higher-paying positions within your company or elsewhere. It doesn't have to play out this way.

You may be thinking, "What if the ethos of my company is not about taking credit?" Still, within that corporate culture, people do get promoted; people do get chosen to be groomed for the coveted leadership roles or for succession candidates. People do make partner. So recognize that even within a so-called we-not-me culture, there is a competition. There are people watching.

One woman I interviewed, Doris, a forty-two-year-old creative director and senior executive at a top New York advertising agency, told me about a former boss (we'll call her Ms. Exploiter) who routinely took credit for Doris's work, both to her face and behind her back. When Doris got her first yearly raise (she was new to this company but was a seasoned, high-profile veteran in her industry), she waited until her boss, Ms. Exploiter, was out of the office for the day, then went straight to her boss's boss (Ms. I Respect You), and said, "Come on. This raise in no way reflects the money I've brought this company over just the past six months alone. This raise is a joke, and you know it." She got her raise tripled. Four years later, when Ms. I Respect You left the company, she took Doris with her, gave her a vice presidential role in which she could shine, and set her ambition bar higher than ever before by letting her work autonomously to define her new division's brand. She also got a fabulous salary—and a corner office that Ms. I Respect You insisted "had Doris's name on it."

Heads-up! Not down. You've got to pay attention in order to get your due.

Credit Extreme #2: I'm the Best Bitch Here! Out of My Way!

On the other end of the spectrum, if we start demanding credit in a way that is decidedly inelegant or nonstrategic, we risk sounding like an empty braggart. Even if what you're saying is true, talking about it too loudly takes away from your credibility. Muhammad Ali can go on television and declare, "I am the greatest," and everyone thinks it's charming, but very few can get away with that. The guy who comes into the office every day and says, "I am the best son of a bitch in this whole company," is the one you want to kill and eat. One woman I interviewed put it this way: "My boss, who is also obviously ambitious and competitive, insists on a 'Go team! We won!' approach. He told a woman I work with that if he heard her say 'I,' 'me,' or 'mine' one more time, he'd send her home." Another potential consequence is that when your performance reviews come in, your reputation as an arrogant, loudmouth braggart is going to bite you on the backside. These days, many companies are looking at feedback not only from supervisors, but also from direct reports and peers, when deciding whom to groom for promotion and whom to boot. Alienate your coworkers, including your employees, by coming off guns a-blazin' and you're going to end up discredited.

Strategies to Be a Heavyweight Contender

Your KaChing! File

Not every manager will give you recognition for your contributions or the credit and remuneration you deserve. Starting now, keep a file on winning projects you've spearheaded. It will be your KaChing! File, filled with your successes. Write a note-to-self summary at the completion of a project while the facts are still clear in your mind—do it right then and there, even if you've just pulled an all-nighter; record it while it's fresh or you risk not doing it at all or forgetting important points. Include dates, numbers, and dollar amounts documenting how your ideas, decision making, and leadership increased revenues, boosted the bottom line, improved customer retention, or led to better employee relations. Keep notes from thrilled clients. Don't be shy about asking a client to call your boss or CEO to relay how pleased he or she is with your performance. It's also a networking, win-win opportunity for the client and the boss to speak. Look at it that way and you'll be less reticent to ask. Visit www.amBITCHous.com to order an amBITCHous KaChing! File.

Be E-mail Savvy

E-mail is a really great medium for taking credit. If you're so good at what you do, then if you've done something great, you should be able to send an e-mail to somebody (boss, client, prospect) that either tells the story or conveys an idea that is sophisticated and reflects the level of skill that has caused you to be successful—without directly saying how great you are. You're showing, not telling; you're showcasing your brilliance by making your thought processes or your decision tree or the obstacles you faced and how you overcame these challenges transparent. Here are some examples: "As I was doing this [name the specific project or issue or interaction], I had this thought, or this insight. . . ." And then be specific, yet succinct.

When you receive compliments via e-mail, don't hesitate even for a moment. Immediately forward away—to your boss, to your team, to your boss's boss, only adding, "FYI." FYI—that's all you say. Put it in the subject line and at the top of the body of the e-mail. The rest—all that needs to be communicated about your creditworthiness—gets communicated in the complimentary e-mail. Here's another new mantra:

FYI—FORWARD AWAY!

Correct a Missed Opportunity to Take Credit

What do you do when you've missed an opportunity and given away your credit? You need to fix that mistake.

Let's go back to Adrianne. When she went back to her desk, she spent only about ten minutes "feeling like crap" before she wrote her boss an e-mail saying, "I don't know why I couldn't tell you this when you asked, but the truth is, I spearheaded that project—and I wrote that pitch letter." The result? He reiterated that it was a great job and Adrianne "felt a million times better."

Obviously Adrianne could have popped back by her boss's office to correct her missed credit opportunity; repairing a credit mistake in person is another option to e-mail if you're more comfortable just turning around and saying what you wished you'd said a couple of minutes earlier.

Bonus Tip: Always ask yourself what you could have done differently that would have kept you from having to sweat, beat yourself up, and figure out how to backpedal in order to claim the credit you'd initially given away. I asked Adrianne what she will do differently the next time her boss says "This was a great job— I don't know who wrote this, but it's fabulous" about work she's been the architect of. She replied without missing a beat: "I'd say, 'Thank you. *I* wrote that. I appreciate your comments.' " Taking credit is the first step to becoming a contender.

Conviction: Creditworthiness from the Inside Out

To accept credit from the outside, we have to be comfortable in our own skin, especially since there are still stereotypes out there working against us—including the 2005 Catalyst survey finding that women executives are still viewed, by both their male and female peers, as less skilled than male executives in " 'take charge' behaviors such as delegating and influencing upward." If we don't stick up for ourselves, we cannot count on others to do it for us. Ways to demonstrate you're a credit contender include:

1. Avoid verbal softeners. Senior law partner Judith Thoyer told me that the most common form of this that she sees with young female attorneys is beginning what should be an assertive

statement with: "Correct me if I'm wrong, but . . ." "You've probably already thought of this, but . . ." "You've probably got a better idea, but I'll say this one anyway . . ." or "I know we're almost out of time, but let me squeeze in this one thought." Using verbal softeners undermines your credibility.

2. Suppress the urge to acknowledge everyone else's viewpoint before you express your own. For example, don't start with "Well, John, I understood you to mean that your preference is to go with plan C . . ." or "Jill, I hear that you feel strongly about this point. . . ." Don't derail the meeting momentum by trying to validate each person in the room—this fruitless search for consensus invites going around in circles. Skip it.

3. Speak in the first person when discussing your proposals: "Here's my idea . . ." "It occurred to me that we should try this . . ." "I think it makes sense to . . ." "My research revealed that this is the best course of action . . ." "I just identified from our annual report two million dollars in nonperforming assets, and here are some notes on my plan to turn that around, which I'll also e-mail a copy of after this meeting."

4. Don't fish for validation after you've made your point by asking, "What do you think?" It makes you seem insecure.

Your newfound self-assurance means that you will naturally speak up when it's called for. You don't have to yell to get attention. With a dignified reserve, you take credit for your hard-won success, projecting to others that you know what you're worth—and so should they. Once you are confident about accepting acknowledgment for your accomplishments, you can more easily share credit with those who deserve it, thus building supportive alliances and finding those win-win strategies for sharing the glory.

Be Disarming

In business, to be a contender sometimes you have to disarm a credit blocker. Do this by going against type. For example, people expect a top litigator in New York to blow into the room, big attitude, big screaming, big swinging dick (yes, man or woman with a dick), with a pound-the-table, f__k-you! kind of attitude. I know a female litigator, a partner in a top New York firm. I've seen her in action in very male-dominated, aggressive environments, including boondoggles where the guys are throwing back Johnnie Walker Blue shots and playing their most alpha-male, frat-buddy, king-of-the-universe roles. When she walks into a fight it is the most remarkable thing: everybody in the room wants to help her, even if they're on the other side. She disarms, while filling up the room. How? She conveys the sense that this is a team enterprise, because she's charismatic and because she's confident. She preemptively defuses a stalemate by coming across as laid-back and relaxed while at the same time capable of and focused on getting to yes. And then she goes to work focusing collaboratively on the issues that are on the table rather than on acting according to how her adversaries expect her to behave. The whole package is professionally attractive and disarming—and very powerful. She uses that atmosphere she's created selectively, not to win every point, but to win—and get credit for—the ones that matter.

Say, "I'll Do It"

Don't ask; just do it: "I'll do the opening description of this project, its outcome, and talk about our team and who played which roles at tomorrow's meeting." Should some other person try to hijack it, just stand up and do it when it comes time to talk about that project, or join her rather than sitting there seething. Also actively look for ways to participate on committees or projects, including ones that no one else wants to handle. Then find subtle ways to let people know on a continual basis, over time, what you're up to, what you've learned that might help the team, the organization, or other individuals. A brief mention at the company coffee bar of a little tidbit of information gets you on the radar.

Before any group project begins, get explicit written agreements that specify how responsibilities, financial rewards, and credit will be apportioned. This doesn't mean that you make others sign a contract. It doesn't mean that you have to call in the head of human resources or your attorney. It does mean that you are instrumental in getting discussions going about roles that will be played and how the spoils will be shared. You can then get it in writing yourself, through memos or e-mails that *you* write and send.

Here's how to do it. After meetings and discussions, be the so-called secretary who writes down what was discussed—focusing on any pertinent information that will protect and credit your contribution. Circulate e-mails to everyone who was there. Send to higher-ups or to clients any relevant big-picture information that you'd like to be sure gets noticed, which will keep them current on what you and your team are up to. Additionally, always, always—make that always—write down what is said in meetings and date it. Relentlessly document. Write down the time and date of someone's voice mail, if it's an important one. Save all of your documentation where you can easily find it, even if you don't need it for a year or two. It doesn't have to be fancy. Just make sure you keep a record of what you did that worked. Facts and dates and numbers are hard to argue with if you find yourself playing hardball with another contender.

Follow Up

Follow up any communications, phone calls, meetings, or information sharing using multiple channels. If you e-mail someone to
update them on a project in progress, say in the e-mail that you're
also going to leave them a quick voice mail. And then perhaps you
also drop by their office, pop your head in for two seconds, and
make sure they got the information. If you see them at a meeting
and exchange an idea, tell them you'll drop them a note or give a
quick call later that day to follow up. If you receive an e-mail and
respond, don't assume the person received your reply; it could get
lost or overlooked. Follow up with a phone call. Joy Machelle
Williams, senior director of sponsorship development for ESPN,
told me that she always uses this strategy because "you never
know how someone processes or takes in information; some people take it in through hearing it; others have to see it in writing to
absorb it." In your multiple-channels-of-communications approach, say things like, "I'm just following up with this e-mail to
make sure my understanding is on target and we're on the same
page. And I'll also leave you a quick voice mail to make sure you
got the message." You get the personal touch when you drop by
someone's office or the coffee bar or run into them in the lunchroom and ask, "Did you get my message about the great news
concerning . . ." Tip: Whatever the message, be as brief as possible; I mean bare-bones. People are busy; they aren't going to listen to a rambling voice message. They aren't going to scroll down
through even a paragraph in an e-mail; sum it up in the subject
line and then start your brief message with "FYI."

Never assume someone is ignoring you or got your message
but didn't return your phone call or e-mail because they aren't interested. I see women do this all the time—they assume the worst.

"He didn't respond to my e-mail or voice mail; it's been five days. That can only be a bad sign." They stay silent and fail to follow up, and then miss out on credit opportunities when they find out after it's too late that the person never received their earlier communication. Sometimes people are just too busy, and a gentle prod can dislodge the answer you're looking for. Don't assume you've been rejected.

Make it easy for people to get back to you. Always state your phone number twice when you leave a message, even if you think they already have it. Include your contact info in e-mails.

Practice Your Penmanship

Learn the nuts and bolts of writing press releases and query letters so that you can get your name and advice in print. Learn to write articles, books, tip sheets, and briefs that have wide appeal and circulation potential. How do you do that? Former journalist–turned–PR expert Joan Stewart has excellent resources at www.thepublicityhound.com. Also check out Dan Janal's wide range of quality PR offerings at www.janal.com.

Write articles for your team or company newsletter or intranet bulletin board. Or step up to chair a publication for your firm or a periodical for your organization. If you're not a natural writer, you can collaborate with those who are. See to it that this gets circulated company-wide, to clients, journalists, friends, and others. (Of course, if your company has strict public relations requirements, you always partner with that department—meaning get the okay—to make sure that you're in compliance.) If you're writing an executive summary, report, or article on a project you spearheaded, make certain you name yourself as chair or whatever title was yours. Own it; don't leave it off of the report for fear of bragging. If someone else is writing the report, let them know you want to take a look before the distribution of the report, and make sure your name (spelled correctly) or title is included and listed in a prominent place. If your name has been omitted, let the author know politely, but authoritatively, that you want it corrected and insist on seeing and approving the final version before it goes to press. Follow this up with an e-mail repeating what you expect.

E-mail colleagues and bosses with information gleaned from a professional conference you attended, chaired, or spoke at. Just drop one juicy industry tip or statistic you learned at the conference—one line, even in the subject heading. Even if they don't read the e-mails, they'll see your subject line—succinct and eye-catching—and your name will remain at the top of their minds, keeping you creditworthy. Follow up verbal suggestions with a written memo summarizing your ideas and recommendations for turning goals into results. Copy everyone who should also know about this information—your great idea. Be pithy, but specific; spell it out—how much money will be saved, or how much will be turned into performing assets, and so on. After a meeting, e-mail everyone who attended with a brief summary of your contributing points and copy anyone who should know that you're the author of these ideas. Save all e-mails and memos that back up agreements and important communications for your KaChing! File, and to prevent credit theft because you're blazing your paper trail and documenting your creditworthiness.

Consider hiring a publicist and creating a PR campaign, or learn to handle your own publicity. Keep your name out there to let others know that you are a consummate pro and that they should seek you out for expert advice, consulting, and business opportunities. Check out these cutting-edge resources: www .PRLeads.com, www.WomensRadio.com, www.eReleases.com, and www.Factiva.com.

Give to Get

One of the secrets of being a successful ambitchous woman—
someone who doesn't make enemies (and remember, this doesn't
mean everyone has to like you)—is that, by and large, your team
and the people who work with you like you. They like you because
you treat them like human beings. And because you find a way to
communicate and make them believe that they are adding value to
the business proposition.

So, one strategy for getting credit is that you develop a reputation as someone who is focused on the team. This may be a bit
counterintuitive—because it's not directly about getting credit
from your boss. Yet being the kind of respectful, strong leader
who praises and recognizes her team, and who sets the bar high
not only for herself but for those who work for her, means that
you do, in fact, end up getting credit—precisely because you've
built team loyalty. Trust me: credit will gravitate to you through
this method of recognizing others who support your—and your
team's—success. Here's how to make this work.

Example scenario: You're working on a deal and there's a problem. You and your team are preparing for a call with a client.
You're kicking around ideas; people have different thoughts,
approaches—some are good, some are bad, some are close, some
are not so close. And sometimes the junior person will come up
with a really good idea that's a big bridge to solving the problem.
You're the leader and you're the one who will be on the phone
with the client and with all the big muckety-muck power brokers.
Your team will also be participating. If you get to a point that re-
lates to the associate's (let's call her Chandra) great idea, you say,
". . . and this was Chandra's idea," rather than embracing it and
taking credit for the idea yourself. That builds enormous loyalty
below. Why?

Typically, the senior person leading the conference call or meeting or pitch will take credit for any ideas. So by attributing the idea to the lower person, you give that lower person credibility with the client or the boss; and you're also communicating to the subordinate that you see the value she or he adds and recognize her or his talent and potential. You communicate to the team that you're not a bitch, you're ambitchous. It's just a great strategy all around.

Orchestrate Celebrating Wins

Take a look again at Adrianne, who successfully led the charge by orchestrating a highly competitive, complicated transactional process of gunning for the new deal. There is something she should have done to get credit for her role, and you, yourself, should do it too: officially celebrate. You've headed up what's been a group process with a lot of different people doing a lot of different things, and you win (*you* as in all of you). Now you should celebrate in order to ritualize—officially recognize—your team's and your company's win.

How and when? You should do it with after-work drinks, or a dinner. It doesn't have to be a fancy restaurant—any steakhouse or local place your company patronizes will be great. It could even be as simple as a toast in the conference room at the end of the day. Organize whatever you can as soon after the win as possible, while your team is still experiencing the afterglow of a fabulous job well-done.

And—this is key—you should invite the boss. So obviously, make sure you schedule the event after you've made sure your boss can make it. And make sure you forward an e-mail to him or her, and your team, to save the date—even if the date is the next morning for a working breakfast.

You should lead the celebration because you led the team effort and you'll be telling the story of the win. And, yes, you need to be able to fill up a room in order to get full credit for your value. Happily, most of what allows you to fill that room involves authenticity coupled with your specific professional skills and substantive knowledge. For example, don't feel pressure to suddenly be formal when you're opening the toast or dinner. Instead, focus on what makes you feel the most empowered. Is it starting off with a joke? Is it launching the occasion by suggesting you all start with a cheer? For example: "Okay . . . ready? Everybody . . . *yay!*" Something that simple can get it rolling—and you're filling the room, the role. Commanding a room has a lot to do with projecting comfort and the ability to communicate and be at ease, along with the ability to work together collaboratively. And, obviously, the ability to get others to feel at ease and start being themselves so that they will talk, joke, and bond professionally even more.

Now—building on developing loyalty from below, it will be even better if the people who are involved like you. Why? If they do, they naturally do a lot of the credit-taking dirty work for you. How? They're talking, storytelling, joking, and laughing, and singing your and your team's praises. It happens naturally. Once you've created that celebratory environment and that team loyalty, your subordinates, your team, will do what you've modeled for them—specifically, they're going to give you credit and talk about how you led the charge and specific things that you did to make this win happen.

And by the way—you don't have to be the boss to organize such an event; you can suggest it to your supervisor, who might think it's a fabulous idea and say, "Great! Go for it! Let's do it." So if you're a junior person, step up and make this happen when you can—especially if your boss or other senior people aren't doing it. Make yourself look good, like someone who has energy.

Ambitchous Course Correction

"Oh, My God! I Could Never Do That!"

You may be thinking, "Wait a minute—it seems presumptuous to set up a celebratory dinner or toast; I don't feel comfortable doing that." Or "I'm only a junior person—I can't offer to organize and lead a celebration." Correction: Yes, you can do this. And it may even end up feeling like second nature to you once you recognize that you already have the skills to do it and need only to learn to transfer this talent to your work role.

You're already skilled at this in your personal life—community building. Believe me, if you can manage a birthday party of fifteen six-year-olds, to which the clown showed up drunk, you can handle this. If you can orchestrate a dinner to cheer up your friend whose divorce was finalized on the same day that her ex announced his engagement to his pregnant girlfriend, who is fifteen years younger than your friend's youngest child—hey, you can orchestrate a business celebration. But the difference is that those community-building skills—transferred to this business setting—are put to use bringing you the credit you've earned for your ambitchous goals and performance.

How'm I Doing?

To avoid looking like a jerk and also get buy-in and support—even from rivals—stay humble and open to improvement by asking for frank feedback from your peers, direct reports, supervisors, and clients. Asking others every so often for candid feedback gives you hard data about how you can improve your performance and your ability to be a contender. Give them two or three specific questions or areas you're seeking feedback on, and you'll be more likely to get a reply. This approach also gets some degree of backing from everyone you work with, even direct competitors: they see you as someone who is open to honest feedback and willing to change—all good attributes in building your contender image. Oh, and when you get great feedback, FYI—forward away. And KaChing! File it.

When it comes to being vetted, lead your own charge. Two months before you go in for your next salary review, look through your recent Ambition Journal entries and sift through your KaChing! File. Write up a one-page self-evaluation for your review. Include all the information from the period preceding each review that demonstrates your creditworthiness. This is like conducting your own performance review before the performance review. Do a bullet-point summary of wins, how you accomplished each one, the challenges you overcame, the decisions you made, the profit added, specific costs saved, and any benefits garnered through your direct contributions. Include opportunities that you didn't get to take on during this period—but that you're chomping at the bit to step up to. Include professional development you've invested in, what you've learned, and how you've strengthened your already solid leadership foundation. Why? Because, as Judy Johnson, executive vice president and managing director of the western region of GolinHarris, tells her employees, "Your own perspective on your strengths and weaknesses and all the tremendous things you've done for this company can be very different than your boss's view—and I want to hear what you have to say."

Visit www.amBITCHous.com to download free templates that you can use for your self-review. These templates include the following: projects completed; clients worked with; new business generated; contribution to the division's and company's bottom line (include specific dollar amount); training and development completed; contacts made; and opportunities on the horizon.

As you do your self-review, can you see how useful your Ambition Journal and KaChing! File are?

Be the In-house Information Broker

Send around periodic e-mails with a newsflash of something important in your industry that just came over the wires (FYI) or something you just found on Hoover's or read buried in the *Wall Street Journal* or the *Financial Times* or your industry publication, something that might not be so obvious. Send summaries of recently completed important team projects with a brief description of who handled which piece (sharing credit), obstacles that the team overcame and how, and the bottom-line fantastic outcome. Don't be shy about showing enthusiasm or talking about the rough spots and how people were, for example, stretched to their limits but prevailed. Sit with people in the lunchroom and don't be afraid to drop juicy facts that you learned at a meeting or conference or lecture you attended the night before. Being the one who tells the team and company stories—and remember, everyone, adult and child alike, loves stories—keeps your name out there. Being in the ring requires staying connected with others in your organization, even if they're in a different division, on a different team, or below you or above you in the pecking order. Stay visible and you'll stay a contender.

Women hate to feel that they're boasting. So storytelling is a great way to get around this. You tell the tale of why you deserve credit—without explicitly bragging. Especially when you've spearheaded a project or accomplished a difficult goal or solved a hairy problem, it's the perfect opportunity to sit down and say, "Hey, this was an important situation. Here's the story of what happened. . . ." You tell the tale, not in a self-congratulatory way, but in a way that makes it apparent, through the storytelling, through the narrative, that you've played a crucial role.

And wait, there's more! While telling the tale of the business adventure, offer a glimpse of your thought process—this weaves in an opportunity to showcase not only the decisions you made, but also smart, clever, alternative approaches you considered. Thus you are again letting the story speak for itself rather than boasting or knocking people out of your way. For example, you've told the story of how it played out, key decisions made along the way, and the outcome. Now you add other courses you considered: "Well, I considered handling it this way versus that way. . . ." (and give some brief specifics about your thought processes). Or, "I thought I might have managed this person this way rather than that way. . . ." Ask for feedback: "I considered going in direction such-and-such. Do you think that would have been feasible?" Leaving the door open for feedback about your decision tree builds in learning opportunities about other courses you might have considered and ways to improve how you handle your next challenging project.

Have Friends in Every Camp

A friend called me one day to tell me she had been awarded a national leadership award from a political party that wasn't her party. Should she accept? "Yes, absolutely," I said. Why? Because you have to have friends on both sides of the aisle. Because you have to think more strategically—not just about your personal ethics or what your colleagues will think. You have to think about what this recognition will allow you to contribute to broader goals, how it will enable you to accomplish what you want to see happen for the greater good, regardless of party. In my friend's case, she works globally with organizations all over the world and also plays a role with the United Nations. A myopic preoccupation with political parties might have blocked funding or collaborative opportunities that could benefit people all over the world; with this in mind, she decided to accept.

What does having friends on both sides of the aisle look like in a corporation? It means building relationships and alliances with people in other departments, divisions, and even competitors within your company, even with people working in competing companies. Of course, you're not going to share confidential, proprietary information or intellectual property with competitors. But you will run into these people repeatedly over the years at industry events, or conferences, or even socially—and it's perfectly fine to get to know these folks, stay in touch periodically, and stay visible in the industry network. It's a smart, strategic way to keep your name out there and your credit currency thriving. You never know when these efforts will pay off.

Accept Awards

All too often I see ambitchous women self-sabotage by refusing an award or title or leadership role for the following reasons:

- They don't feel entitled or worthy enough to accept such a nomination or role. For example: "I'm not really an expert in this area. They made a mistake. My colleagues would laugh. I'd be viewed as a braggart. I'm not up to the challenge."
- They overthink the politics involved and the potential motivation of the search committee. For example, "I'm not going to accept on principle. I know they picked me only because I'm one of the few women in this industry and they are just using me to make themselves look good." Or, "They just want someone from my political party in their lineup. I'm not going to play that game. And besides, what would my colleagues who share my politics think?"

- They want to avoid the spotlight. For example, "I don't want to have to give an acceptance speech in front of a thousand people—especially given that it's going to be televised."

They end up shooting themselves in the foot by doing so. I'm not talking about accepting an award from The Baby-Seal Killers of America for Gender Equality if your beliefs are pro–baby seal. But be reasonable, not reactionary.

Exploiting organizations' interest in recognizing visible women is a perfectly respectable way to keep yourself in the game. These days, companies and organizations want to be viewed as women-friendly. Sometimes the mandate comes from a sincere desire from the powers-that-be to recruit and develop ambitchous women. Or maybe the goal is to turn around a reputation of being unfriendly to women. Other times the motivation may be to undo a tarnished image after having been sued for gender discrimination. Or sometimes it is a public relations and investor strategy to become known as leaders in the race to attract and retain talented women:

> I was given an award—and it was an important award—from Columbia Law School. There was no question but that I wouldn't have received it if I weren't a woman. The award committee was, that particular year, looking to give the award to a woman alumnus; it was the seventy-fifth anniversary of the admission of women to Columbia Law School. I was in the company of some great luminaries, other people who received other awards. I didn't for a minute focus on the fact that it was because I was a woman. So what?
>
> —Judith Thoyer

Bottom line: It doesn't matter what the motivation is—exploit it. How? Be alert to companies or organizations that seek to appoint women to their boards or that wish to recognize women as award recipients. Nominate yourself. Ask someone else to nominate you. And by all means, if an opportunity falls into your lap, accept it with confidence and pride, knowing that you've earned it.

The Competitive Stance

This is business. And business isn't like some big commune where everyone is going to be friends and holding hands in a sun circle. It's not a place where you are den mother, where you have to process the minutiae of everyone's feelings. Business is a game. Business is a competition. It's not bad to compete. It's not bad to try to be different and better and more deserving of power and recognition without worrying about whether someone else is jealous or nursing hurt feelings because of your successes.

The reality in life and in business is that some people are better than others: some people are leaders, some are managers, some are decision makers, some people are born to go the distance—and other people aren't. They're followers, or they're just flat-out not as good as you are at the work you do. The fact that you act creditworthy at work doesn't mean that this marketplace posture has to translate to how you deal with the rest of your life. You can still be warm and fuzzy outside of work. But at work, strike a competitive pose.

Visualize yourself as being among the top earners in your industry. You are a contender. You make sure to get the credit you deserve. And as a result, you earn your worth. From today forward, don't limit yourself because you just can't quite see yourself as making not just more money—but a lot of money. Consider Barbara Corcoran's words of wisdom on this subject:

> I sold my business two years after it was ready for me to sell. I waited because I didn't feel comfortable getting several million dollars. I think it was because I had this sense that if I sold the business, I would be rich. And I worried what people would think of me if they thought of me as rich. So I had to get out of my own way in order to sell when it was right for me.

When Barbara did sell her company a couple of years later, media reports indicated that the selling price was about $70 million.

Barbara told me about going to an ATM machine after the sale and printing out a hardcopy of her account balance. She was "stunned seeing all of those zeros." She immediately phoned her mom, whom she credits with teaching her the most important lessons about being effective in business. Her mom congratulated Barbara and reassured her that it was just splendid to have all of that money.

Start today being okay with being a rich woman. Do not wait.

As a bright, capable, ambitchous woman, your job is to speak your mind when you've done your homework and have a strong opinion. You must learn to do this regardless of how powerful the boss or client you're dealing with seems to you to be, and regardless of whether or not you see yourself as a rookie. Show what you've got brewing in that big mind of yours. Your view may be the correct one. Your knowledge and great idea may be the one that ends up blowing away the competition. But you have to be willing and able to get in there, to challenge, to throw your ideas on the table, and even to interrupt, whether at group meetings or at a one-on-one meeting with your boss. Otherwise, how will you make it known what you know, what you've done, what your ideas are, and thus get recognition and remuneration for your contribution?

Now you're fit and ready to hurl yourself into the ring. You're going to stand out immediately as a serious contender. People will recognize your contributions. Watch how you start racking up credit, power, and money as you use your newly developed heavyweight muscles for getting in there and shining along with the best of them. When it is time to take your due, just own it. I promise you this: it feels great once you get the hang of it—and it only gets easier the more you exercise your credit-taking muscles.

seven

■ ■ ■ ■ ■ ■ ■ ■ ■ ■ ■ ■ ■ ■ ■ ■ ■ ■ ■

Am•BITCH•ous Rule 2
Get More Power from Powerful Advice

■ ■ ■ ■ ■ ■ ■ ■ ■ ■ ■ ■ ■ ■ ■ ■ ■ ■ ■

The single most important thing I learned through my participation in the Women's Business Alliance is that it's okay to ask for help.
—Barbara Weldon, chiropractor, Marin County, California

I'm a part of a peer advisory group. I call it my Dream Team.
—Andrea Henderson, thirty-seven, founder and executive director of The Basketball Academy in Newark, New Jersey, and managing director at Strategic Management Group, an executive search and diversity consulting firm in New York

THE majority of ambitchous women I've worked with over the years initially express a reluctance to ask for help or guidance. They don't pick up the phone or send an e-mail to ask for advice from people they know could brainstorm with them when they hit a tough professional problem. They don't spend the money hiring a lawyer or a certified public accountant to look under the hood of their business strategy and give them diagnostic information about what's working, what's not—and how they could be more effective and profitable professionally. If they hire an executive coach, they hide it; they don't ask their company for reimbursement even if they could get it. My male coaching clients brag about the fact that they have a coach; they definitely take advantage of any company benefits that would pay for their executive development work. If I meet them at their office to do our coaching session, they'll tell their friends and colleagues on the walk to their office, "Hey! I want you to meet my coach"; my female executive coaching clients wouldn't think of having me come to their office unless I promised to wear a disguise or say that I'm their cousin. And I thought it was the guys who were too stubborn to stop and ask for directions!

One twenty-eight-year-old investment professional now on partner track in a midlevel private equity firm described to me how she'd found it hard earlier in her career to ask for help: "I like to rely on myself to get something done. Asking for help is a very difficult thing for me to do." When I asked her to elaborate about why asking for help was hard for her, she had difficulty answering.

> I'm not really sure why. I guess partially because of a lack of confidence that the other person is going to respond in a way that's positive to my request for assistance. Also because only recently did I finally learn that asking for help was a smart way to be more effective professionally. Before then, I had it in my head that relying on my own merit without asking for help had always gotten me where I wanted to be, so why expose myself to looking foolish or weak by asking for someone else's advice?

The ambitchous woman's unwillingness to ask for help is rooted in this socially sanctioned self-sabotage:

Sheep's Clothing (overt message): Women should be self-sufficient—especially in today's marketplace. They need to present themselves as unwaveringly confident, tough, and equal in order to hold on to respect in the professional arena.

Wolf (covert message): Asking for feedback and advice exposes a weak, feminine underbelly. Asking for help is shameful, something to hide. It means they don't know their stuff.

Socially Sanctioned Self-Sabotage: You isolate yourself professionally. You believe your colleagues always know how to handle business dilemmas and you're the only one who needs help. You berate yourself for not having all of the answers. You don't take advantage of professional development opportunities—even those your company will reimburse you for—because you're ashamed or embarrassed. Or you don't invest the time, effort, and money into assembling unpaid or paid steering committee members to turn to for expert advice or feedback because you think you should be able to figure everything out on your own.

No Need to Reinvent the Wheel

From time to time, every ambitchous woman needs feedback and advice. We need a sounding board. If we don't ask, we risk putting ourselves through unnecessary work every time we attempt to advance our ambitchous goals. False pride stemming from the fear of looking incompetent only serves to slow us down professionally, financially, intellectually, and creatively. No matter how objective you try to be about your career decisions and strategies, you are going to be quite subjective simply because you are the subject. Others can always spot something about you and your situation that you yourself will miss.

Used effectively, a board of advisers can be a high-yield, cost-effective, and fast-track resource for advancing your professional objectives. Its sole purpose, from your perspective, is to educate and mentor you in your quest to open your horizons. The members can offer fresh and diverse perspectives as well as steer you in the right direction. It will dramatically increase your overall business acumen because its focus is geared to your specific career situation, it operates on your own level of knowledge, and it aims directly at your goals. It can quash a strategy that is headed over a cliff.

Strategies for Convening Your Advisory Board

Your initial task is to identify five to seven movers and shakers to advise you. You'll need to keep a few things in mind: They'll have to agree to advise you; you'll have to establish a relationship with them; they'll be the ones offering advice and moral support; and they'll be the ones you'll celebrate your thrilling wins with. The ultimate goal is to surround yourself with an uplifting, inspirational team. It may be just as rewarding for them as it is for you.

When assembling your first-round draft picks, make sure the people you select are smarter and more experienced than you and won't hesitate to tell you when you're headed in the wrong direction. Each person's expertise and knowledge should complement another's. By choosing people in varying professional areas, you will fill in all sorts of information gaps. Your goal is to create a group that can offer expert advice in as many professional areas as possible, depending upon your needs: leadership and performance development, management, business plan development, public relations advice, long-term strategic career planning, marketing, finance, strategies for profitability, budgeting, accounting, sales, customer service, or legal advice. Keep in mind, though, that for complicated and time-consuming legal and professional advice, you're also going to develop a second advisory committee of paid experts, including lawyers, certified public accountants, agent representatives, and others. People who are just smart are a dime a dozen. Select wise professionals with business savvy who are also aggressive movers and shakers. These are the people who can make things happen for you and can show you how to be more bold and creative. After all, your ambition is what these people love, or will come to love, about you. Don't be intimidated about approaching the best and brightest—even if you've never met them. What's the worst that can happen? They say no, you thank them, maybe ask for referrals to a couple of colleagues they know who might have the expertise and availability you're looking for. Don't forget this step.

And remember to write down all of these contacts in your Ambition Journal; write down the trail of who referred you to whom and when, or how you found a potential adviser through reading an article on him or her and in what publication, etc. Your list will grow over the years. And trust me, you will forget how you ended up on this person's doorstep, so document, document, document.

Ambitchous Course Correction

"Oh, My God! I Could Never Do That!"

You may be thinking: "I wouldn't even know where to start. Who would I call? I don't know anyone. What if they say no or humiliate me? I've lost touch with too many of my old colleagues; how can I contact them without being embarrassed that I dropped out of sight and am now only appearing to ask for assistance?" Correction: You *can* do this. Work through the following ten brainstorming steps in your Ambition Journal. You'll have your dream team in place in no time.

Identify Your First-Round Draft Picks. Then Recruit Your Team

1. You want people who will give you frank, hard-hitting advice, even when it may be tough to hear. This is a key reason you rarely or never have friends or family members on your steering committee. Though well-intentioned, they are too close to you to be objective, or their desire to protect your feelings will override their ability to give you accurate, wise advice.

2. Write down the areas of expertise you think you may need help with. Keep these in mind as you are compiling your candidates. Remember—you want your board to have diverse backgrounds and knowledge.

3. Think of the person you'd be most afraid to ask. Write him her or down.

4. List a second person you'd be almost as nervous to ask.

5. Who else do you find too intimidating to ask? Write down those names.

6. Think about whom you've lost touch with and are reluctant to contact now because it's been so long. Write down these names. This will jog your memory of other potential people you'd forgotten about.

7. Whom have you read about in the media who inspires you? Write down these names. No, you don't have to know them. No, it doesn't matter if they are high-profile—that's better, in fact.

8. Who would you never consider asking because they are too powerful or intimidating or, you're guessing, too busy, but who would be perfect for your team? Write down their names.

9. Go through your contacts. Which people pop up as ideal candidates for your board?

10. As you contact potential steering committee members, ask for and write down additional people they recommend and add them to your candidates list.

Start Contacting Your Candidates Today

Now, start phoning. Start e-mailing. Start talking to people face-to-face. Work your way down your list.

What do you say? If the person doesn't know you, but you've been referred by a mutual contact, start by reminding her of that referral person (who hopefully has e-mailed or phoned to say you would be getting in contact). Tell her very briefly who you are and what your job is. Did I just say be very brief? This bears repeating. Remember, to say that people are busy is always a colossal understatement, so keep it to one short sentence.

If you have a specific question, ask it succinctly; be crystal-clear about what you are asking for and how she can help you. If you get her voice mail, or if you are e-mailing, leave an even shorter, to-the-point message, including exactly why you're contacting her and how she can contact you.

Remember to leave your phone number twice; leave your contact info each and every time you contact this person, even if you've had an ongoing relationship with her for years by this point. I know I'm repeating myself, but I can't tell you how often highly accomplished women—and men—don't leave their phone numbers in a voice mail because they assume I have it handy. Dumb, dumb, dumb. Rarely am I going to take the time to dig up their contact info. And I might be traveling and without my database. Who knows? Also worth emphasizing: If you are e-mailing, always make sure that with each and every e-mail you use an e-mail signature that includes your contact info. Make it easy on people and they're much more likely to get back to you.

If you are calling a potential board member to ask for periodic mentoring, but aren't seeking immediate advice, tell him briefly who you are, what your job is, and one or two macrolevel bullet-point career goals. Keep these succinct, like sound bites. Simply ask if you might periodically contact him for a quick question. Say: "I know you're extremely busy. I also know that so-and-so (your mutual contact) has emphasized what an expert you are at what you do." Or you may say that you've read about her— mention the story where you got her name or the piece you saw her interviewed in. "I'm sure I could learn a lot from you. And I would love to occasionally contact you with miniquestions." We all have egos that enjoy periodic stroking. What better way than to serve on the board of an eager up-and-comer?

When to Wait to Contact Potential Advisers

It's easiest to get people on board if you contact them with a specific question or clear goals and a strategy rather than a vague request for mentoring or advising. With this in mind, you may want to compile your list, and then wait to contact people until you have a very specific question. Oh, and never, ever call someone and say, "I would love to pick your brain and ask how you got where you are." That's an automatic disqualification where most potential advisers, myself included, are concerned.

Sometimes you begin in a more organic way. You e-mail for a quote for an article or book you're writing. Or you phone to check a reference on a potential employee or to do some due-diligence digging on a company culture you're looking into. Or perhaps they even contact you first, a stranger out of the blue, for a piece of information or a quote. Then you keep their information, and maybe six months, maybe two years later, whenever and however it plays out, you get back in contact and ask for your piece of advice.

If you are contacting someone who is at about the same level as you in your industry, suggest that you might serve as each other's peer advisers as questions and issues arise.

If you are still reluctant to ask for help, consider this: in my experience, about seven out of ten people will be happy to share their knowledge because they want to give back in some way, especially to someone in whom they feel invested—which will happen over time as you build a relationship with them, assuming you do it the right way. As for the other three, they might have reasons for rejecting your request that have nothing to do with you. Don't take it personally; just move on to more enthusiastic supporters.

Be Willing to Pay for Expert Advice—Line up That Team Now

> *I usually prefer to pay for my steering committee advice. It keeps it cleaner that way. And also I then don't feel like I have outstanding debt that I owe to someone, which can be hard to pay back, especially now, when I'm managing my demanding career and also parenting a one-year-old and a three-year-old.*
>
> —Janet Scarborough, Ph.D., forty-one-year-old licensed clinical psychologist, certified coach, principal of her own consulting firm

We all occasionally need legal advice or information from other professional service providers. Don't wait until your feet are to the fire to assemble your paid advisory committee. Make a list of providers you might need at some point: An intellectual property attorney? A transactional attorney? A bookkeeper? A certified public accountant? A computer/tech support person? A publicist or media trainer? A coach? An editor? A Web site designer and e-commerce team? A financial adviser? A marketing strategist? An agent?

Especially when you move higher and higher in your industry, you want to play like the serious contenders. You may be offered a high-powered position after rounds of vetting, and when your compensation package is on the negotiating table, you'll already have the contact information of an attorney or agent who can handle the contract and salary negotiations. Simply say, "At this point, I'm going to pass over the contract and salary negotiations to my representative," and you'll be able to say it with cool confidence, knowing that this is what the players in the big leagues do and that to do otherwise would actually undercut your credibility and bargaining position. Never tell them how much you're making at your current job. Let the experts do their work for you.

Start your list now. Start asking around—word-of-mouth referrals are best. And when you need expert advice, don't scrimp, don't hire a cut-rate service provider. Pay top dollar; investing in expert advice will save you time and money, and you won't end up having to fire an incompetent adviser.

Be Willing to Pick Up the Phone or Send an E-mail

Learning to deploy a team of expert advisers helps you kick it up a notch where your professional self-reliance, knowledge, and power are concerned. Look how learning this technique has empowered twenty-eight-year-old Lisa Taylor to achieve goals for herself and for her company and its investors:

> We ran into a snag with this particular investor's attorney and our company's attorney. And our attorney said, "Look, I can't get past this investor's attorney; the investor's law firm is not willing to fix this issue." So I went to my CEO, Deborah, and she said, "Well, I can't call this investor—you're the only one who knows him. So here's where you have to use your relationship skills to

make this happen." And I asked her, "Can I do that? Can I just call an investor and ask for help?" And she said, "Absolutely." So I called and explained to him what was going on and he said, "Yeah, let me talk to my attorney." And it was super easy. He fixed it, just like that. And Deborah said, "See—I told you."

I asked Lisa how having learned the skill of leveraging her steering committee has helped her with her ambitchous goals. Before answering, she first corrected me: "I'm still learning it!" Then she explained how getting into the habit of feeling comfortable turning to her network to ask for help has made her more effective:

It's definitely changed how I'll approach a problem. It's made it easier for me. Just yesterday we were working on this complex deal, and one of our investors is involved, and we had an issue come up that might affect this same investor. And so somebody said, "What are we going to do? How are we going to know what to do?" And I said, "Well, let me call Rick"—one of the investors I have a good relationship with—"and let me ask him what he thinks about it." And I don't know if even a year ago I would have so readily thought: "Oh, here, let me use this person that I have a relationship with to find the answer." And now I feel like I turn to that as a solution more often.

This willingness to ask for help builds on itself; it shores up your network and reciprocal relationships. As Lisa described it to me:

I've also found that it then is reciprocated—people are more willing to call me for a question. A couple of weeks ago, one of our investors called and had hired someone new to their team and said, "Hey, would you mind taking this person out to lunch to talk about your industry?" Our industry is pretty unique, and now he needed my help.

There's an added benefit to your professional self-esteem, credibility, power, and marketplace value. Having people feel freer to call upon you for your advice and expertise begins to neutralize your sneaking suspicion that you might be a fraud and strengthens your sense of competence. It also brings new people into your network—to exchange advice and resources with, or perhaps to hire, or to turn to for fresh perspectives on your own opportunities. You begin to see yourself as the real deal.

Active Sponging—Observe Mentors and People You Admire

I have so much respect for my boss—the CEO—and this firm. It's a fabulous place to work. And I'm her direct report, so I'm trying to actively sponge up everything that she does and pick up on strategy. And I try to just kind of feel her business and negotiating and client instincts.

—Christina, twenty-nine, junior associate,
leading New York architecture firm

Every meeting you're in, every interaction you have with a dazzling boss or peer or advisory member, is a chance to be a keen observer. Be a diligent student of what it is these people do that makes them so successful. Study their processes. Break them down. Dissect in your mind just how they handled a tough negotiation, corralled a meeting that was getting offtrack, defused an explosive client matter, handled a tough sales pitch, or closed a deal. What worked? What didn't work? Pay very close attention—this is your opportunity to gain more power by learning from powerful, brilliant people. Don't squander any opportunity. Reflect and take notes and then think some more about what went down after the fact. Ask questions whenever you have the chance to do so: "What made you decide to take that course of action with that employee?" "How in the world did you calm down that angry client?" "What were your decision points in constructing that winning pitch?" People like to have their egos stroked—and asking questions shows that you admire their skills and expertise. And many folks like mentoring and teaching and grooming a talented employee or peer. Don't be shy about asking for information. You'll get powerful insights—and demonstrate that you are a serious contender.

Conducting a Group Steering Committee Meeting

Some people prefer a live individual or group steering committee meeting. When thinking about how to conduct a live board meeting, be sure to set it up so that it is a pleasant experience for everyone involved. If it is a group meeting, you can arrange for a one-hour conference call. If you don't have conferencing capabilities on your phone, you can arrange to rent a bridge line for a very small fee. This is a number you use once, or only for the time you rent it; your committee members will have to phone in long distance if they are geographically diverse, but you can thank them later with a fabulous gift or some other sort of payback.

Some people prefer to take their board members out for a working breakfast, lunch, or dinner, individually or as a group. Splurge on a top restaurant with a private meeting room. In exchange for commanding their undivided attention for the couple of hours that the meal lasts, your contribution is to wine and dine them. They will enjoy the food, the company, and the intellectual stimulation, as well as the knowledge that they're mentoring a high-aiming protégée. You will, of course, benefit from their pool of wisdom and knowledge. Within only a few hours, you will be amazed at the gold mine of fresh, innovative ideas you've amassed.

If you are doing a conference call, purchase in advance a simple, inexpensive telephone recording device that can be hooked up to any nonportable phone and plugged into a tape recorder (check to see if your tape recorder requires an adapter). Be sure you ask permission to tape your conference call; explain that you want to be free to focus on the meeting rather than trying to scribble everything down. If you are having a live meeting, bring a battery-operated tape recorder to record the entire session. Note: Don't forget extra batteries and blank tapes if you're using a nondigital recording device. Practice beforehand so that you can seamlessly record your meeting. Tape recorders are also useful over working meals. People talking over wine and food have a tendency to get offtrack, so you have to be prepared to pull the conversation gently back to the subject whenever necessary. It is in your best interest to brainstorm with the others, not sit there like a potted plant. While someone is talking, questions and ideas will spring to mind. Don't interrupt; jot them down on a notepad and bring the subject up later.

Another step in the preparation process involves mapping your own informal business plan in advance and making copies for everyone on the board. The plan is a written summary of short-term and long-term objectives and ideas, goals, concerns, and dilemmas. This kind of preparation will spare you from wasting valuable time being tongue-tied, confused, or directionless. You don't want to head into your meeting announcing, "I have a big problem. So, what do you think?" and then leave it wide-open for comment. The more you are able to identify in advance what you are specifically looking for, the more precise the advice will be. With your business plan in the board members' hands, you will be free to focus the meeting and maximize precious time. Then, except for necessary questions and comments, just listen attentively. Take in the rich pool of brainstorming, expertise, ideas, cautionary tales, encouraging words, excitement, and inspiration that will erupt with the free-flowing passion of a think-tank environment.

In the weeks that follow, return to your audiotape and notes frequently, especially during transitions or planning phases. This process may sound repetitive, but it isn't. Each pass-through will yield additional information that you may not have absorbed yet. Also, different ideas will resonate more strongly at different times, depending on the goal or dilemma you are currently facing.

In addition to the live board meeting, you can build in longer-term and more consistent contact. Ask your advisers if they are amenable to periodic e-mails or phone check-ins, during which time you can succinctly ask for clarification of fine points; you can also keep them up-to-date on your progress or ask for their counsel on new barriers to your career advancement.

Reconvene your board meeting quarterly. Think of it as your own mini-M.B.A. crash course that will keep you on an ongoing career education track. The information gathered during these meetings shortens the time between the inception and the implementation of your professional objectives and business ideas. And the people on your board will not only enjoy themselves, but will often walk away with new information to help them advance their own careers or to disseminate to other protégées. You're creating a win-win situation, solidifying professional contacts, and building new friendships that may last a lifetime.

Don't forget to give your board members "bonuses" at the appropriate times—a handwritten thank-you note (e-mails don't count), a nice bottle of wine, or a grander gift in recognition of your achieving a grander goal.

When in Doubt, Don't Act Before You've Contacted at Least Two—Preferably Three—Board Members

Always speak to at least two, preferably more, board members before taking action—especially when the stakes are high. Clear your head. Wait to hear back from advisers you weren't able to reach; delaying making a move for a day isn't going to make a difference in many cases, and you'll be armed with more ammo. Or you can have someone else—an attorney or other representative—step in for you and handle the situation, which frees you up from the stress of dealing in an area out of your realm of expertise.

Forget "Yeah, But . . ."

Remember the young protégée in the mentoring group who countered every recommendation with, "Yeah, but here's why I can't do that"? I've seen this dynamic in countless Women's Business Alliance meetings and workshops with women. There's no faster way to turn off interest in giving you advice than to outright reject and close your mind to the opinions of those who are taking the time and making the effort to help you. Even if you disagree with what they are saying, even if their advice may be hard to hear, keep your mouth shut and listen. Think about what they have to say. Force yourself to ask yourself hard questions about why you are being so resistant to their perspective. Often, it is the most dead-on recommendations that we initially recoil from. Pay attention to your defensive reactions and be willing to peel away some of your pessimistic or negative attitudes and you might find a pearl of an idea that you otherwise would have thrown out without further consideration.

Know When to Fire a Board Member

One interviewee told me this story. Randi, forty-four at the time we spoke, told me that she'd had as one of her first mentors a very prominent tenured professor she'd studied under at the Ivy

League M.B.A. program she graduated from. When Randi was thirty years old, she was working at a miserable job as the vice president of product development at a small private software company in Austin, Texas. She was then offered an amazing opportunity with a publicly traded company, one of the industry heavyweights in Silicon Valley. She was offered the job to launch a product line and lead it. She was to receive double the salary she was currently making, stock options, a bigger title, and moving costs. When Randi phoned her adviser, one of the most powerful people in her academic circle, to tell her the good news, the woman said to her, "It'll be tough to make back all that money. I don't think you should do it. It's too much exposure, too much risk. You're better off where you are." Randi described to me how, after she'd initially panicked, she mentally fired this woman from her board. She took the job and it launched her career. I pointed out to Randi that this woman was a saboteur. She said:

> Absolutely she was a saboteur, but you can imagine how I was fooled. I was twenty-seven when I met her, and she seemed to take me under her wing. I was so flattered to have such a powerful woman seemingly behind me, you know?

The lesson: Know when to give someone the boot—even if they are a powerful industry leader. In my professional life, I've made sure to surround myself with people who are supportive and who are not trying to bring me down. There are definitely people who, truth be told, behind their smiling personas, do not have our best interests at heart. You need to learn to walk away from them, literally or figuratively.

We've covered proactive ways you can take credit for yourself by building a credit platform, plus strategies to get the recognition you deserve by learning to be a real contender in a competitive work environment. We've talked about getting power by tapping the support and wisdom of heavyweight advisers. Now you're ready to get your hands dirty. In the next chapter, we're going to tackle the icky stuff that's probably going to make you cringe, like what to do when all else fails and you have to bust a bald-faced liar or a jerk. I'm going to teach you how to do the odious deed am-bitchous women most hate doing—confronting people.

eight

Am•BITCH•ous Rule 3
Don't Be Afraid of Confrontation

■ ■ ■ ■ ■ ■ ■ ■ ■ ■ ■ ■ ■ ■ ■ ■ ■ ■ ■ ■

OKAY, what if all of this lovely advice and the best-laid plans don't work? Sometimes getting power, respect, money, or credit that belongs to you doesn't work out like a polite British tea party, no matter how hard you've tried to be fair-minded and strategic. So, what if some unscrupulous person—or persons—flat-out lies or sabotages you?

The short answer is: it depends. It's always situation-specific. Sometimes you let it go. Sometimes you talk behind their backs, letting it be known to others what really happened. Often it's usually someone who's known for doing this sort of thing, so no one is surprised.

But sometimes you have to bust the person. Even if it goes against every fiber of your being, you've got to take them to task. Consider Rachel's story.

Rachel, thirty-nine, joined a company as chief financial officer (CFO). She found herself in the midst of a situation common to small, fast-growing companies, where several people rise up through the ranks but do not have the skills for the jobs. Being a seasoned veteran, Rachel came in expecting her team to behave the way people with their job titles would normally behave. This was highly threatening to Rachel's new direct reports because they were used to doing things the easy way rather than in a complete, thorough manner. And this was in the pharmaceutical industry, where that type of shoddy work ethic could get the company in a whole lot of trouble; the compliance laws demand that the work be done right—or the regulatory agencies will shut you down.

Her staff began trying to get rid of her. They were undermining her on multiple fronts: by complaining to human resources (HR), by taking the CEO out for drinks and talking about her, by being disrespectful to her face in team meetings and in one-on-one interactions.

By the time Rachel came for coaching, the CEO was pretty convinced that she needed to be fired. But the more she related to me these stories about what was going on at work, the more it became clear to me that these employees were out to get her. She'd had a very good track record with previous companies, and she was very competent. Yet she was becoming more unsure of herself than she'd ever been. She was having a crisis of confidence. The CEO had already told her straight out, "If you don't turn things around, you're out of here." And HR was leaning on her as well. She was being called a micromanager, when everything she was asking these employees to do seemed reasonable to me.

In her coaching work, she found her center again and became confident that she was not micromanaging or being unreasonable. What she ultimately came to realize was that she wasn't the wrong CFO; she had the wrong staff. Of making this discovery, Rachel said: "That was very hard for me—because I did not ever want to fire anybody. I always thought you could mentor and rehabilitate and develop." My message to her was, "Hire for attitude; train for skill. If the attitude isn't there, you do not want to keep investing all of your time, because frankly these people are out to get you."

Rachel started to clean house selectively. She hired people who were willing to step up, willing to do their jobs the right way.

Unlike Rachel, who did a one-eighty and began to get comfortable firing back, I've seen many women wait until it's too late. Why? Because they avoid confrontation at all costs. Evidence abounds that a woman is being gaslighted—meaning people are hiding their true intentions and acting in sleazy, manipulative ways to cause her to begin doubting the reality of her perceptions. It would be apparent to any objective observer that people are trying to sabotage her at work. Even in the face of this, all too often she is reluctant to challenge destructive or counterproductive behavior; her self-confidence and sense of competence are eroded by her environment. The crowning humiliation may be losing her job, her financial security, the respect of her industry peers, and her self-respect.

The ambitchous woman's unwillingness to stand up to people who are out to get her is rooted in this form of socially sanctioned self-sabotage:

Sheep's Clothing (overt message): There is usually a civilized way to deal with a conflict. Women should exhaust all peaceable measures before calling into question the negative behavior of others. It is important for a woman to give people the benefit of the doubt, to give second chances, to see the best in people, and to try to help them to change rather than face off with them.

Wolf (covert message): Resorting to a showdown is akin to launching an unwarranted attack on someone who might not really be as bad as they seem to be. Confrontation is uncivilized and counter to womanly values.

Socially Sanctioned Self-Sabotage: You doubt yourself and the objective evidence alerting you to what is really going on. You ignore how it is hurting you professionally and from a mental health perspective. You wait too long to take action. You risk losing your job. Your credibility, your reputation, and your earning capacity may end up compromised.

At work, people have their own little area or territory. It's marked off just like it is in the wild. If some person passes over into your area inappropriately, you're going to react aggressively—and you should. How to tell when the line has been crossed is very situation-specific, so it's hard to lay out hard and fast, black-and-white rules. But if you have to knock someone upside the head and set the record straight, here's how to do it without being a bitch.

Busting a Credit Thief

A legal team is doing due diligence on a company before an acquisition. This due diligence involves teams going out and really kicking the tires of a business, which may require sitting in some windowless conference room in Toledo, Ohio, or spending endless hours on the Internet. The whole point of that exercise is to identify issues that determine the right valuation for the acquisition. You're basically trying to identify problems—things that could mean that the company isn't worth so much. The seller is not required to point out the problems, so the onus is on the buyer to figure it out. So you have teams of lawyers to investigate.

Then there's an internal meeting (no clients present), where they present their findings to the partner (their boss) so that the partner can decide what's important, what's not so important; what to tell the client, what not to tell the client. Say you're in this meeting and one of your peers blurts out to the boss, "I uncovered this critical piece of information that's going to be a deal point."

You know it was you who busted your butt to dig up that arcane piece of law, not the jerk who just tried to steal your thunder. In this situation, what would you do?

Here are a few options, assuming that the stealing of your idea or contribution was significant enough that it mattered to make it into a confrontation. I would recommend doing one of two things, depending on the dynamic of the room and the nature of your relationship with everyone present.

You should either say right then and there, in that meeting, in a matter-of-fact, firm—but nonhostile—way: "Wait a minute; that's just not what happened," even briefly laughing while you say it. Communicate with your tone in a respectful but authoritative way that it's ludicrous to suggest that the would-be credit thief was the author of that idea. Say it publicly, with a calm, matter-of-fact tone.

And if it doesn't feel right to you, for whatever reasons, to do that, then you should tell the boss afterward. Go in and say succinctly, nondefensively, "That wasn't true; here's what happened." And I would add, "Look, I don't want to make too big a deal of this, but I think it's important to let you know that this is the way it happened. It just didn't feel right to me that it was presented a different way at the meeting. And I wanted you to know. Thanks." Or: "I was surprised to hear Jack say that he uncovered that information. Actually, it was me who handled that." Then get out of there. Don't linger. Don't process. Remember—it's business, not a therapy session.

Keep in mind that if you've followed my advice and built loyalty with your subordinates, colleagues, and boss, people will know your track record and trust your integrity. So in those rare instances where you do have to set the record straight, you've already minimized your risk of sounding like a whiner with a chip on your shoulder, because you've worked hard to establish your professionalism and ethical way of doing business.

Weigh When, Where, and How to Bust a Jerk

It's all about tone. And it's all about choosing the right time and place, and not just letting it go when you should be sticking up for yourself. It's about calm, mindful strategy, and feeling strong enough inside to make these determinations on the spot—and then not berating yourself afterward for having had the balls to do what you did.

Here are a couple of example scenarios to add to your mental repertoire:

If you were in a meeting and a decision had to be made within, say, an hour, I wouldn't recommend saying something then and there; the focus of that time-sensitive meeting can't be on your individual issue. It has to be on the broader goal of meeting the deadline and getting the right answer. So you'll deal with theft later.

But if you're sitting around a couple of days before in an internal meeting and time isn't of the essence, and somebody says something false, respond to this credit theft right then and there. Use a firm tone, not hostile. Be direct and honest. On *Everybody Loves Raymond*, the characters spend a lot of time fighting. They say really hostile stuff. But the actors are aware of tone—it's always confined so that it doesn't make the characters, or the viewers, feel that it's vicious. Use your voice and your intonation to say things that are very biting, or critical, or confrontational, but in a way that doesn't make people recoil. You have to say it without feeling or conveying intense irritation.

Here's an example. Use the person's first name—the person who has just blatantly tried to steal your credit. "Bill . . . what, are you kidding me?" Or: "Are you nuts?" Or: "Come on!" Then, especially when it's really clear, follow up your biting-but-comical-edged comment with a phrase like this: "*You* know"—chuckling again for emphasis—"that *this* is what happened. And let's not get distracted—let's keep the meeting focused on getting the right decision. But, come on!"

Don't Repeat Yourself, Don't Ask for Backers—You'll Look Defensive

So whenever you must confront someone, your goal is simply, declaratively to say, "No, that isn't what happened," and then move on. Don't linger on the conflict. Don't repeat yourself. The best way to get people to listen to you, and to pay attention to you, is to say as little as possible and to make whatever you do say really f____g count.

Here's the next important strategy to add to the mix. You've engaged and said, "Come on!" or whatever you've said with the right tone. Now, if there are other people in the room, do not say, "Isn't that right, Jon?" Or "Isn't that right, Ann?" Seeking affirmation from others in the room makes you look defensive. And what's worse is that it puts others on the spot, which is never a good strategy. When it comes to really successful people, they state the facts. They make the point, they make it quickly, they say it *once*, with conviction, and that's *it*. The more it's repeated, the more it undercuts you. If you can say it the right way once, and if you have the attitude and all of the ingredients above, you're going to be more capable of getting the credit you deserve.

Think about How You Confront People You're Comfortable With

Here's another way to think about setting someone straight in a work environment. If you were with a close friend, or your husband, or your sister, and he or she said something to you one on one, or in front of a group of family or friends, that was clearly bulls__t, how would you respond? What if your teenage son told some story that just clearly misstated something? How would you react? What would your tone be when you responded to what the person had just said? You wouldn't feel defensive or threatened—you'd give it to them straight and then get off it, right? You might say, "What, are you high?" Something like that. That's the right kind of tone to set. You're not being emotionally reactive or volatile. But you are letting it hang out a bit. So they've said something absurd. You respect this person, love them even, but you're communicating that they've just said something that's ridiculous or insulting. It's that kind of authentic, direct reaction that will guide you in getting your tone just right in a business confrontation. Go with your gut in a social setting. Then quickly segue to a succinct, declarative statement about what really happened: "You know I was reading the contract that had that problem in it, not you," or "I was the one who gave the client X advice, not you," or "I was the one at the meeting who came up with the idea." And if that's true, and if you're surrounded with other people who were there and who know the truth, then they will respect you for calling the person on it.

But if it's just you and the other person who know what really happened, then it's riskier. So that's another thing to consider as to whether you confront somebody then and there or if you wait to do it later.

Don't Avoid Confrontation Because You Fear You'll Make an Enemy

Maybe you're reluctant to confront. Maybe you're thinking, "If I bust someone, doesn't that mean I compromised my integrity? And made an enemy?" No. When a person attacks you and you protect yourself, and that angers or offends the attacker, you haven't made an enemy—the attacker has created this situation, not you. And you've preserved your integrity by protecting, rather than compromising, yourself.

Don't Avoid Confrontation Because You're Being Ganged Up On

Deciding to confront can be even harder for a woman when she is being ganged up on—especially when those ganging up on her are attacking her by suggesting that she is being emotionally reactive or acting out of fear or psychological baggage. Jackie, thirty-eight, a senior executive in the biotech industry, was ambushed by a board that wanted to make a very risky financial decision without consulting either a transaction attorney or a certified public accountant. When she raised the warning flag of "Hey, this could be bad," the board members piled on and said, "Oh, we know how conservative and fearful you are." They made her professional prudence into an emotional-baggage issue. But because there were so many of them and only one of her, she faltered a bit and thought, "Is this really a fear-based concern on my part? Am I not willing to take the big financial risks to get big financial returns?" And this caused her some anxious hours until she had a coaching session. The advice? Insist on a transaction attorney and a CPA. Insist that this board should not be making huge financial decisions without due diligence. Jackie realized that the fact that they were rushing to do so made it suspicious. And so, after the coaching session, she decided to stand her ground, and she insisted that they run it by the appropriate financial professionals.

It's hard for women to stay centered in the face of being belittled, particularly by a group. It's easier for them to feel that maybe there is some emotional thing going on that's keeping them from thinking clearly. Don't let this dynamic cause you to doubt your instincts, your expertise, or your willingness to confront.

Confronting Passive-Aggressive Jerks

Passive-aggressive behavior is one of the most difficult behaviors to call someone on precisely because it is indirectly hostile. Passive-aggressive people will never admit to what they've done.

Beat them at their own game; don't confront on their behavior—because they'll never cop to it. Instead, learn to pose questions geared to right a specific wrong. Deborah K., whose boss changed her time sheet and docked her pay for the amount of time it took Deborah to attend an award ceremony at which she was being recognized, confronted her boss about it. She said to her, "I turned in my time sheet this week and included the time I spent accepting my award at the breakfast conference, as you and I agreed I should do. Then I saw that you changed my time sheet without telling me. I should be paid for that time, and I wasn't, so how can we fix this?" Deborah's initial instinct was to avoid conflict, to avoid confronting her boss. Had she done that, she would have lost power and credit on many fronts—in terms of cold, hard cash and in terms of self-respect—and she would have even lowered her professional standing with her boss, who, on some level, knew that she'd put the screws to Deborah and deserved to be confronted. To save face, her boss pretended there had been an oversight. Deborah got paid what was owed her on her next check.

Sometimes the wrong you're trying to right is to get the passive-aggressive person to stop behavior that, unchecked, can undermine your ability to effectively lead or participate in a group meeting, or that can eat away at you if you don't know how to confront their individual nasty remarks. Here are a couple of examples of stopping passive-aggressive behavior in its tracks:

Scenario 1: Someone says something to discredit you, but in a veiled, indirect, passively hostile way: "Well, that was a waste of ten minutes" in a group meeting. Calmly say, "Why do you say that?" Or: "What makes you think that?" If he answers sarcastically or with other cynical remarks, calmly repeat, "Tell us more so we can be sure we understand why you are saying that." Or: "What specific data led you to that conclusion?" Won't this invite confrontation and criticism? Unlikely. More often, these jerks want to get themselves out of the hot seat quickly by backpedaling with something like, "Oh, I didn't mean it that way; forget it." Don't worry—if, for example, the jerk does come up with a rationale for why you just burned up ten minutes of his precious time, you've made him speak to the group, revealing his negative attitude. And if he does this, don't let it go on for more than a couple of sentences; simply interrupt, in a slightly amused, slightly sarcastic, yet upbeat tone (remember—no chip on your shoulder!) with something along the lines of: "Okay, then! Thanks for clearing that up for us. We must not have gotten the memo!" followed by a one-syllable chuckle and a dismissive shake of your head. Then, "All right! Let's move on. Clock's ticking."

Scenario 2: One of your direct reports has been stirring up trouble lately by spreading her sour attitude and hostile opinions of you behind your back. She's gone to HR to complain about how you micromanage, put undue pressure on your team, and are just, in her opinion, a lousy manager. You're leading a team meeting in which she, once again, mutters something under her breath. Rather than let it go by unnoticed, you say, using her name, "Sorry, Jane. We couldn't hear what you said. Could you repeat that please?" She'll likely say, "Nothing." You press her once more: "No, it must have been important if you said it. Go ahead. Let us know what's on your mind. We're interested." She'll say something like, "No, really, forget it." Then you move on. But each time she tries this behavior, you confront it right then and there. You can use slightly different wording each time you call her on it; she'll quickly lose interest in harassing you once she learns it's going to make her look like a jerk, because you're not afraid of confrontation and you will hold her accountable.

You should put passive-aggressive troublemakers on the spot rather than feel like dirt later for failing to call them on their thinly veiled attacks. Make them accountable for their hostility. Often, simply asking a direct, challenging question will cause the passive-aggressive person, who is basically a yellow-bellied blowhard, to back down.

Elegant, Subtle Strategies for Correcting Mistaken Identity

Let's say you find yourself in a situation where you need to set the record straight—and it must be done then and there—or you're going to lose. But you've got to tread lightly. For example, if your boss jumps up and appoints herself spokesperson for your baby and doesn't credit you as the driving force at a big meeting, what can you do? You stand up. Immediately. As soon as it's become clear what she's doing—don't sit there and wonder "Should I . . . shouldn't I?"—stand up! Extemporaneously join her—in a collegial manner, of course—in reporting on the challenges you and she—your boss—and the team encountered, and how you all tackled them, while moving this project to a successful conclusion. You will leave people with the unmistakable impression of the key role you played. If you handle it skillfully enough—for example, praising your boss, yes, your credit-thief boss, on specific roles she played and make her look good in front of this group of her muckety-muck peers and superiors—it will be hard(er) for her to drop the hammer on you later (unless she is just a complete jerk, in which case it might be time to start thinking about looking for a different job opportunity).

Still, you have to be prepared for retribution or backlash. It's happened to me, and it isn't fun. But letting my credit be stolen would have been way less fun—so it was worth it to stick up for myself. I once called a former boss on credit theft in a group setting, when my hand was forced. For three days afterward, she would stop by my office to say, "I admire that you stood up for yourself. I should have followed through on my promise." Then an hour later she'd be there again, saying, "I am outraged that you went over my head like that in that meeting! That was completely out of line." Then back twenty minutes later to say, "I have mixed feelings about it, but you did the right thing; you're a good role model. I wish I could have been so bold at your age and at this early stage of your career." Then an hour later: "I should fire you." I felt like I was watching Linda Blair's head spin around in *The Exorcist*. I just listened. I'd already done what I needed to do to protect myself.

There is always a possibility of conflict. If you hate friction and confrontation, you've got to fight the tendency to sell yourself short just to avoid them.

Sometimes You Leave the Environment

If you've exhausted all reasonable, diligent efforts to get the recognition and credit and money you're due, and have been thwarted at every attempt, it's time to start looking for new opportunities. Here's how Pat Lynch, CEO of Women's Radio, described her take:

> If I didn't already have a good enough relationship with the people that I work for, with my team, my boss, with my colleagues, where I could go and say the truth, then it would be time for me to leave and look for other opportunities where I would be valued

and given the respect and credit I deserve. Moving along. I don't believe in working in any location, in any environment, for any people with a lack of integrity.

If this time comes, and you determine it's time to move on, remember—don't come off as having a chip on your shoulder or appear to be arrogantly focused on self-advancement. Just know that sometimes you simply have to leave. And knowing when to do this for yourself, and trusting your instincts, is part of being an empowered, ambitchous woman.

nine

■ ■ ■ ■ ■ ■ ■ ■ ■ ■ ■ ■ ■ ■ ■ ■ ■ ■

Am•BITCH•ous Rule 4
Make 'Em Pay

■ ■ ■ ■ ■ ■ ■ ■ ■ ■ ■ ■ ■ ■ ■ ■ ■ ■

> *Women do two-thirds of the world's work. Yet they earn only one-tenth of the world's income and own less than one percent of the world's property. They are among the poorest of the world's poor.*
>
> —Barber B. Conable Jr., former president of World Bank

I CHAIRED a meeting of the Women's Business Alliance attended by Dr. Tania L. Weiss, scientist, president, and CEO of a leading biotechnology and pharmaceutical company. She recalled hiring two advance-degreed, equally qualified consultants: one man, one woman. The female scientist submitted her bill, querying, "I hope it's all right that I charged my ninety-dollar-per-hour fee?" Dr. Weiss replied, "Of course." The male consultant—with identical credentials—later submitted his bill for the same services, stating, "My fee is one hundred and seventy-five dollars per hour," to which Dr. Weiss replied, "Of course."

This is a theme I've seen countless times over the years:

professional women who are complacent about earning far less than the marketplace will bear for their level of skill and expertise.

Here's the life fulfillment mantra for this chapter:

I DESERVE TO EARN MY WORTH.
I WILL TAKE CONTROL OF MY OWN
ECONOMIC EMPOWERMENT.

I want this to be the touchstone message you tell yourself, whether you're still in high school looking at colleges and career options; whether you're a young woman in her twenties just starting out in a career or looking for your right career; whether you're in your thirties, forties, fifties, sixties, and beyond; single, married, divorced, widowed, with or without children; in your dream career, between jobs, going back to school for an advanced degree, still figuring out what you want to do when you grow up. Whatever life phase you find yourself in, I want your mind-set always to be: "I deserve to earn my worth and to feel independently in control of my financial situation and security at all stages of my life."

But in order to earn our worth, we have to feel entitled to make more money, and we must feel good about making a lot of money. This is a hard concept for many women to wrap their minds around. Would you answer true or false to the following statements?

- You've never visualized yourself as being wealthy, financially secure, and fully in control of your money, assets, and investments, no matter if you are single or partnered, and no matter what stage you are at in your career.
- The idea of earning a lot of money—as much as the highest earners in your industry earn, or maybe more—makes you cringe. It makes you feel greedy. Or morally bankrupt, because

money is tainted with incorrect values. Or you feel you aren't qualified to earn that kind of money.

• You don't know what the highest earners in your industry or profession earn.

• You have no clear sense of what the range of total compensation packages is for people with your training and expertise— including performance incentives, stock options, early salary reviews, and signing bonuses. You don't know how to go about finding this information.

If any of these statements mirror how you think about money and earning your worth, then we have some work to do. But don't despair; you're definitely not alone.

> I know I undercharge compared to my colleagues. It's just that they always seem like they know more than I do about being current on professional journals and the latest industry information. I have eight journals stacked up on my desk right now that I can't find the time to get to. You know what I think it is? The others don't really know more— it's just that they know how to drop a factoid here and there and appear as though they're really on top of things, when, truth be told, I know a hell of a lot more about this job than most of them.
>
> —Annabeth, thirty-four, Ph.D., Washington, D.C.,
> one of only one hundred board-certified
> experts in her specialty in the United States

> I tend to be a little nervous about charging what I think the job should be bid at, and it falls into two areas: I do a lot of work with women-owned start-up businesses, and I always feel as though I shouldn't be charging them huge amounts of money because they don't have the budget for it. Then I go into a larger organization, and I have that same sensation of not wanting to charge what I'm really worth because I'm afraid I'm not going to get the bid. It looks like so much money to me when I get to the bottom line—even though it represents a tremendous amount of hours and a whole lot of expertise that I bring to the project.

I look at those numbers, and I start to get really nervous—it doesn't feel like me; that money doesn't feel like me.

—Jacqueline, fifty, former computer engineer;
currently graphic artist and member of the
National Speakers Association

[For] what I do, I'm told I can charge two hundred and fifty dollars an hour. I say that, I know it for a fact, but it's very difficult for me to integrate that. I can manage saying to people that my fee is a hundred and twenty-five an hour, and I can almost manage to say it's one-fifty an hour. But to say two-fifty . . . I wonder who doesn't work with me because it's two hundred and fifty dollars an hour? Am I really worth that? What do I really know? I worry that I don't know enough. And I have an M.D. and a Ph.D. I am educated sufficiently for this work, but then I begin to imagine there isn't anybody out there who can afford me, that there's no marketplace.

—Jenna, thirty-one, single, licensed M.D., Ph.D.,
building her private practice while continuing
as a contractor at two hospitals

The word deserve *comes up for me: Do I really deserve this executive position, do I really deserve this fat salary, do I really deserve to make this amount of money? All that comes up. And the idea of puffing myself up—because I'm educated, I think this or do that—that somehow by saying who I am in order to sell myself in the marketplace . . . well, I don't like people who have overly inflated egos. So in order to not even get close to being labeled as someone who might be a person like that, I will understate who I am because I don't really want to do that.*

—Lauren, thirty-five, vice president for quality
improvement, large-cap, publicly traded
preferred-provider organization

One of the most common topics to arise, during my Women's Business Alliance and other women's conferences, centers on how an ambitchous woman demands to earn her worth: "How can I get comfortable negotiating a raise or a bonus I know I've earned?"

"How can I stand up to my boss and say, 'I'd like an accelerated salary review, given this quarter's results'?" "How can I get comfortable charging more money for what I do?" "How can I earn what I know I'm worth?" "How can I know just what I am worth?"

Women constantly tell me that they leave money on the table when negotiating, including backpedaling on a demand or point they've basically already won, or would have, if they'd kept their mouths shut. That's if they negotiate at all. They tell me all the time that they accept less money than a man doing an identical job, don't negotiate salaries, and are afraid to ask for more. According to economist Linda Babcock and journalist Sara Laschever, authors of *Women Don't Ask: Negotiation and the Gender Divide*, men ask for what they want twice as often as women do and open up negotiations four times as often. My executive coaching experience and interviews confirm that women still have enormous difficulty admitting and owning their own excellence—and this makes it almost impossible for them to demand they be paid what they're worth.

Why is this so? Because women are raised to believe that we're all equally deserving, and thinking that you're better than someone else—including that you've worked hard and should be paid well for the level of expertise you've achieved—is conceited.

Sheep's Clothing (overt message): Women see the good in everyone; they believe everyone is equally worthy.

Wolf (covert message): Seeing themselves as exceptional smacks of arrogance, even disrespect for others.

Socially Sanctioned Self-Sabotage: If you find yourself in a position of power, you feel like an interloper who doesn't deserve your place at the big table because, after all, there are so many other worthy candidates for the spot.

This generous outlook makes us women overlook our unique talents and capabilities and forces us into an ambivalent approach/retreat relationship with power. We want it, but when we get it, we back off out of guilt or fear. We then don't fully partake of the spoils of success; we don't hold ourselves out as experts, taking advantage of the publicity, marketing opportunities, and the higher salaries and fees that go with success and reflect our true worth.

My challenge to women is to recognize where you're stronger than anyone else and make 'em pay for it. To paraphrase George Orwell, all people are equal, or should be in certain regards; but in business, in the marketplace, some are more equal than others. That *some* includes you. This chapter outlines strategies for helping you recognize and own your unique abilities, enabling you to negotiate fees that reflect your true value.

REALITY CHECK
Am I Making 'Em Pay — or Giving It Away?

- Do you charge less than you know you're worth?
- Are you being paid a salary or total compensation package that you know is below industry standards, but you consider yourself lucky to have this position anyway, so you say or do nothing to correct the situation?
- If you're self-employed, do you raise fees with current and new clients at least once a year?
- If you work for someone, do you ask for yearly salary reviews? Or if yearly salary reviews are standard, do you ask for a six-month performance review?
- Would you have the guts to ask for a review at three months if you'd just delivered dazzling results that were directly responsible for boosting your company's (or division's) earnings unexpectedly for that quarter?

- If your boss holds out a carrot promising a promotion, do you check in regularly to ask, "How am I doing?," reminding him or her that you're gunning for it?

- If you received a raise or bonus that was far below what you knew you'd earned, would you challenge it by taking it up with your boss, or even going over your boss's head?

- Do you pass on referrals to colleagues rather than saying, "Hire me; I'm the best at what I do"?

- If you are a consultant, do you charge your fees up front?

- Do you take advantage of opportunities to position yourself as an expert who can command higher fees? Do you jump on chances to be recognized at industry meetings, in the media, or among potential clients?

- If you're attending a conference or a team meeting, and you have something you'd love to say or a question you'd like to ask, do you stand and speak up? Or do you keep your mouth shut because you prefer to fly beneath the radar when you're around colleagues?

- Do you write and publish articles, books, tip sheets, briefs, and so on, so that your expertise gets circulated among potential clients, colleagues, and industry leaders?

If your answers made you wonder whether you are comfortable being better than others at what you do professionally, and if your answers made you wonder if you're earning your worth, you're in good company. One top litigator, a partner at a top New York law firm, recognized among her peers as a superstar, echoed a theme I've heard countless times when she said to me that while she's perfectly comfortable negotiating "like a shark" for a client, or for anything that will benefit her firm, she has a very difficult time negotiating on her own behalf.

On a similar note, I've lost count of how many women over the years have told me that they'd be willing to fight to the death on a matter involving their child, but they roll over immediately if they're fighting for money to put in their pocket. Marilyn, a twenty-seven-year-old who has her master's in psychology from the University of California, Berkeley, came to me for advice because she found that she was reluctant to negotiate for a three-month salary increase that she and her new-hire boss had already agreed upon at the time of the interview. She said, "It makes me feel demeaned to have to be at the mercy of his authority to say yes or no, so I'd almost rather not even bring it up."

The Cumulative Effect of Seemingly Insignificant Decisions Costs Us Big-Time

In cognitive therapy, there's the well-known concept of seemingly insignificant decisions: you make one decision after another and they add up to a huge decision. So you decide, "Oh, I'm not going to negotiate that salary they offered because it seems fine—and besides, I don't like to negotiate." Or: "Sure, I'll cut my rate for that client; it's better than risking losing the project." Or: "I have no idea what my value proposition commands in the marketplace in terms of salary, but I don't have the time or luxury right now to find out; I'll get around to it later." All these decisions may seem relatively unimportant in isolation. But where making more money is concerned, the pattern pretty much adds up to this: "I'm not going to bother earning what I'm worth or caring about making more money, at least not for now." But *now* adds up; you end up selling yourself short in a huge way—today, and over the course of your lifetime.

Following this logic of what seemingly insignificant decisions cost women, Dr. Evelyn Murphy, author of *Getting Even,* asserts that the gap between what women and men earn "isn't some

meaningless abstraction. It adds up. It takes a personal toll."
Failing to fight for their worth is costing women the paychecks,
pensions, and security that they need and deserve. Dr. Murphy's
Wage Project surveys warn that "we are missing almost a quarter
of our rightful earnings—money that few women can afford to
miss." Consider Murphy's figures as well as statistics compiled
by *Women Don't Ask* authors Babcock and Laschever that expose
the huge cost of settling for less than we are worth:

- "By not negotiating her salary, a high school graduate
loses $700,000. A young woman graduates from high school this
year and goes straight to work at $20,000 a year. Over her life-
time, she will make $700,000 less than the young man graduat-
ing with her."
- "A college graduate loses $1.2 million. A young woman
graduates from college into a $30,000 starting salary. Over her
lifetime, she will make $1.2 million less than the young man get-
ting his diploma in line right behind her."
- "A professional school graduate loses $2 million. A young
woman gets a degree in business, medicine, or law and graduates
into a $70,000 starting salary (along with staggering student loan
debts). Over her lifetime, she will make $2 million less than the
young man at her side."
- "Women frequently don't negotiate their salaries. What it
costs us: By not negotiating a first salary, an individual stands to
lose more than $500,000 by age 60—and men are more than four
times as likely as women to negotiate a first salary. One study calculated that women who consistently negotiate their salary in-
creases earn at least $1 million more during their careers than
women who don't."
- "20 percent of adult women (22 million people) say they
never negotiate at all, even though they often recognize negotiation as appropriate and even necessary."

- "Women often don't know the market value of their work: Women report salary expectations between 3 and 32 percent lower than those of men for the same jobs; men expect to earn 13 percent more than women during their first year of full-time work and 32 percent more at their career peaks."

I would like for all of this to change. I would like for you to wake up each morning consciously thinking: "I am going for economic empowerment. I deserve to earn my worth and to feel financially strong and secure."

Financial Muscle Gives You a Lifetime of Options

What's economic empowerment got to do with it? It buys you time when you need it: "Do I take this new job in this new city, even though relocating is going to cost me?" "Now that I have a baby and am strongly feeling that I want to be in charge of my own scheduling and whom I answer to, can I really afford to start my own business, can I afford the time between launch and profitability, or should I return to my old job after my maternity leave runs out just to keep a steady income for now?" "Do I figure out a way to stay in this house after I get through the emotional and financial devastation of this divorce, or do I just get it over with and move into an apartment that I don't own?" "Can I afford to support my husband while he pursues his M.B.A.?" It buys you the ability to afford good child care so that, should you decide to keep working or return to your career, you have some relative peace of mind knowing that your babies are in good hands because you can afford it. It buys you more confidence when you're negotiating— say, for a salary and total compensation package on a new job. If you have a good package at your current job (because you negotiated) or if you have assets or money in the bank to allow you to float for a few months, the pressure to take whatever is offered is not there as you negotiate to earn your worth.

Be more discriminating about how and what you spend your money on. Do you buy clothes, skin-care creams, and makeup? Or do you pay your way to an expensive, high-powered conference? Do you spend your cash on an advanced degree, or pricey legal or tax or other service provider advice that will profitably inform your business or professional decisions; or a new state-of-the-art laptop you need; or even a subscription to the *Wall Street Journal*? Honestly, many women wouldn't think twice about forking over money for socially sanctioned girlie choices—and don't get me wrong: I pay the price to have a great haircut and highlights and quality cosmetics. But, all too often, we spend too little, or simply don't invest at all, ever, in tools that will advance our careers and economic security.

Strategies to Make 'Em Pay and Earn Your Worth

Never Let Them See You Sweat: Learn to Negotiate Your Value

Generally, any deal is negotiable. Women just don't tend to do it—especially for ourselves. Negotiation is part of the game. And if women don't negotiate, those who do look at them as fools.

Part of the solution is to learn basic negotiating skills. For example, put your number on the table and then shut up. Women who are afraid of negotiations will put a number out and then keep talking until they talk themselves out of it. They don't even give the person time to say yes. Here's an example of how this works:

*I'd tell my protégées to make up a cardboard sign that said, "Shut up,"
and position it prominently on their desks, so they'd learn to make an
offer and stick by it, rather than cave in to pressure during negotiation
by lowering their bid.*

—Betsy Rapoport, writer, editor, and life coach;
twenty-two-year veteran of trade publishing,
most recently as an executive editor at a
division of Random House

Sometimes you shouldn't name your number first, no matter
how hard you are pressured to do so. Try tactics like saying,
"What's your budget?" And if the person says they don't know,
press further. Say, "Give me a range so that I can come up with
some options for you." If you work for yourself, submit to clients
three options with different services and prices; clients will be
more likely to engage your services if they have options. If you are
interviewing or entering salary negotiations, and are asked what
you expect to earn, answer, "That depends on the opportunity.
What is your range?" And if you've done your homework, you
know what you should be making.

At certain levels or in certain situations, bring in that lawyer or
agent from your paid steering committee to handle your negotiations. Just make sure you don't cede control to that person. Make
sure you've read thoroughly and understood any contracts, and
have discussed your views on key issues with your adviser, including what your deal points are and what issues you're willing
to concede. Act like a pro and you're more likely to earn the worth
of a pro. One woman I interviewed, who was offered a top position in her industry, hired a lawyer who called others in the industry to find out what the traffic would bear. Once she'd agreed to
accept the position, her soon-to-be boss said, "Do you want to tell
me what you're making?" She said, "No, my attorney will take it
from here." Of course, she had her attorney's card with her and

handed it to her new boss, saying that she was thrilled to be moving into this exciting new opportunity. See how she wasn't a bitch, but ambitchously managed to make sure she was making the amount of money she was entitled to? And she came off like the pro she was being paid the big bucks to be; had she not handled her salary negotiations in this way, it would have raised eyebrows, as in: "Hmmm . . . is she really a big-league player if she doesn't know how to fight like a pro for her own interests?"

Be More Entitled: Ask Yourself, What's in It for Me?

Before you take on a new job assignment or client or agree to a promotion or career move or title change, do you explicitly ask yourself, "What's in it for me?" Do you thoroughly research this question, think about it, get information and hard data, and then back all of that with a gut check? Many women do not do this. For example, Dr. Ann Demarais related this observation to me:

> When I hire NYU students to do things for me I'll tell them I'll give them some training in this or that. And the men are always much more specific about what they want: "They'd really like X, Y, Z from me; they want the opportunity to do this or that." And they want to know how it's going to help their career. Whereas the women are thrilled to have the work. They're like, "Great." They never ask for anything more. I sometimes think these guys are ballsy—I'm thinking, these guys are twenty-five years old, I'm paying them. I'm paying all of them—women or men. And only the guys want to know what else it's going to do for them, and they're very up-front the first time they meet me about what they want in addition to the money.

Whenever you are considering a new job or a promotion or taking on a project, you should always be thinking, "What's in it for me?" Always remember that you are entitled to ask outright, "What's in it for me?" The subtext getting conveyed is: "I'm a highly trained professional, I'm ambitchous, I'm a hard worker, and I want to make sure I'm getting what I need out of this situation. Plus, I want to make sure I'm getting the most I could be getting out of this opportunity. And I want to make certain that I'm earning my worth."

Do Your Homework So You Know Where You Stand

Do salary researches using sources like Hoover's and LexisNexis. Call alumnae from your university or graduate school and ask who knows someone else who might have some insider information that will help you know what you should be asking for. Do a thorough review of industry publications and track what others are reportedly making. Contact an executive search firm or attorney familiar with your field and be willing to pay for the information that will let you stand on a solid foundation of accurate and current industry information about what your value proposition is and what the market will bear. Don't ever go into a situation without being fully informed.

Don't Just Take the First Offer

If you don't get a higher salary, negotiate stock options or a guaranteed salary review in three months instead of a year, or incentive bonus options, or specific promotion opportunities you'll be able to work toward—and be sure to find out how long you can expect these advancements to take if you work hard and prove yourself.

If you can't get the salary you want right off the bat, negotiate for a job description. Check out possible titles at sources like www.wetfeet.com. Having a job title that looks impressive can work to your advantage over the longer-term course of your career, especially if you're a young professional building your résumé. Even if you're a seasoned veteran you should be going for the most prestigious title you can. And you've done your homework, in any case, beforehand, so you know precisely what industry titles are out there and you can make very specific recommendations about what title would benefit you the most.

Conduct periodic updated reviews of current fee ranges in your profession and in your geographical location, particularly if you work for yourself and feel clueless about what you should be charging. This is a common trap ambitchous women unwittingly fall into. Consider these two examples:

I never went to business school; I don't have a big background in that. I've taken some courses on how to be a more profitable small business, but still I do everything myself. And I'm a smart woman—but maybe I'm not even sure how I should price it? And I'm just so busy, it's not on the top of the list to research it, even though I have a sense that, yes, I'm underearning.

—Shona, thirty-two, certified financial planner,
solo practitioner, San Francisco

I just found out there is a similar program to mine, and I was stunned to learn that the owner is charging more than double what I'm charging. He's a colleague, a competitor. And when I talked about it with him, he even said, "You're not charging enough."

—Alex, twenty-nine, personal trainer and gym
owner, Los Angeles

Do your research. Find out what your competitors charge. Ask around. Eliminate the guesswork. Stop selling yourself short—and start earning your worth.

Always Ask for More

Raise your fees or ask for a salary increase at least once a year, if not twice. If you are a small business owner, do you raise your prices at least once a year? Your physicians and all other service providers all increase their rates at least once a year for cost of living. Women often feel we have to justify doing so. Don't make this mistake—you're ambitchous, and an ambitchous woman understands that she is entitled to earn her worth, remember?

If you work for someone else, think about multiple ways to boost your earnings: Aggressively ask for what you would need to accomplish in order to earn an accelerated salary review. If you believe that your bonuses don't reflect your value proposition, back up your claim with hard, cold facts and specific numbers. Go back to your Ka-ching! File. Then go to your boss and advocate for a more appropriate bonus. If he or she is nonresponsive, hems and haws, and never gets back to you, go to your boss's boss. When you're considering a new job, research everything you could and should be asking for in your total compensation package—including not just the actual salary, but stock options and bonus incentives, signing bonuses, vacation or sabbatical time you'll be eligible for and when, what the policy is on outside freelancing or consulting, when you can expect a salary review, and how much of a raise you can expect. What growth opportunities and promotions are available within the company? Does the company have professional development incentives, including paying for all or part of an M.B.A. or advanced degree or executive training or coaching?

If you are a consultant—even a brand spanking new consultant—set your rates in the upper range of what your colleagues are charging. If you are just starting out, don't fall into the trap that so many of us women do of charging below market value simply because you feel that you aren't good enough yet, or that you'll be cheating your clients; start out setting your prices low, and you will forever struggle to get to a point where you are commanding the fee you ought to be making. Set your prices high from day one of launching your consultancy, and you'll bring in more serious clients who are enjoyable to work with, who are willing to pay you for a job well done and will refer other serious clients to you, your work will be more challenging and rewarding, and you'll be rewarded financially, from the get-go, for your hard work and brainpower. Make 'em pay.

If you are a seasoned veteran consultant, charge what you are worth, even if this is in the upper end of the market range. Tanya Styblo Beder spent many years heading up her own risk management firm and leading the charge as one of the very few women in that industry. She now serves as CEO of Citigroup Alternative Investments' multi-strategy proprietary hedge fund unit, Tribeca Global Management LLC. I asked Tanya if she'd ever felt reluctant, even as a young professional, to charge top dollar for her services. She laughed and said:

> No way! When I had my own business for thirteen years, I knew people didn't hire us because we were a cut-rate service provider. They hired us because we were the best at what we did—and they were willing to pay market rates for that expertise. So we did charge top dollar, but only because we delivered the best.

Consider the pros and cons of bundling your services and pricing them as project-based fees, rather than billing by the hour. Be sure you set up merchant service capabilities with your bank so that you can accept all major credit cards from clients, making it easier for them to pay for your services—and to pay your fees upfront. Negotiate with your bank and shop around for the best rate you can get on what percentage you are charged when you accept credit cards. Always be on the lookout for ways to increase your revenue streams—do you have products you can include if you are a service provider, such as books, tapes, booklets, downloadable reports, etc.? Make sure you have a current Web site that has credit card and shopping cart capabilities. Learn about how to buy ISBN numbers for the products you create so that you can list them on Amazon.com and increase your sales.

Rosalind Resnick, CEO of Axxess Business Centers, Inc., and a former business and computer journalist, built her Internet marketing company from a two-person home-based start-up to a public company that generated $58 million in sales. Here's what Rosalind posts on her Web site about the company she heads up today:

Corporate Principles We Live By:

If you're looking for free advice, you've come to the wrong place. At Axxess Business Consulting, we don't give away anything for free. And we don't accept payment in equity, livestock, or fruit baskets. If you want to come in and sit down with one of our experienced small business consultants, you'll need to fork over cold, hard cash. (We also accept checks and credit cards.) There are two reasons we do this: 1) We're a for-profit company and we need to make money to stay in business, and 2) People who get things for free generally don't take them as seriously as things they've got to pay for. (Just ask our friends at the U.S. Small Business Administration.) So, if you don't have enough money for serious business advice, come back when you do. We'll be waiting.

Use Rosalind and Tanya and other women who aren't afraid to charge what they're worth as inspiring examples of ambitchous women who are *explicit* about knowing they are more talented than others in their area of expertise—and they make it *explicit* that they're going to make 'em pay.

Become Your Own Benefactor—Take Advantage of Company Benefits

From day one in your company, find out and take advantage of all professional development opportunities that are available to you. Lisa Taylor described to me how she started becoming her own benefactor early in her career by using this strategy:

> With my first job, they had an educational program that was very lucrative for the employees. I signed up for that as soon as I started with the company, when I was twenty-two. As a result, at age twenty-five, I received my CFA [Chartered Financial Analyst], which is a designation well-known in the finance community. And in the back of my mind, one reason that I thought about receiving that designation is it's a great thing to have if you want to open your own business. And I've always enjoyed financial planning and working with people and being involved in investments. It didn't make me popular with my young peers who were going out and partying and bonding while I was studying; they shunned me. It bothered me at first, but I figured that someday maybe that CFA would be helpful to me on the personal front as well as on the career front—and that trumped my desire to be one of the cool kids at work.

Start right now getting information about each and every opportunity in your company. Take full advantage of all resources to advance your professional standing and career opportunities. This is part of your total compensation package—if you don't use these resources, you're throwing away money that belongs to you.

Study Stalled Lives

Read about or talk to women who weren't able to express their own ambition and fight to earn their worth. What held them back? Read stories about what happened to women who waited too long to ask for or to take a position. Or who failed to invest in property or in a better education or career development for themselves. Or who undercut their salaries by not negotiating, or undercharging when they worked for themselves. What do they say about it now, as they move from their thirties into their forties, fifties, and sixties? What would they have done differently? Read about women who figured out that they could have been far more savvy in their approach to spreading risk in terms of how they invested their earnings. What do they say now about what it cost them because they couldn't be bothered to take classes, or to learn how to study Ibbotson charts, or to read investment books, or find out the best way to invest their hard-earned money strategically? What would they do differently? What can you learn from their stories?

No Matter What Your Long-Term Dreams Are, Commit Yourself to Being Financially Sovereign and Economically Empowered

Stay in control of your own financial destiny, no matter where you are in your life. I am not saying that you shouldn't dream for or eventually team up with a great partner, soul mate, or husband. I am saying that you should not, under any circumstances, relinquish control of your own, individual economic empowerment. Don't hand over money management, spending, and financial investment decisions to your spouse; don't slip into the role where you fail to look at how your individual career choices and decisions impact both of you. Don't be afraid to earn more than your spouse. Start out right now, wherever you are—and especially if you're young, especially if you're single—telling yourself, "I am going to begin today to plan in all ways possible to become financially empowered—including focusing on making sure that I always earn my worth. And I will no longer leave money on the table."

Consider Investing in Property as a Single Woman

Don't wait for your life to catch up with you. Research how you can get into the real estate market now. This is a piece of advice that is not obvious, yet it is a critical foundation that never gets pointed out to women. It is a factor that is directly linked to getting paid what you ought to be making. How?

If you are planning to buy a house, then you feel empowered enough to save up for a down payment—including investing and managing your portfolio yourself. You feel empowered to get your credit in order, to figure out just how much of a loan you will qualify for, what the financing options are, and what the smartest mortgage package is for your particular circumstances. Then you'll go out there and find a Realtor who you feel is earning his or her worth in terms of serving you as a client. That's a huge accomplishment, and one that requires you to get your hands dirty—in ways not so many single women do, particularly younger single women—with money and finance and marketplace research and financial planning and strategizing. You've taken charge of a major purchase. You've planted roots while at the same time investing in those roots rather than renting them.

Making all of this happen will increase your ambitchous confidence in your workplace skills as well—your take-charge attitude will transfer to your professional confidence in the market-place in any of a number of ways. You will feel more confident in negotiations that involve money. You'll feel more powerful in your overall ambition goals. You will feel comfortable and confident to wait and not settle where either your job or life partner is concerned.

Buying real estate when we're young and single also gets us into the housing market early on—a positive move because, generally speaking, real estate tends to be a fairly stable long-term investment and a good way to diversify risk in your investment portfolio. Granted, if you are in the Los Angeles or San Francisco Bay Area or New York real estate market, it is very difficult to get into that market as a single person unless you have a giant nest egg or the ability to borrow from family to help with a down payment. However, once I started talking with women about the fact that so few women invest in property when they're single, I uncovered the invisible barriers.

First, single women don't invest in property because they are waiting to catch up with their lives: "I'm not going to buy property now because who knows, I may be partnered in three years." Young women, more than young men, seem reluctant to buy property when they're single, almost as if they have an unconscious or irrational fear that, by doing so, they'll sabotage their chances of finding their soul mate. Or they don't even consider it an option when they are single, because we just don't get the message that, as single women, it's something we should investigate or aim for. And we're afraid of making such a huge decision on our own.

Thus single women—especially those in their twenties and thirties—don't think about investing in property; they don't even investigate what it would take, what it would look like on paper, what tax write-offs might benefit them, how that move could give them a long-term return on investment.

When we last spoke, Elizabeth Mizrahi was preparing to buy her fifth property. She bought her first home when she was in her second year of graduate school and in her early twenties. She acknowledges that she was very lucky because she received a small inheritance that she used as her down payment. Elizabeth described to me how she "kept trading up in cities" as she took different jobs and relocated over the years. She needed only fifteen thousand dollars for the down payment on her first property. With this current move she's preparing for, some ten years later, she'll need a couple of hundred thousand dollars. So while the initial risk was not so great, each time she sold she made money, so she was able to stay and move up in the housing market.

Make Enough Money for Good Day Care

There are many ways in which you are more skilled and accomplished—and should make 'em pay. One of the key reasons is that earning your worth will allow you to provide your children with excellent day care and educational opportunities.

> I make enough money for good day care and after-school care so that I can work at a career I love. I get a lot of help from friends and family. But basically I just do it, just do what has to be done. I desperately wanted to have my children. I worked very hard to have them.
>
> —Wilma Wasco, Ph.D., single mother by choice of two young children; associate professor of neurology at Harvard Medical School and Massachusetts General Hospital

You value your ambition and your children. You want to work and you want the best for your children. Earning your worth is essential to giving you peace of mind about the quality of care and education your children receive while you are minding your ambition.

Have a Long-term Strategy for Making 'Em Pay over the Long Term of Your Ambitchous Career

Occasionally float your résumé, which you can do anonymously through trusted people in your network, or by putting out feelers with headhunters or taking their calls when they contact you and asking questions about what's out there in terms of better earning opportunities. Even if you don't want to make a move, this will arm you with information that you can leverage within your current company.

If you work for yourself, raise your rates today, right now—at least with new clients. Send out notices to existing clients that you will be increasing your fees effective the first of the upcoming month.

Offer yourself up for a promotion—don't wait to be asked. Create a new business plan for your division or a product idea; write up your job description and what your value proposition would be. Ask—and see what happens. Or try this same approach with a company you're not currently working for. Take a proposal to them and they may just create a position for you—it happens all the time.

Always, always stay current in terms of knowing the range of salaries—or consultant fees, if you work for yourself—in your industry. Continually strategize ways to negotiate, make a job move, increase your revenue streams—whatever you can think of in order to keep yourself in the top percentile of earners in your industry.

Earn your worth. Make as much money as you can. This doesn't make you a greedy bitch, but a smart, strategic ambitchous woman who is planning ahead, starting today, to get paid what she's worth. You've earned it!

ten

Am•BITCH•ous Rule 5
Be More Irresponsible to Others—
And More Responsible to Yourself

It's taken me six years to make the huge decision to delegate some of my client service delivery. I had to get pretty miserable first, to the point where I was always exhausted. Before I began delegating, I was boxed in and couldn't do everything I wanted to do. I now have a professional résumé writer and two psychologists. I envisioned that delegating would be much more painful, but now that I'm doing it, it's wonderful. It's such a relief knowing that I am not the sole resource for my business. And I think clients are enjoying having multiple perspectives and the benefit of more sources of wisdom than they had when it was just me trying to do it all.

—Dr. Janet Scarborough

I've learned the hard way that some people—even a person I've just met or barely know—won't hesitate to ask me to spend time serving up accounting advice at a social event and then parasitically gorge themselves on as much information as I'm willing to give away. It took me a long time to get comfortable with the idea that I didn't have to let myself be taken advantage of that way. It took longer to learn to ignore the shocked expression on their face and seeing them stalk away after I started saying, "I don't give free advice, because you get what you pay for."

—Sarah, thirty-two, certified public accountant
and Chartered Financial Analyst

I used to feel like I always had to answer an instant message at work. I know it's stupid, but I felt like my friends could see that I was there and if I didn't reply, they'd feel hurt or ignored. Then one day, I just started letting people know, one by one, that "I'm not doing IMs anymore because I find them too distracting—nothing personal." It worked like a charm. No one encroaches on my time at work now, and if they do, I just ignore it, because I've set my policy.

—Caroline, forty-five, senior managing director,
advertising agency, New York City

Melody is the founder and president of an acclaimed national publicity firm based in Los Angeles. She left a successful career as a television anchorperson to launch her own business venture. When we last spoke, she had on her staff nine full-time publicists working out of her large home-based office. In recent years she'd hired an architectural and construction team to build on rooms and expand her office space to accommodate her growing business. She'd also just opened a second office in San Francisco.

Melody is a great example of an ambitchous woman who understands this paradox: By being responsibly irresponsible, she ends up being more responsible. I talked with Melody about how she manages being a single parent of four who also runs a highly profitable, fast-growing firm. I wanted to know: What's her secret for making it all work smoothly? She's learned how and when to be responsible. Plus how and when not to kill herself, by being irresponsible and delegating—at home and at work. "When I figured this out I saw that what ends up happening is that everyone's needs get met—my own professional and personal goals, the needs of my talented employees, and those of my amazing children."

I have to have a thrilling and profitable career. It's in my blood. I believe women absolutely can do what we love, but our aspirations and expectations of ourselves sometimes need to be adjusted to fit the reality of the situation. For example, the reality is that children need care; they need to have someone there when they come home from school. At the same time, I need to be free, at all times, to be at my desk, to be on the phone for a breaking client news story, or to devote myself to some other business issue that requires my full attention, right then and there. That's how it's got to be for me to be able to run a successful national PR firm—and love every minute of it rather than feeling exhausted and drained. But I also have to know that my kids are well cared for and that they know they're loved and that their needs are always going to get met. So even though I have a large office in my home, I don't for a minute think that I have to run myself into the ground being all things to all people. I delegate and I feel just fine about doing so.

Sounds great, but how does she manage? I asked for more specifics.

For example, even though my office is attached to my house, I have a full-time person employed to be there after school to take care of my kids' needs. Say my daughter comes home and has a question. She needs to have someone there to answer it for her. With my current setup, sometimes it's me; sometimes it's the person I have in place to give her the care she needs. So, it's funny that, even though I run a major PR company, sometimes my younger kids are asked, "What job does your mom do?" and they say, "Oh, nothing." Still, I set a fabulous example of a mother and a career woman, and my older kids already admire that.

I raised the issue of how so many women have a hard time delegating. And about how so many of us feel guilty about being responsible to our own needs by being irresponsible—irresponsible according to how some people in our culture, and even many ambitchous women, might view it. Melody suggested another way of looking at being more irresponsible:

> Think of how great the kids feel—knowing that there's always someone there to take care of their needs. Think of how great I feel having this fabulous business and knowing that I love my work and I'm building a nest egg and real financial security for all of us. And I get to work with creative, inspired employees and fascinating clients. I'm making a contribution on many fronts. I wouldn't be able to do that if I put my needs on the back burner.

We women are far too generous with our time and resources by helping others—particularly other women—when we ought to be more mindful that we're in the minority of people at the top of our fields and need to use those resources to reach our own ambitchous goals. We have absorbed the cultural belief that being nurturing is actually the key to our success, and perhaps it does bring some perks. But it comes at a price. When we focus on others' needs at the expense of our own, we're losing focus on ourselves and on our work, both of which suffer as a result. Women put their own needs last when they've metabolized the following:

Sheep's Clothing (overt message): Women succeed because they're nurturing and maternal.

Wolf (covert message): It's a woman's job to take care of everyone's needs—even people she doesn't know that well or not at all—along with her own needs. On the other hand, if she asks for something for herself, or if she asks for help, that's selfish.

Socially Sanctioned Self-Sabotage: You neglect your own needs and sabotage professional success and personal happiness out of a sense of guilt and overresponsibility to others. You give, but you don't take. You end up feeling resentful, overextended, burned out, exhausted. Your overall quality of life suffers.

Ambitchous women need laserlike attention to do our jobs well. Worrying about everyone's feelings is one big distraction. You can do your necessary worrying in the off hours. There's a difference between being responsible and being unwisely responsible. I'm going to show you the difference.

REALITY CHECK
Do I Find It Impossible to Be Irresponsible?

In order to be more responsible to yourself, you need to take a good, hard look at the following questions. Do you:

- Make haircut appointments for your teenagers?
- Agree to finish up loose ends for colleagues?
- Agree to be responsible for dinner whether cooking or ordering in?
- Take responsibility for household chores or micromanage the cleaning person who does them?
- Make all the travel arrangements for your family?
- Do the work of one of your reports because it's easier than teaching them?
- Say yes to dinners that overextend your schedule?
- Absorb another colleague's workload without compensation?
- Do your own tax returns to save a few bucks on the CPA?

- Convince yourself to delegate, and then hover over the person to make sure he does it right?
- Take phone calls from friends and loved ones anytime at all during business hours?

If you recognized yourself in any of the above scenarios, you are shouldering far more than your share of responsibility—at work and at home. You need to start making some serious changes in both environments. It's time for you to learn how to put your own needs at the top of your priority list, rather than at the bottom. You need to learn how to start setting better limits.

Strategies for Becoming More Irresponsible

Being Overly Responsible Attracts Straggler/Stalkers

Being responsible first and foremost to your ambitchous goals sometimes means that you have to be more *ir*responsible to the needs of others. If you don't do this, you make yourself vulnerable to what I call Straggler/Stalkers. Straggler/Stalkers are people who hang around just waiting to hit you up for something they want from you, something that will make you immediately regret having said yes. These may not be bad people, but they are pressuring you to tend to their needs or goals at the expense of your own—and that's not good for you. Renee, a thirty-seven-year-old vice president of an executive search firm in New York City, described to me how strangers at parties, as soon as they find out the type of work Renee does, often say, "Oh! Let me just run out to my car and grab my résumé so that you can take a look and tell me what you think." Or someone at her daughter's back-to-school night or at her son's weekend soccer match will ask to pick her brain about a particular corporate culture, or fish for insider contacts. Before Renee learned how to quickly set limits with people who hit her up for professional advice when she was off the clock, she paid the price. She would end up agreeing to do work that she didn't want to do, for free, during what was supposed to be her time. As a result, Renee suffered: "I would drag myself back into work on Monday mornings feeling absolutely drained."

Like Renee, if you don't learn to be responsible to your own needs by learning to set limits with people who don't care about them, it will deplete you in one of these ways:

- You end up spending your precious time and energy doing something you wish you hadn't agreed to do.
- You waste energy backpedaling after you have gone ahead and said yes.
- You do say no, or you do set boundaries, but then later waste your time obsessing over how you said no and whether you hurt someone's feelings.

Learn to Say No to Straggler/Stalkers— Even the Most Persistent Ones

See if you recognize yourself in the following stories of women who stopped Straggler/Stalkers in their tracks. Think of similar instances when you have had to confront a Straggler/Stalker, how it made you feel, how you dealt with it, and how you would handle it differently—or not—if it happened again tomorrow.

I was at a yoga retreat. A stranger there found out that I was a literary agent. Her eyes bugged out of her head as she told me she had a book idea she'd been working on and that I should read her manuscript, which she happened to have with her. I said I wasn't interested, thank you very much. She kept on and on and on, at different points in the day, whenever she'd run into me—at lunch, at dinner. Finally, I'd had enough and said, "No. I told you I'm not interested. And I'm here on retreat, so please respect that." Later that night, in the community gathering room, she had an ally with her—someone who happened to be an acquaintance of mine—and she brought him with her, cornering me to say that what I'd done had made her feel like a door had closed for her. I said that closing a door was my intention. Her ally said that he had to agree that my actions had been counter to spiritual principles. It was really outrageous. I said, "You know what? We're just going to have to disagree. I'm on retreat, and this feels like an assault. I'm going to bed. And I don't want to talk about this again."

—Morgan, forty-one,
San Francisco literary agent

You can see why Morgan felt stalked. She was on a much-needed yoga retreat, away from her sixty- to eighty-hour-per-week job. Yet if the Straggler/Stalker had had her way with Morgan, she wouldn't have been able to get away from work at all. And, as it was, the Straggler/Stalker ate up way too much of Morgan's downtime.

I do want to point out one excellent part of Morgan's response that illustrates a subtle yet critical distinction between what you should and shouldn't say. Morgan said, "We're just going to have to disagree." Morgan did not qualify her limit-setting by saying the more commonly used phrase that adds just one bad word: "We're just going to have to agree to disagree." Do you see the difference? The other person does not have to agree with you. And whether or not that person gets the distinction, you will. You'll feel far more grounded and powerful if you simply eliminate the agree qualifier when deploying this limit-setting statement. Mantra: We're just going to have to disagree.

Christina, forty-five, a principal of an East Coast private equity firm, told me that she once refused to pay for a teeth cleaning after the dental hygienist—a woman—asked her what she did, and then spent the entire appointment talking about her business idea, what she'd run up against so far trying to get a small business loan, an interested partner, and on and on. She obsessed about the virtues of becoming a not-for-profit versus a for-profit venture, and whether she needed a brick-and-mortar storefront or should save the overhead and have only an online Internet presence. She talked loudly and rapid-fire for the entire, interminable forty-minute appointment, holding Christina hostage. She wondered what Christina thought, since she saw so many business plans. At the end of the appointment, the hygienist said, "I'll get your contact info from the front desk and call you to see if we can have coffee or drinks—I'd love to pick your brain when you're not having your teeth worked on and are able to really chat!" Christina said, "I was so angry. I said to her, 'Hasn't anyone ever talked to you about boundaries? I'm sure you deal with many people who are much more high-profile than I am. You should learn about not crossing professional lines.' Then I told the woman at the front desk, 'I am not paying for that service. That was outrageous.'"

Liz, a forty-one-year-old executive producer for a high-profile television program, described to me how she was cornered at a small baby shower ten minutes after arriving by a woman who wanted to pitch a script idea. Liz told the woman that she worked only through agents, and went back to focusing on the mother-to-be. Liz saw the woman leave the gathering shortly after this exchange and afterward told the host—a mutual friend—what had happened. The host reacted by suggesting that Liz's behavior had been "well, sort of rude . . ." and that "you could have told her to talk to me, or something." When I asked Liz how she felt about this, she said, "I felt I'd done the right thing—it was a huge imposition to have this woman hit me up at a baby shower the second I walked in the door."

"I Don't Do Lunch"—How to Spot and Stop Step Skippers

"For some people, the only taste of success they'll ever have is the bite they take out of you."

—Dr. Janet Scarborough, recalling a saying she'd heard

New York Times bestselling author Nicole Shapiro was the featured speaker at a standing-room-only meeting of the Women's Business Alliance. When her presentation was over, I witnessed her walk the talk about standing your ground and refusing to let people bleed you dry. Many women crowded around Nicole after her presentation, asking intelligent questions, buying her books, complimenting her on her inspiring words, taking a business card in order to set up an appointment later, networking, or enjoying the post-seminar adrenaline buzz. One person hung around until the crowd had thinned and then said to Nicole, "I'd love to have lunch with you and pick your brain." Without missing a beat, Nicole replied, "I don't do lunch, except with my family or friends. We have very little time together, so I save downtime for them." The subtext of her message was, "My time is valuable—I don't give it away, and certainly not for the price of lunch." Had the workshop attendee asked to set up a consulting appointment with Nicole, her response would have been very different.

That exchange always stuck with me as an example of pure limit-setting at its best. I know another woman, an architect at a large San Francisco firm, who makes it her personal policy not to do drinks after work—because "inevitably it bleeds into dinner-time; I'm dying of hunger and exhausted by the time I get home."

So often, women have trouble simply saying no, and that can be a real problem, because there are always encounters with people who are willing to take advantage of your weakness. People who want to take you out and pick your brain are what I call Step Skippers—they want to bypass the steps hardworking professionals take to achieve their ambitchous goals. They want a free pass. These are the ones who corner you at a party, or hang around until everyone else has left your speaking event to ask for free advice, or they somehow find themselves face-to-face with you, find out what you do, and immediately hit you up, talking nonstop about what they do and how you can help them—for free, of course. It's your obligation to yourself to say no to these people, run from them, hide, get them out of your face, and stop letting them make you responsible for their needs.

Women are often told, and I even advise you in this book, to form a steering committee—and to support other women by serving on their boards. So isn't this advice counter to that mission? Aren't people who come to you and pitch you or ask to pick your brain or ask for free advice just being ambitchous? No. Step Skippers are people who try to skip the accepted protocols that truly professional people understand and follow, in order to ride on the back of someone else's success. Here's an example to illustrate the difference.

Bestselling author Karen Salmansohn told me about dining out in Los Angeles and spotting Madonna at a nearby table. Karen waltzed over to Madonna's table and said, "I really respect your work." She purposefully used the verb *respect*: "I knew I had to compliment her work first, but not go overboard, to keep it from being sycophantic and to keep me businesslike and somewhat at her level." To immediately establish credibility, Karen then stated, "I'm a bestselling author." She then shut her mouth and showed her stuff by plopping down two of her books. "Knowing we live in a visual culture, and that she was visual, putting down books for her to see conveyed so much more than I could say. They had great covers—I designed them; I got her instant opinion rather than throwing more words at her." Isn't that ballsy? Yes. But it's not step skipping—and here's why: Salmansohn was already a recognized, published author. And what happened next was that, according to Salmansohn, Madonna said, "You wrote this book? I own this book. I love it. God bless you." Karen's publisher got this story into the *Daily News*'s equivalent of the *New York Post*'s Page Six, then sent her to England, where she immediately sold out the fifty thousand copies her publisher had in stock. Karen is the opposite of a Step Skipper: "My publishers see me as their 'one hundred and fifty percent author'; they know I always go above and beyond to make sure someone hears my tree falling, and that I'll work tirelessly to sell my books."

Now here's an example that would have been step skipping: someone invaded Madonna's dinner space, saying, "Oh, my God! Madonna! I have a book idea . . . or a song I've been kicking around . . . and I'd love to sit here with you and tell you about it." Do you see the difference?

Here's another example of this distinction between step skipping and being collegial. A literary agent I know told me two stories. The first is an example of someone who understands appropriate professional boundaries and doesn't try to step skip. The agent knows a woman who designs very high-end jewelry, hand-selecting only the finest gemstones; her work is highly regarded. The gemologist had gotten to know this agent over a period of a year of so; then one night, they were having drinks and this woman said, "I've been thinking and wondering if there would be a market for a classy little book on how to buy stones for the general consumer that I could package and market." And the agent recounted to me how she thought about it, and pretty immediately said, "Well, yeah, actually I think there probably could be, and I think there's someone I could hook you up with." Now example number two, same literary agent. She is at a party, and a woman she's just met says, "Oh! You're an agent? Oh, well, then I should get your card, because, as you know, I myself am a lawyer who represents all these high-profile clients— but I've been wanting to write a book myself; not sure on what, but let me get your card." Step Skipper? Right.

You'll know when someone is treading inappropriately in your space. You'll feel your gut tighten; you are suddenly on edge, on the defensive, and are looking for the nearest door.

It can be even harder to say no when you've got someone indirectly manipulating you. They know they're gunning for you, but they're being so sneaky about what it is they want from you that you're left feeling put-upon, angry, annoyed, stressed, and stalked. You feel confused and unable to figure out how to address it. Their behavior puts the onus on you to cut them off at the knees—and if you directly confront them on what they are doing, they'll deny it ("I have no idea what you're talking about!"), or act shocked ("Well, excuse me—I had no idea you felt that way!"), or act hurt to make you feel guilty ("I was only trying to express my admiration for you and just get a little morsel of advice").

Don't let them get a free ride on your back. Be irresponsible— just say no.

"No Can Do"

Scenario: someone asks to take you out for breakfast or drinks to pick your brain. Pretend that you say this: "I'd be happy to consult with you if you'd like to set up an appointment. My fee is two hundred and fifty dollars per hour." How do you imagine yourself feeling? Do you feel like a heartless bitch? One woman I recently interviewed asked, "Isn't it greedy of me to charge someone rather than to cheerfully offer to mentor them?" My answer: "Why is it you who are being greedy, rather than the person who is trying to hog your precious time and energy—and all for free?" She had never thought of it that way.

Same scenario: this time you say, "My plate is full, so I don't do outside consultations." What if you say no? How does that make you feel? Stingy? Irresponsible to someone who's earnestly trying to learn? Do you feel you have to explain yourself? Do you imagine yourself immediately feeling self-imposed pressure to reconsider ("Well, maybe next month I'll have more time . . .")?

Same scenario: this time you've agreed to something that you didn't want to do. How do you feel? Do you immediately feel like kicking yourself? Beating yourself up? ("Why, oh why, did I say yes? I'm swamped at work already, I have no time for my husband or friends as it is, I've promised myself I wouldn't get backed into a corner like this again, and I did it anyway. I'm so stupid! Damn it!").

How Can I Say No? Let Me Count the Ways

To implement this, you need stock phrases and tacit tactics for when you're getting hit up for free advice. Try out the following silent responses to common situations that threaten to compromise your ambitchous needs:

• An e-mail from a stranger; she is cryptic, at best, about what she wants. Don't respond. Deliberately not replying is a conscious action! Don't feel guilty that you haven't responded— you have. Now forget it and move on.

• A voice message from a stranger leaving only his name, with no reason why he's calling or why he wants you to return the call. Or saying he wants to network, or pick your brain. Don't respond. Again, many women feel guilty about taking this action—I see it all the time. Delete. Done. And the Step Skipper moves on to some other easy target.

- An instant message while you're at work or anytime. If you hate IMs and find them disruptive and intrusive, don't respond. Tip: Don't imagine that the other person sending the IM can magically see that you're there, even if you're online. You could be away from your computer, on the phone, who knows? No need to explain.

Sometimes you have to speak. Here are some phrases you should practice and have at the top of your mind ready to use when you're put on the spot.

- "Actually, no. I don't work that way." (Do not say, "Sorry.")
- "I don't have coffee, drinks, or dinner—I spend all my free time with my family and friends. I do consult at two hundred and seventy-five dollars per hour, if you'd like to set up an appointment with my assistant."
- Someone asks you why you never answer their instant messages: "I don't IM. E-mail works better for me."
- "That doesn't work for me." Use this for anything you don't want to do. Remember this mantra when you're working out your No Can Do muscle:

> ## I DON'T HAVE TO AGREE TO DO ANYTHING THAT I DON'T WANT TO DO.

However you manage to communicate it, don't say yes when you want to say no.

1. EXPLANATIONS NOT REQUIRED

Remember—Straggler/Stalkers and Step Skippers alike are parasites who want to suck you dry. They cross professional boundaries they know they shouldn't cross. When you spend time explaining, it gives them ammunition to tell you why you should help them. They are being professionally disrespectful of you. Remembering this will help quash any knee-jerk reaction you may have to explain your no. Don't do it. Don't overexplain, or don't explain at all. These folks don't deserve an explanation.

2. STOCK EXPLANATIONS

Feel that you just have to give some type of explanation at first, as you practice using your No Can Do muscle? Then try these stock phrases:

- "No can do; it's against my company's policy."
- "I'm over my pro bono limit this year."
- "I have a strict policy of not talking about work when I'm not there; it keeps me sane."
- "My schedule is just packed for the next six months."
- "I don't IM. I find it distracting, so I stick with checking e-mail twice a day."

3. "YOU NO LONGER HAVE A BACKSTAGE PASS"

Sometimes people will figure out a way to get close to you without revealing a hidden agenda. At some point you realize that they're really using you, draining you, or are just not someone you want to deal with any longer. Then you have to figure out—and feel okay about—how to communicate to them, "You no longer have a backstage pass." Examples of communicating this: not returning calls promptly, declining invitation after invitation, etc. Slowly it will sink in, and they'll stop trying to get an audience with you.

4. DON'T BE THROWN IF DOING THE REJECTING SOMETIMES FEELS THE SAME AS BEING REJECTED

Setting boundaries sometimes requires us to reject someone's request. As a result, when we are doing the rejecting, which should be a good, positive feeling, we feel we've just been rejected ourselves. That proactive rejection may feel like we've been rejected because active rejecting is so unfamiliar to us as women. If we get tripped up by this unfamiliar emotion or body sensation, we may be tempted to backpedal on the limit we've just set. Don't do it. And don't worry—you'll get used to setting your boundaries and doing your own fair share of rejecting.

Bonus "No Can Do" Tips

- Do not say, "I wish I could, but I can't."
- Do not apologize with, "I'm sorry, but I can't."
- Pass the buck: "You can try calling this other company—maybe they know someone." "You can check with my executive assistant on Monday, but I'm quite sure she'll tell you I'm not taking on any new clients and that my schedule is absolutely closed."
- Stand your ground.
- Don't be thrown by the sugarcoating on the request or your own fear of being rude. Take a couple of slow breaths, then say, "I don't do that." Or a simple no. Then let them, not you, stumble over the awkward three-second silence before you say, "Excuse me. Gotta run. Take care." Be nice, to a point, but don't end up giving yourself away and then later regretting that you failed to set limits. It gets easier to say no.

Recognize That Sustainable Ambition Requires Being Irresponsible

Real success in some professions requires a person to build and develop expertise and a track record over a ten- or twenty- or thirty-year period. Think about careers in which you really come into your own power the longer you're in them, like consulting, law, medicine, or the upper echelons of corporate America—these careers tend to reward longevity. People who are in careers for the long haul have to pace themselves like a runner in a marathon or they'll burn out or never achieve the level of ambition they are aiming for. So the conservation-of-energy concept is really vital for an ambitchous woman to understand and value. You've got to learn how to set really good boundaries so that you have a sustainable career as opposed to a burnout/give-it-all-until-you're-spent career.

Ambitchous women who pace themselves achieve excellence—and boundary-setting is integral to reaching the highest levels of success. Keeping this in mind will help you set those boundaries when your feet are to the fire and people are pressuring you or putting you on the spot to spend your energy on them, instead of on your own ambitchous goals.

Hire People

For all of you out there yelling, "I need a wife!," you actually don't. You need an executive assistant, and a tech butler, and a cleaning and organizing team, and a bookkeeper, and a CPA. You need to delegate the little jobs you can't handle to people like these and do it without micromanaging.

I've seen many ambitchous, incredibly busy, and successful women do battle within themselves—"I feel guilty; I shouldn't pay someone to do work I could do. I feel like a prima donna." You need to get over that. One tax attorney in Washington, D.C., told me of how she did battle within herself on this issue:

> I always walk a fine line between neglecting my child and committing malpractice. I made a decision when my daughter was

born that she would come first, but it's a hell of a lot harder to do than to just say that's what you're going to do. But less so now, because I no longer have that martyr thing: I'm neither a martyr nor a superwoman. I'm just a regular, ambitious woman trying the best I can to make it work. I used to have a problem with having someone organizing my underwear drawer and doing my laundry and stocking my fridge. Then I realized, I didn't go to school for nineteen years to wipe butts and snotty noses while my husband is becoming a star lawyer. So my solution is outsource, outsource, outsource. And now I get more quality time with my daughter and with my husband. I'm less of a bitch because I don't have too much on my shoulders. And I even have time again to do things for myself now, like running and yoga.

If you have a built-in resistance to delegating responsibility, it may help you to consider that the worst-run businesses, large and small, and the worst-run divisions and teams, are those where the head honcho—be it the CEO of the company, the small business owner, the senior executive, or the middle-level manager of a team—does not delegate. Whenever he or she is out of the office or leaves the company, things fall apart. It's no different for you— whether you are at work or at home. If you don't hand over responsibilities to others and then let them figure out how to fulfill their roles, you will be stretched way too thin, your ambitchous goals will be stifled, and your morale will suffer.

To be the best you can be, to do everything you aspire to do, you not only have to finish the work in front of you; you also need time to think deeply about future possibilities. Delegating will give you more time for deep thinking. But tolerating frequent interruptions is a form of selling yourself short. Delegate, turn off the phone, close your door—when it's time to focus, shut out all interruptions and laser in on your ambitchous goals.

Do the Math

Just how do you figure out what you should outsource and what you would be saving yourself by doing so?

First, cut to the bottom line about what it really costs you to hire someone else to take on some of your chores. Let's say you clear $100,000 a year operating a small consulting firm; that breaks down to $48 per hour. Now let's say you spend six hours a week going on low-skill errands that anyone with a car and a sense of direction could do. Plus you spend at least six hours a week doing household chores. That comes out to $576 (12 hours × $48/hour). You could hire a competent person to do the same work for $18 per hour ($216). So a very logical argument could be made that you are losing $360 a week by doing the work yourself.

If you are a salaried person, each and every one of the hours you burn up doing these kinds of chores is time you could be investing in your career, moving up in your department, taking on exciting new project opportunities, positioning yourself for advancement, or networking with your colleagues and supervisors.

I've worked with hundreds of women who have trouble rationalizing the expenditure involved in outsourcing domestic duties, and it doesn't matter how much they earn. They just can't convince themselves to do it. If you do the math, however, you'll have objective figures to alleviate your guilt and to realize, once and for all, why it makes sense to free up your time for what really counts. Ask around and find yourself a good cleaning person, a part-time or full-time executive assistant, or other people to call to come in and take care of tasks you don't have time for. Often, they're even faster than you. For instance, a computer support person (the Ritz-Carlton calls them tech butlers) can identify and fix a technical problem in a fraction of the time it would take you to track it down. They come out to your home or office and bill you a reasonable fee to quickly and painlessly troubleshoot a crashed computer or a jammed printer. If you fail to take advantage of services like these, you are probably going to fail yourself.

Systematize Your Processes

Now that you've made a firm decision to change, how do you go about it? Assess. You can't hire the right person for the right job if you don't know what the job is.

First write down your job description, everything you are responsible for on a daily, weekly, monthly basis at work. Carry around a notebook and record everything you do, as you do it, for a week, a month—whatever it takes and however long it takes. I know this is adding one more task to your already full plate. But trust me—it will pay off. Write it down. Be specific. Don't try to keep it all in your head.

Second, repeat the same procedure for everything you are responsible for on the home front; write it down; don't leave anything out.

Third, sit down for an hour and type into your computer two checklists—one work job description, and one domestic job description. No time to make the checklists? Can your secretary do it? Can you pay your teenage son to do it? Can you unplug the phones for one whole night so that you don't get interrupted and offtrack?

Include everything you have to take care of every week. Once you've quantified everything you do, you'll be amazed at how much work you shoulder. And you may find it less outrageous to think about getting a team in place to shore up support, rather than carry it all on your own.

Outcome: You'll have two detailed, specific lists of what needs to be done.

Announce a Domestic Ho-Down Embargo

Assume there will be resistance when you refuse to go on shouldering more than your share of responsibility. Assume you might have to go on strike first in order to make a point. That is, you will have to stop doing the tasks and let them go unfinished, so that people can see what a mess will pile up if somebody doesn't get busy. Dishes will fill the sink and trash will overflow, but stick to your guns.

So far, you've found it easier to get things done yourself than to take the time to rally the troops. Now that you have your lists, start with the domestic checklist. Make an honest appraisal of tasks and responsibilities that others can assume and then start assigning daily and weekly jobs. There should be no confusion about who is responsible for what. Make your checklists available to everyone so they can see the total picture.

To get your spouse fully on board, talk to him about the importance of lightening your unpaid workload so that you can focus on your paid workload, which will benefit not only you, but also the relationship and the family. If you've got a good relationship, you should be able to talk about this issue openly. Communication will help ensure that you don't end up sounding like a bitch just to get all the work done. Once you get a verbal agreement, it's much more likely that you'll make it all happen without the need to nag.

Delegate without Hovering

At work, are you afraid to let others do a job because it will take too long to tell them how to do it? Or because they won't do it right and you'll just have to do it over? No problem now that you've created an accurate job description. Print out pieces of that JD and give it to subordinates to whom you're assigning projects. If you are a small business owner, use the same technique to eliminate communication problems and crossed wires. When people know exactly what's expected of them, they are much more likely to do it or to come back to you with succinct questions that will help them deliver the goods. You'll be a better manager, streamlining your workflow and getting better results from those you've delegated or outsourced to.

Sometimes, to be a good delegator, you have to let others fail a little. Failure is good; it means things are moving forward. It takes about seven failures for every one success. If people aren't failing, they aren't trying, they aren't taking risks, they aren't challenging themselves enough, or they aren't stepping outside of their own comfort zone. If you let them fail more, you will actually see them shine more. So learn not only to tolerate others' failure, but to embrace it as a sign that you are doing a good job managing and delegating. Don't fire the person until you've given him a real chance to succeed. It's better to manage and develop him.

Adopt a new mantra about being more responsible to yourself:

BEING IRRESPONSIBLE IS GOOD FOR ME, FOR MY AMBITION, AND FOR THOSE I LOVE.

Just start being irresponsible and others will catch on. You will benefit from the huge weight lifted off of your shoulders. If you put yourself first, I promise you that all of your relationships will improve, because you will be happier.

. . . .

eleven

Am•BITCH•ous Rule 6
Be a Power Broker

. . . .

Marguerite, a new junior associate at a leading private equity firm in San Francisco, was given an opportunity to take on a new challenge, something she'd had little experience doing previously:

> I completed work on a deal spreadsheet. Then I went to a senior associate and said, "I'm doing this for a partner, and I'd like it if you could check my number." He came back later and said, "Your number was wrong." I said, "This is how I got my number." He said, "I don't care how you got your number; your number was wrong." Meeting over. Twenty minutes later, he comes to my office and goes, "Oh, by the way—yours was the right number." I thought, "That must have been hard for him—to come to me and say that."

But Marguerite was too quick to trust that the senior associate's intentions were to help her:

> Later, I was meeting with a different guy, the CFO, going over some numbers, and that same senior associate came in with a

smirk on his face and said, "Are you sure that's the right number?" I was thinking, "Isn't that weird that he keeps coming around, suggesting that my calculation is wrong?"

Another of Marguerite's missteps came from trusting the validity of information verbally given to her by the senior associate—information she relied on to work up her calculations accurately:

While doing the spreadsheet, I didn't have the actual hard-copy breakdown of the acquisition of the stock—I was given the information verbally, and I wrote it down, but I wasn't going to pass that verbal information back to the partner, along with my number. Which now I know for next time—I'm going to get all the facts, get the documents in hand, and work directly off the documents as opposed to what someone has told me. But, based on the verbal information he'd given me, a number of other people had also looked it over and said my number was right.

Then she found out that she'd failed—in a big, humiliating way with lots of witnesses:

Then it all blew up in my face. Another partner came in later and just reamed me, because I hadn't calculated in the cash value. He didn't even give me a chance to explain—he was done with me; there was nothing I could have said. I shouldn't have been handling projects like this, as far as he was concerned.

Marguerite hadn't failed because she'd done her calculations wrong—she failed because she'd blindly fallen into a deliberately set trap:

I think it was clearly a booby trap. The senior associate who kept asking me, with a sneer on his face, "Are you sure that number is right?"—he set me up. He knew what the terms of the deal were, and he withheld certain information from me, which caused my number to be wrong. If it had been a team effort, it would have never happened. As it played out, I think people were snickering at how I'd walked right into a trap. I think it's because everyone there wants to be a star, so some of them don't mind setting up others for a fall, or sabotaging someone else, or making someone else look bad.

Caroline, a forty-five-year-old internationally renowned bio-medical researcher with an impressive list of well-known colleagues and contacts in her network, described a situation she was hit with fifteen years earlier as a fresh-out-of-grad-school professional. She was sitting in the greenroom preparing to go live on national television to discuss her controversial first book. A woman who was also waiting and whose professional position was famously in opposition to Caroline's point of view said to her, after Caroline had misguidedly confided having had the misfortune of having just gotten her period along with a bad case of cramps, "Oh, that's too bad; I just read a study that found that a woman's IQ actually drops twelve points during the first few days of her menstrual cycle." Caroline recalled being "knocked off balance" by the comment, despite her usual strong, confident, professional sense of self. She described feeling somewhat shaky during her live interview a few minutes later. She said that, in retrospect, her first mistake was to let down her professional guard to this woman who had given the false impression of being supportive before Caroline's first-time media appearance. Her second trip-up was letting in the woman's attack, rather than recognizing it for what it was—a hostile effort to undermine a perceived competitor.

· · ·

Women give away power because we fail to stick up for ourselves or fight back against hostile criticism or below-the-belt attacks on our hard-earned reputation and power position. Face it—people get jealous. People get territorial. And when they do, they will fight dirty. And they won't hesitate to try to make themselves look better by making you look bad. Why don't we fight back? Because we don't know how to spot power thieves and ne'er-do-wells who cross our paths in the workplace. We don't see the warning signs and the red flags, so we get blindsided. The am-bitchous woman's myopia in this area is the result of the following socially sanctioned self-sabotage:

Sheep's Clothing (overt message): Women are trusting and fair. Women have an innate ability to see the good in people who may not, on the surface, exhibit their best selves. We model ethics and integrity and showing respect toward others.

Wolf (covert message): If you accuse someone of trying to cheat you or bully you, you are being disrespectful and unethical. You are robbing that person of their dignity.

Socially Sanctioned Self-Sabotage: You place your trust in those who are really out to get you and whose objective is to steal your power. You don't see them coming. They sucker punch you and make themselves look good by making you look bad. You don't stick up for yourself, or you do so too late, after the damage has been done. You end up feeling and looking powerless and ineffectual.

I've observed these common reasons ambitious women don't become power brokers:

• We don't know how to spot naysayers. We don't see the warning signs.

- We don't trust our instincts when we're under attack or when someone is trying to undermine us, because of a false belief that everyone else plays as ethically and fairly as we do.

- By failing to trust our own powerful intellect, professional expertise, judgment calls, and instincts, we let either intentional saboteurs or well-intentioned but misguided folks plant a seed of doubt in our hearts and minds that shakes our resolve. This allows others to penetrate and shake our confidence.

- We cede our desire to fight back to our desire to keep the peace.

- We're not careful enough about the people we let into our inner circle, and therefore we allow ourselves to be negatively influenced by detractors.

- And most important, by undervaluing just how precious our hard-earned power is, we are stopping ourselves from fighting to preserve our power, our professional reputation, our earning capacity, the recognition and respect we deserve, and the sanctity of our ambitchous dreams.

Learn to Spot Naysayers, Attackers, Detractors, Critics, and Underminers

There are several garden varieties of naysayers, attackers, detractors, complainers, doubters, critics, and underminers. Their tactics are diverse, and whatever you call them doesn't matter. What's important is that you understand the key thing they have in common—if you let them get away with it, they will sap your strength, make you look and feel weak, render you less powerful in the marketplace, and drain your internal power and self-confidence.

Take, for example, what I call a nasty naysayer. These are critical, pessimistic, irascible, emotionally volatile, jealous, hypercompetitive, or insecure people who hit below the belt, don't play fair, and strive to bring others down. They go for the jugular. They don't care in the least about you or how you feel or what you think or how you are impacted by their behavior.

A powerful woman in the workplace who values and guards her hard-earned power will cut a nasty naysayer off at their knees, even if it requires being heavy-handed. Then she will move on— and won't waste time or energy second-guessing her actions or feeling guilty. And the women I work with who confront in this way are actually nice, decent, professional people who treat their colleagues and employees with great respect. It's just that these same decent women are not going to let the office jerk run roughshod over them.

By failing to fight back when we're being attacked in the marketplace, not only do we lose power in terms of how others see us; we also set ourselves up for letting an underminer's criticisms eat away at our sense of internal power and confidence. We ruminate about what happened, what we should have or could have done, and the consequences of having done nothing. What a waste of time and energy.

Recognizing previous experiences with power thieves can prepare you to spot the next saboteur. Recall a time when you were attacked—either in a group or one on one, by a boss, a peer, a client, a competitor, or even by someone who reports to you—and you failed to stick up for yourself.

- Where did you let your guard down? How did you feel during and after the attack?
- What kept you from sticking up for yourself? Was it that you couldn't think of the right thing to say in that shocking moment? Were you afraid that fighting back would put you at risk

for an escalated attack and further humiliation? Were you afraid your voice would shake because you were so angry, or that you'd tear up and look weak? Did you secretly feel that the attacker was right?

• How much ruminating did you do about what you could have said, what you should have said, the ramifications of not having done so, how others who witnessed the encounter had changed their opinions of you? Were you distracted that night at dinner, with your husband or kids, because you were absorbed in replaying the tape of the attack? Did you find it hard to fall asleep that night because you couldn't stop thinking about what had happened, and also because being so pissed off—both at your attacker and at yourself—kept you awake?

• Did you spend precious time worrying about when and where and how the next sneak attack would be? Did you especially dread team meetings he or she would be attending because you feared that you'd again be knocked off guard and made to look powerless, weak, or stupid? Did you obsess about all the possible ways that your power position in your company—with your team, with your direct reports, with your boss, and across divisions—had been weakened? Not to mention your reputation in your industry at large?

See Them Coming and Protect Yourself

I feel like I've had my fair share of being set up and beaten up at work, enough of being a rock battered by the tide. But I'm learning a lot, because you know what? The people who play dirty are all showing me their cards; they're showing me how they work, and I'm watching. So, okay, now I'm onto you. Now I can predict how you're going to do it next time and I'll be prepared. Now I can see you coming from a mile away.

—Tam, thirty-one, investment banker in a
leading New York City firm

Use the following exercise to power up by learning to spot power-draining people in their various incarnations:

- The Heckler Underminer. Take a moment right now and think of your least favorite, most draining coworker—that person who can never restrain himself for longer than five minutes into a team meeting before voicing a negative, sarcastic comment.

- The Mind-Game Power Thief. Now think of someone in a senior role who loves to play mind games with you. She'll say, "Are you sure you're going to hit your quarterly target? Are you sure? What if you overshot your projections?" But you know you're right—and you think she knows it too.

- The Nasty Naysayer. Identify that division head—your peer in a different department of your company—with whom you and your team must work in order to achieve larger objectives, including regular product rollouts and promised client deliverables and deadlines. For example, you're senior VP of sales and marketing; he's senior VP of engineering and new-product development. He constantly yells in meetings, bullies you and everyone on your team: "That's an impossible client demand and a ridiculous strategy and time line. What is this company paying you %$# people top dollar for? What do you do with your days—surf the Internet for new porn? As far as I can tell, you've accomplished absolutely nothing since our last joint team meeting. Is anyone in charge here?" It's not uncommon for your direct reports as well as his to end up in tears after reading an e-mail from him or taking one of his barking phone calls. You don't cry—you're just outraged, yet uncertain how to handle this volatile, closed-minded person.

- The I'm-Just-Concerned-About-You Naysayer. Think of a person in your life—be it a colleague, family member, or someone else outside of work—who always thinks they know, better than you do, what's best for you; that person who often questions the decisions you make and subtly tries to plant seeds of doubt in your mind about those choices. "Are you really sure this choice is in the best interest of your career, your family, not to mention your own well-being?" Or: "Are you really sure you should accept that promotion? It's going to require you to travel fifty percent of the time. Aren't you concerned that all that time away from your husband will jeopardize your marriage?" Or: "Are you certain you want to take that job? It seems very risky—it's a start-up company; what if they go under?" Or: "Are you really confident you have the capital to start your own business? What if there's another terrorist attack and the economy crashes again? How will you pay the bills?"

• The Passive-Aggressive Power Detractor. Identify someone you work with, or someone in your personal life, whose style of being critical is never to explicitly say the words conveying that you've made a misstep, but their tone signals shock or doubt and that maybe you should rethink your position. After you've told one of these folks a big goal you've just set, they say, *"Really? By such-and-such a date? Oh. Well, good luck. But I'm worried that you won't be able to make it on your own."*

All too often, we ambitchous women allow ourselves to be overly influenced by detractors, because it never occurs to us to question motives or do a quick mental fact-check about whether or not this person knows what the heck he or she is talking about. Time to pull out a Reality Check tool to nip this tendency in the bud.

REALITY CHECK
Detractor Vulnerability Quiz

Are you giving too much airtime to naysayers, saboteurs, doubters, and underminers?

1. If someone puts down my idea, my first reaction is, "Maybe they're right."

   True _____

   False _____ My first reaction is, "They're wrong; they just don't get it. Too bad, so sad for them."

2. When someone reacts negatively to something I've just shared about my work, I become flustered and can't articulate what I've already mapped out in my own head.

   True _____

   False _____ I am clear and verbally confident when it comes to succinctly laying out what I've already figured out in my own mind and fact-checked, even when someone disagrees or criticizes.

3. When I first get a sense that someone is subtly trying to undermine me, I immediately think, "I must be imagining it; she (or he) is definitely on my side."

   True _____

   False _____ I have pretty good instincts when it comes to spotting passive-aggressive or hostile people and identifying them. As such, I trust my gut.

4. I've just shared my latest, greatest ambition and strategic plan, and the first words out of the listener's mouth are, "But how are you going to fund it? There's no room in the budget." I immediately go into fear mode.

   True _____

   False _____ My first thought is, "This listener hasn't seen my balance sheet"; my second, "He is thinking small." My third thought is, "There is always a way. I'm ambitchous, after all."

5. If a colleague smirks and mutters something under her

breath after I state an opinion in a team meeting, I worry that I've just sounded stupid.

True _____

False _____ I think that the colleague looks not only unprofessional but inappropriate, and am confident that others in the meeting regard her similarly. And I take quick action to call her on it publicly, such as, "Jane, you just muttered something under your breath that I didn't catch. Was it important?"

6. I am particularly likely to be knocked off balance when an undermining comment is made by someone who holds a powerful or prestigious job title.

True _____

False _____ I recognize that not everyone in a power position has good people or leadership skills. This person's negative attitude will come back to bite him. I don't let it affect me or my self-confidence.

7. If someone says to me, "Oh, no, you don't want to do that, do you?" my first reaction will likely be to doubt my own idea or goal.

True _____

False _____ My reaction is to say or think, "How do you know what I want to do?" Or I might say, "Thanks for clearing up for me what *I* want to do," chuckling and shaking my head dismissively. And I'm thinking, "What do you know about this, anyway?" And then I move on with my plan, leaving this negative person behind.

8. If a colleague responds to my ambitious idea by observing that, "Competition in this area is fierce, and very, very few people succeed," my confidence takes a nosedive.

True _____

False _____ I recognize that this person is probably jealous or highly competitive, or maybe even an underachiever, and isn't self-aware or strategic enough to keep it under wraps.

9. If I'm turned down for a conventional bank loan to help capitalize my business, I have second thoughts about moving forward with my venture.

True _____

False _____ If I can't initially finance the venture through traditional means, I am confident I will be able to identify innovative ways or find other creative, bootstrapping interim methods.

10. If I've failed on a first attempt to launch an important new project, I falter and feel shaken inside.

True _____

False _____ I know that failures come with successes. An Ivy League business school study found that the key difference between start-ups that succeed and those that fail is that the successful companies shifted gears and changed ineffectual business strategies and ditched false-start products as many as five or six times in as many as five or six years before hitting on a winning model. I'll be all the wiser the next time out.

11. If a colleague says to me, "Don't do it that way; do it this (my) way," I feel shaken in my conviction about the right course of action.

True _____

False _____ I say aloud or think to myself, "I am confident that my way is the right way."

12. If someone says to me about a goal I've set for myself, "You're too old (or too young) to do that!" I want to crawl into a hole.

True _____

False _____ I understand that age is irrelevant. Or, more accurately, age gives me a particular developmental vantage point and perspective, wisdom, maturity, and experience that I can leverage to achieve my goals.

If you answered true to two or more of these statements, you need to beef up your detractor-defense strategies. Not to worry. It's perfectly normal for your confidence to take a hit when a negative person assaults your idea or something about you. The important thing is not to let those feelings linger or get you down. Recognize it as a detractor situation. Feel the impact for a minute, or for an hour, or for a day (and yes, of course, it's sometimes painful), and then let it go. Keep yourself moving forward, optimistic—and most important, armed with strategies to protect yourself and your power from further attack.

twelve

Am•BITCH•ous Rule 7
Disable Detractors

IF you're like many professional women, you find it hard to break the habit of giving underminers or nasty jerks the power to take away your power. You may find that you give these detractors more credit and influence over your career ambition and self-respect than they deserve. If this is true, you're not alone.

Sheep's Clothing (overt message): Women are natural-born peacekeepers. They hold families and communities together.

Wolf (covert message): Women shouldn't be fighters. They shouldn't fight back, slap back, push back. Engaging in a fight means that they are failing at their role as coalition builders.

Socially Sanctioned Self-Sabotage: You let people steal your power. You feel weak, impotent, ineffectual, and powerless to make your most ambitchous dreams happen. You feel like a wimp in the business world.

The key here is to step back and look objectively rather than emotionally at what's happening and at what's being communicated to you—either directly or indirectly. If you can train yourself to do a fact-check in these situations instead of letting the attack impact you viscerally, you'll be able to call it when you experience it. You'll be positioned to protect yourself from a painful mental or emotional hit. In fact, you'll get so good at doubting the validity of what detractors hurl your way that you'll be able to deflect their negative energy immediately and elegantly put them on the defensive: "Hmm . . . What would make you say such a negative thing?" Better still, you'll become so skilled at neutralizing their intended impact that you won't feel the need to respond at all: "Oh, wow. Look at the time; gotta run."

After getting into the habit of responding in this way to detractors, you won't waste a moment analyzing why they said what they said or whether there's any truth to their comments. We're not talking about discounting constructive feedback, which can, of course, be invaluable. But there is no such thing as constructive hostile criticism. Positive brainstorming questions or ideas have a very different feel to the recipient. And the intention on the part of the person delivering the information is very different. It's supportive rather than destructive. Think of how liberating this new mind-set will be and how much energy will be freed up to focus on your goals, rather than on people who aim to bring you down with their negativity.

Strategies for Disabling Detractors

Trust Your Gut

If you sense that someone is doing something to you, then they probably are. If you feel it in the pit of your stomach, or wherever else in your body you experience instincts—a tightening in the chest, a heavy feeling in the shoulders—then pay attention. Don't try to talk yourself out of your own perceptions. And don't bother trying to reason with detractors. It's a waste of your time and effort—they won't admit to their behavior, and they'll keep tying you in knots about your own.

Keep going back to what your instincts are telling you and you'll feel an almost palpable release from what could have been this person's power grip. You'll be untouchable. You'll see what the detractor is all about. This protective boundary shuts out anyone who would undermine your self-confidence. This will give you a detached perspective on the situation and enable you, finally, to walk away unscathed.

Be Armed with Snappy Comebacks

How many times have you thought of a perfect retort after a detractor incident has come and gone? A snappy comeback after the person who invalidated you with a below-the-belt sarcastic comment in a team meeting has already left the room? You'll probably agree that there's nothing more frustrating than to be shocked speechless during a naysayer's onslaught, only to think of the bull's-eye, back-at-you rejoinder when it's too late.

By contrast, an elegant, understated, well-aimed, and perfectly timed retort neuters the negative naysayer, rendering him harmless and making you feel less vulnerable and exposed. It takes care of it right then and there. You'll also benefit from an enormous amount of saved energy and emotion.

This detractor strategy involves having five or six or more snappy rejoinders at your disposal—these are one-size-fits-all, repartee wardrobe essentials just waiting for you to flash in those situations when a critic sidelines you with an unexpected verbal attack. It's like having your pair of great black pants, that basic, fabulous white shirt, and the way-too-expensive, always-in-style boots that you can whip out of your closet in a snap. This is an outfit you can build on, dress up, dress down, and accessorize to quickly tailor to any number of professional or social situations.

Example 1: Detractor says in a team meeting with six of your senior VP colleagues: "I worry about you that you're in over your head with this project." In a mildly amused, slightly sarcastic tone say, "Good point." Translation, "You should worry about yourself, not me." Follow this by saying—to the rest of the group, not facing the detractor—"Okay. Let's keep moving." Or, "Next person's *serious* comments?"

Example 2: Detractor: "I worry about you, that you'll never be able to make it on your own." With a chuckle and a superficial smile you say, "Thanks for thinking of me!" Continue with a head-shaking amused laugh and walk away.

Example 3: Detractor: "You're being unreasonable." You reply, "Thanks for clearing that up for me! Okay, then. I've got a meeting to make." Then you head off to your next appointment without looking back.

Example 4: A detractor jokes to you in a group meeting, "Is it that time of the month?" Several women I've interviewed have described this as actually having happened, and recently, too. Without missing a beat, you say with a disdainful laugh, "What, are you nuts?" Then stare at the naysayer for a couple of seconds— seconds that will be painful for him, not for you—with a direct, clear-eyed gaze tinged with a slightly amused, condescending edge. Then turn to the others and say calmly, "Okay, moving on to our next point."

Or you could deploy this fun Option 2 for responding to the is-it-that-time-of-the-month? bomb. You would use the same approach and same facial and body posturing I just described, but instead laugh and say, "*Jack!* I think it's actually you who has his

period! It's okay. Take a Midol or a time-out if you need one."
Then, turning back to the group, "Now let's move on! We're
making great progress."

Sure, you could have said, "I can't believe you made such a sex-
ist remark!" Sure, you could have escalated it by going to HR, and
maybe sometimes you do this behind the scenes, if the harassment
continues. But can you see how this strategy nips it in the bud right
then and there so you can let it go, rather than letting it sap your
energy and focus and drain your internal sense of power?

A wonderful added feature of this in-the-moment approach is
that, if you're in front of other people, a skillful, refined comeback
actually makes the invalidator look bad, not you.

Alternative power techniques: Try the simple, silent rejoinder
strategy. This is an inscrutable, poker-faced stare, artfully timed
to last a few uncomfortable (for the detractor—not for you) seconds, and it's a very powerful tactic. You don't raise your eyebrows, you don't frown, you don't give any facial expression at
all—you are utterly unreadable, such that your invalidator
doesn't know if you are hurt, angry, befuddled, or amused. This is
unsettling for a naysayer, who feeds on others' emotional reactions to the surprise attack. Your power here comes from the fact
that you are betraying no reaction; your face is cryptic, a blank
canvas—he or she is left to wonder what you're thinking, robbed
of the sense of having gotten your goat. Silently count one, one
thousand, two, one thousand, three, one thousand, four, one
thousand, five, one thousand. This will give you a bit more internal leverage by passing the time in your head. Then, after that
fifth second (don't cut corners and stop at four seconds!), simply
say, "So, then—see you in the meeting at four o'clock." Flash a
brief smile and walk away. Your detractor will be left scratching
his head, wondering what just happened.

Silent Rejoinder Group Example 1: In a group meeting, a detractor says, "I can't believe you just said that!" You can use the

five-second silent, inscrutable stare (no frown here, just a clear-eyed, indecipherable look), then pleasantly turn to someone else in the meeting and say with an upbeat, confident delivery, "Keeping up our focused brainstorming, I'd love to hear about your thinking this week on Project X."

Silent Rejoinder Group Example 2: I call this the group hit-and-run detractor incident, given that it occurs at the end of the meeting or when people are standing up and almost out the door. The detractor says: "Phew, that was a waste of an hour." You, without missing a beat, say, "This has been a highly productive meeting. Thank you, everyone, for such inspired thinking today!" Use names and fast, bullet specifics, if it's a small group: "Ben, great job spotting that beta test glitch. Jill, congrats on your client win. . . ." Don't include the detractor's name as someone who just contributed. You walk away cleanly, while the detractor is revealed as the difficult person she is. Take my word for it that no one (except another detractor—and luckily there's usually only one per room) enjoys negativity. The balanced people in a group setting will respect your limit-setting as well as your refusal to engage. They will, in fact, be secretly delighted—impressed, actually—that you silenced the heckler. So you also win points in the leadership-skills department. People will remember your elegance in the face of an invalidator.

Practice these Detractor Rejoinders at home alone in front of the mirror, or while you're on the treadmill, or after a missed opportunity has you fired up. You've got to practice over and over again until these strategies take up permanent residence in the front of your awareness, at the top of your mind—where they then become powerfully second nature. Take on a detractor on your own timetable, on your own terms. You don't have to resolve everything right away. And be fit physically. Nothing makes you feel more powerful in the room than knowing that your body is strong.

Like the peak-performance athlete who understands the delicate, interdependent mind/body relationship and regards the task of tending to her body as being equally important as minding her mental state, you too can gain a competitive edge over naysayers by being strategically mindful of your nutrition, sleep, and exercise needs.

Honest Communication Can Turn a Detractor into an Ally

Delia, forty-two, had been offered a promotion to vice president of business development heading up a new division in her company, an industry-leading, publicly traded pharmaceutical company. As she was considering the job offer, she asked one of her colleagues, a chief scientist whom she had beaten out for the position and would soon be supervising, how he felt about working for her. She described his bitter response: "He let me know that he didn't think I could handle the job. He said, 'I don't think you're ready for this. This job is too tough for you. And I told the CEO that he shouldn't select you.'" Delia said that once he let her know how he felt about her promotion, he proceeded to give her what she believed to be an honest appraisal of what was going on in her soon-to-be department and what the challenges were as he saw them.

Delia recalled to me that his initial reaction was "brutally honest" and "painful to hear." But now he is her go-to, right-hand person. How did this happen? She explained it this way:

His initial reaction was, I thought, an honest reaction—and I expect honesty. My instinct wasn't that he was trying to sabotage me; he was disappointed that he lost his shot at a great promotion. After I'd been in my new role for a month or so, I went back to him and asked him to explain himself to me. And he said, "I

> was really shocked. I wasn't expecting you to say that you'd been
> offered the job; I hadn't known that the decision had been made."

Yes, Delia recognized that his disappointment and how he'd responded to it was a normal, human reaction. But she also thought that a few weeks was a reasonable amount of time for him to get over those raw feelings. So after that initial period of time in her new role, she went to him and asked him to explain why he'd said what he said—and communicated to him what her expectations were:

> I met with him and said, "I want to go back to what you said to me
> a few weeks ago when you learned I'd been offered the job. This is
> what you said to me. I need to know what you meant by that."
> Then, after listening to him explain himself, I said, "Your initial
> reaction of being disappointed that you weren't offered the job
> was normal. But now I need to know that you're on board. I need
> you to know that when you go out of this office, I need for you to
> carry the party line; I need you to endorse what I'm saying. You
> cannot go against me on issues—so we have to be on the same
> page." And he agreed with me. And now we have a great working
> relationship. And he's very knowledgeable and a great asset. So it
> was worth going through that painful process to keep him on my
> team.

Gather Data

By backing your opinions and recommendations with hard facts, you have far more power to control a meeting and its outcome. Contact anyone you know who may be able to give you behind-the-scenes information. Do your research. Go online and dig around. Pound the pavement. Get the data you think you'll need.

Before you walk into a meeting, think about the hot buttons, soft spots, and deal breakers you already know about. Think about the players' styles of negotiating. Anticipate points of inter-section—where you already agree, where you could potentially agree if things keep moving in the same direction, plus what you're willing to compromise and why. Be prepared for both log-ical and emotional arguments. Do the best you can to be ready for everything.

Before Debra Pryor walked into her new role as the first female city fire chief in Berkeley, California, she gathered a lot of infor-mation. For example, before she actually started work, she came to meetings that the city manager held. So she learned, before starting her new job, that certain budget deadlines were going to be upon her immediately. She also spent some time with the fire-fighters' union. She said that doing all this gave her power when she walked into a very tough position. It allowed her to build rela-tionships and to let her expectations be known very quickly. She said that doing all this was very time-consuming. But there was a big payoff: when she walked into her new leadership role, she was empowered to lead the charge.

Feel Empowered to Take Control of the Room

You can empower yourself in your day-to-day work life. Before you walk into that conference room, sit in your office—or a toilet stall if you're out of your territory—wherever you can find a quiet space to ground yourself, take some deep breaths, pull your thoughts together, briefly visualize the key bullet points you want to cover, points of agreement, points of disagreement, and open questions. Plant your feet on the ground. Get centered. Then brush your teeth or your hair. Pull up your socks, straighten your suit jacket, tuck your shirt into your underwear so that you know it will stay in place. If you can be the first person in the room, all the better; get there early, sit in the room, size up the surroundings, and visualize the meeting and the outcome you hope for. And you'll have a sort of home-team advantage, having already gotten the lay of the land before the other team arrives.

Whatever makes you feel strong and calm and in control before going into battle, do it. Take those few moments to get grounded in your power.

By the way—wear your power suit for important meetings, even if corporate casual attire is acceptable. Arming yourself with your most forceful clothing does impact how you are regarded. I was recently asked to observe a meeting. Of the three people there that I did not know, two were women and one was a man; I knew that one of those was a lawyer, one was a paralegal, and one was an executive assistant. I just didn't know who was who; nor did this become clear during the meeting. Afterward, I did a reality check with someone in the room I did know. I had pegged the guy in the suit and tie as the lawyer, and the woman in the sweet-looking short-sleeved, spring green cardigan set and white pants as the paralegal; I got it exactly backward. Ms. Cardigan was the lawyer, and a senior one at that; Mr. Suit was the paralegal, and younger and far less experienced than Ms. Cardigan. Power lesson? Armor up; you'll feel empowered and come across as powerful.

Make Transparent Your Thought Processes

Others can't see what's going on in your head or why you make the decisions you make or why you choose certain courses of action. Sometimes playing show-and-tell with power detractors who would otherwise try to derail you will provide them with an *aha!* understanding of what you're thinking and why. And in some cases, they will stop trying to push you off course. Here's what Christine Comaford-Lynch had to say about the process:

> When I've been faced with blockers who threaten to create an impasse, I show my decision process and walk the others through it. For example, if I'm leading a board meeting and we've hit an impasse, if I spell out my thinking to the dissenters, we may reach an agreement. So I might say: "Here's my thinking. I've felt this way before when I was working at such-and-such company heading up this-and-such a product rollout. And the result was X." And I map it out. Then I compare and contrast for them: "On the other hand, I've seen projects heading in this direction before, and avoiding swift action resulted in Y." Sometimes this turns things around and we move forward rather than hitting a wall.

Debra Pryor says that if she provides the leadership and direction her people are hungry for, would-be detractors become invested team members:

> They want to know where they're going as a department. They truly do the work—it's as if we're on a river rafting trip and I'm the guide in the back of the boat and I'm just steering; they're the ones that have the oars in the water and are actually doing the paddling. Therefore I need to know where that boat is going. It is truly them that get us there; I just have the vision and I steer the process. And I've found that if they know where they're going, and they have the tools to get in that boat and paddle down that river, they're going to work with me, not against me.

Make your decision processes and expectations clear. Let people in on what your style is and what your thinking is. They'll learn what to expect from you, and they'll come into a meeting or a project prepared to get to work. And they're less likely to block progress—yours, or the organization's.

Disarm Detractors with Strategic Humor

Let's not forget humor. Franci J. Blassberg is a partner at Debevoise & Plimpton LLP and was named by the *National Law Journal* as one of the 100 Most Influential Lawyers in America. Franci said to me, "Sometimes you can change the tone in the room in a minute—defuse it—with humor and a tiny amount of self-deprecation." Well-placed self-deprecating humor is a hallmark of emotional intelligence—the ability to interact effectively with others.

Sometimes you get hit with an insult. That isn't the time for self-deprecating humor. But don't swing in the opposite direction and look like a woman with a chip on her shoulder. I see many women with this attitude. They don't accomplish as much as they could. Others don't want to assist them with their concerns. Instead, if you've taken a hard hit, learn to use aggressive yet disarming humor—humor combined with "a slap without a hand," an idiomatic expression from Uruguay meaning "a dignified act of revenge." Here's a great example.

Franci told me about something one of her clients said to her early in her career, when she first began representing his firm:

> He said, "I never would have thought that I would have a radical, Jewish feminist as my lawyer." I thought that he, at the time, was just getting acculturated. I thought that he meant it as, "My goodness, you're a really good lawyer, and even for someone like me I can see beyond all that other stuff." So it wasn't intended as a put-down, although one could have interpreted it that way. So I said, sort of jokingly: "I resent that; I'm not a radical." I think

using humor aggressively and both offensively and defensively, if you would, is a key strategy for women to use. It's not clear if that response was offense or defense. But you can take a lot of tension out of a room with humor. And women need to learn to do that, rather than seem to be uptight and ill at ease.

Humor is one thing we all enjoy. And it can be a great tool for disarming would-be detractors. Plus, nothing feels better than laughing—unless it's getting a hostile opponent on your side because you've shared a guffaw together. Laughter really is powerful medicine.

Avoid Negative People—Especially During Critical Ambition Ramp-up Periods

I can't emphasize enough the importance of putting a barrier between yourself and critical, negative people, particularly when you are in professional and creative critical periods of development. You know who they are—the people who give you the sense that they're thinking, if not outright saying, "Who do you think you are, anyway?" in the face of your expressed ambitions.

Avery, a forty-year-old working-class mother of two who'd never finished college, but who'd long had the dream of going back to school to complete her degree and had diligently worked her way into a top-tier West Coast university at the age of thirty-five, told me how a distinguished professor referred to her, to her face, as "a retread." This same detractor later discouraged her from raising her hand in class by saying, "We've heard enough from you—let's let others respond." She dropped the class that day, only after privately calling the professor on his inappropriate and unnecessary attempt to publicly humiliate her in class. She said, "There were plenty of other world-renowned finance professors in this program; I determined on the spot that I needn't put up with that kind of treatment and that I was entitled to get professors who were as invested in my educational and career pursuits as I was." Avery went on to secure a coveted slot in the school's master in finance engineering program and an exciting corporate internship opportunity.

It is vitally important to your ambitious endeavors, as well as to your sense of self and peace of mind, that you feel empowered to protect the purity and integrity of your productive, optimistic, and creative thinking. And it's crucial that you shield your planning, execution, and strategic focusing efforts from people who are so dark that you can feel negativity emanating from them before they've even opened their mouths.

Don't Put Yourself Down

This chapter wouldn't be complete unless we talked about ways that we act as our own worst detractors, undercutting our worth and competence with relentless negative self-talk.

Think of ways you bring yourself down by saying to yourself, in your own head, disparaging things about your capabilities, your accomplishments or lack thereof, your work ethic, your stamina, your looks, the way you present yourself, the way you speak, your weight, your decision-making skills, your risk-taking strategies, your emotional reactivity, or . . . you name it. It's as if we have this little judge inside of our heads who has the potential for being just as castigating, just as much of a power drain as our worst real-life detractors.

Even the most successful women among us battle this internal, power-sapping naysayer. When I interviewed real estate magnate Barbara Corcoran, she was in the middle of a book tour for her business book, *If You Don't Have Big Breasts, Put Ribbons on Your*

Pigtails, which has become a national bestseller. She told me that she is still occasionally prone to being her own worst critic: "My best advice to women is this: Learn to spot one of your least obvious enemies, which is yourself. And rise to your own expectations by thinking how you'll feel if you doubt that you have the power to do what you really want to do. Learn not to accept no as an answer—from yourself, to yourself." To underscore her point, she recounted this self-detracting, power-draining struggle she waged with herself:

> I did a TV appearance recently and I couldn't watch the tape of the interview because I knew I wouldn't be happy with my physical appearance. I'm fifty-three and having to come to terms with the fact that, at this point, our bodies start going to s____t. Finally, my assistant made me watch it, saying, "Don't look at yourself—just listen to yourself." So I did and I realized that I sounded great, I had important, wise, powerful things to say that I wouldn't have understood or been able to articulate years earlier (when I looked better). And I had the realization that day that God does play fair—your outside goes to s____t but you get smarter—and more powerful—on the inside.

B. L. Ochman is known as someone who understands her stuff and who has the guts to be wildly creative in order to deliver the results. She is an internationally known Internet marketer and blog strategy consultant to Fortune 500 companies. When we last spoke, B.L. had just completed her blog-based viral marketing campaign for Budget Car Rental. Using no traditional marketing whatsoever, B.L.'s strategy generated 1 million unique visits to the Budget Web site, and more than 10 million page views in only four weeks. B.L. laughingly described to me battling her own internal naysayer: "Of course I periodically get that little nagging voice of doubt inside my head yammering, 'You're not really as great as you think you are.' It's hard, man, but sometimes you have to just beat that little f____ker down!"

As ambitchous women, we can gain more internal power by learning to look at ourselves almost from the perspective of an outsider. Taking a whole new vantage point helps to quell the voice inside our heads that would otherwise cause us to stumble and to keep from revealing just how great—and powerful—we truly are.

When you hear yourself tearing yourself down, try to become aware of it. The next step is to pretend you care as much about advocating for yourself as you do for others. Tap into the abundance of goodwill and moral support—heretofore reserved for friends, colleagues, and loved ones—and incorporate it into your own positive self-talk. Put this reservoir of encouragement at your disposal and use it liberally. Eventually, a great habit replaces a bad habit—and that great habit will bring you even more power and self-confidence to be the ambitchous woman you know you can be.

thirteen

Am●BITCH●ous Rule 8
Stop the Fraud Police—
You Deserve to Be Here

O to have the gag remov'd from one's mouth!
O to have the feeling, to-day or any day, I am sufficient as I am!
— Walt Whitman, from "One Hour to Madness
and Joy"

*I think that successful women, when pushed, would admit that
sometimes they worry that they've overshot their abilities. I tend
to personalize it by saying to myself, "Who do you think you are?"
And when I say something like that to my husband—why should I
expect that kind of reward or success?—he always says, "Because
you're great at what you do. Because you should win. Because you
deserve it."*
— Mary Lou Quinlan

MANY an ambitious woman periodically experiences a sneaking
suspicion that she hasn't really earned her professional position
and that the bottom is going to fall out one day. One Pulitzer
Prize–winning journalist told me she could get a hundred and

ninety-nine letters that were full of praise and positive feedback and one letter that was negative. She remembers the bad letter for days; it haunts her; it's the one she believes is true. She secretly fears this letter writer may be onto something. Even though she possesses certified credentials and knowledge in her field, has shown her ability and intelligence, and has ample educational background and dazzling prior success, she still tenders the thought, "If they only knew . . ." By any objective standard she deserves her position and recognition and the paycheck that goes with it, but somehow she feels she is undeserving. Her professional veneer seems like a false persona. She is like a person who has just made footprints in the sand but does not recognize them as her own when she looks behind her.

> *Oh, my God! Every time I get on a conference call, I still think, "They're going to find out the truth about how much I don't know."*
>
> —Sara, forty, executive vice president,
> Fortune 500 financial services firm

In 1998, Liz Roberts, first vice president, wealth management, Smith Barney, San Rafael, California, and one of the first women who came on board when I founded the Women's Business Alliance, said to me:

> I've rarely talked to a woman client, no matter how accomplished, who didn't express that sense of it's-all-going-to-blow-up. Someone is always going to find out that they don't know what they're doing—even if they're running Hewlett-Packard.

Liz's comment was both prescient and ironic. Carly Fiorina didn't step up to lead HP until the following year, in 1999; six years later it did all blow up for her, at least within that corporate culture (I'm confident Ms. Fiorina's got plenty of fresh ambitchous goals on her long-term horizon).

Even the most highly accomplished women among us harbor this guilty secret. Researcher Peggy McIntosh, observing women who speak from the audience at professional conferences, says that many of them preface their remarks with statements like: "I'm not sure I know what I'm talking about, but here goes. . . ." Or: "I don't know enough to cover the whole subject, so I'll just restrict my comments to . . ." The disclaimer is a preemptive strike on the part of the speaker; she disparages herself before anyone else can leap up to do it to her. McIntosh's subsequent research revealed that most professional women felt, at least periodically, that they had not really earned their position or that they did not deserve their educational or career credentials. No matter what the level of accomplishment, most of the women I interviewed reported that they occasionally had the sensation that they might be revealed as frauds by colleagues.

Sheep's Clothing (overt message): Women are the more innately humble gender; they don't take their professional brilliance for granted. Looked at in this light, authentically questioning one's ability to fit into the ambitchous big leagues is wise, even a virtue. Women's nature is to be more willing than their male counterparts to self-reflect and to question, in a positive way, how they can continually improve themselves—or even if they want to compete in the marketplace as it's laid out. Underlying women's sense of professional fraudulence is actually a healthy awareness: it's not that they can't play the game of business; it's that they choose not to do so because they have more authentic values and worthy priorities than those the business world offers. Women's willingness to be introspective and to sincerely devote themselves to lifelong learning and self-improvement is a positive attribute—especially in light of the fact that they are so new to the game of business. They can figure out what they value according to their own standards.

Wolf (covert message): If women sacrifice their down-to-earth, unpretentious nature, they'll get too big for their breeches. After all, women in business are not all grown-up yet; they are still relative newcomers to the marketplace. They mustn't overshoot their mark and forget their place. If they do, they'll be humiliated and exposed as card-carrying members of a not-fully-formed stirp of the grander, more mature, and more successful professional species. If they just stay humble, they'll eventually earn their place—maybe as soon as the next century.

Socially Sanctioned Self-Sabotage: An it's-all-going-to-blow-up-in-my-face alarm is constantly going off in the back of your brain. This robs you of enjoying your ambition and the spoils of your success in a relaxed, life-affirming way. Moments of calm confidence that give you pleasure are frequently compromised by sudden, heightened terror alerts, warning you to ready yourself for dodging yet another fraud bullet aimed squarely at your professional credibility. You fear that you're never going to come into your own as a fully developed ambitchous woman who can simply appreciate her accomplishments and love where she is in her career and in her overall life.

My challenge to you is to allow yourself to feel like the real deal. And why shouldn't you? You've worked hard. You've had the guts to dream big and the stamina and determination to chase your dreams. You should enjoy yourself as you move through your ambitchous career. Let's start with a Reality Check to see if, and in what ways, you may be prone to feeling like an interloper. How many of the following statements apply to you?

REALITY CHECK
Are the Fraud Police Banging on My Door?

- You adopt an apologetic stance because you secretly fear you have something to atone for (i.e., being a fake.) For example, before you give an opinion, do you say, "Forgive me if I'm speaking out of turn, but . . ." Or: "I may be out of my league, but here goes . . ."?
- You are afraid to come right out and say you don't know something, because then the truth will be revealed: you don't know anything.
- You read maniacally every professional publication just in case someone hands you a pop quiz one day.
- You try to work into every conversation the fact that you went to Barnard.
- When somebody else praises your accomplishments, you blush.
- You avoid standing up in a crowd if you have to speak— even if the group leader has asked people to stand before speaking.
- You use a weak, willowy, or high-pitched voice when making your point. For example, when you say something in a group meeting, especially in front of a larger crowd, people often interrupt you with, "We can't hear you in the back!"
- You avoid challenging an idea you disagree with. Or you decline to state an unpopular opinion.
- You rush through and cut short what you wanted to say so you can slide quickly out of the spotlight.
- You punctuate your statement with a shrug or a dismissive gesture at the end, as if to neutralize it and render imperceptible what you've just stepped out on a limb to say.

- You look for consensus immediately after speaking. For example, you seek validation that your listeners agree with you by saying, "Don't you think so?" Or: "Right?"
- You don't speak up at all, though you do have an opinion and would like to state it.

If you identified three or more behaviors above, you may be rendering yourself invisible when you should be standing out. Staying out of sight to avoid being spotted as a fraud has consequences.

It limits your ability to cope with the external obstacles to earning your worth. In a conflictive situation where you need to be aggressive, your self-defeating inner dialogue puts you in a one-down position. You think, "Maybe they're right and I don't really know what I'm talking about." The minute you think that, you're toast. It prevents you from speaking with professional righteousness and situationally appropriate arrogance: "I know what the facts are; I've read the law. The options are crystal-clear. You're paying me good money to give you expert advice; here it is." It keeps you from sharing your knowledge and experience with larger groups of people for fear that you are falsely positioning yourself as an expert. For example, you decline public speaking opportunities that could bring you recognition and power. It blocks you from presenting yourself in the media as an authority in your area of expertise because you are afraid to publish articles and books, write guest columns, offer or accept an opportunity to be quoted, or become a guest expert speaker. It affects your ability to compete for awards or contracts by limiting your willingness to advertise what you have to offer. It restricts your competitive edge by keeping you from energetically selling your knowledge, goods, or services as the best the market has to offer.

In all of these ways, hiding out for fear of being exposed as a fraud prevents you from commanding your full salary, getting more power, and receiving the recognition and credit you deserve. And what is the sum total effect? It undermines your determination to go after your most ambitchous dreams and to reap the rewards that you are very capable of earning. Feeling, at your core, that you want to be, but don't belong, in the ambitchous leagues compromises your overall quality of life.

Counteract the Fear of Public Speaking

One of the most common problems that women face is the reluctance to speak up in a group. You would think that professionals would have gotten over this, but a study found that 50 percent of the professional women surveyed, compared with 20 percent of their male counterparts, said they would decline a public speaking opportunity if given the opportunity. This fear of standing out in a group is a symptom of a deeper fear: that of being visible. It is rooted in the following feeling: "If I am too visible, people will see my faults and I'll be a moving target. They'll criticize me for not knowing enough. I will be found out."

There are simple things you can do to counteract the fear of public speaking.

Ask Yourself, What's the Worst Thing That Could Happen?

Some fear of exposure is to be expected in public situations, but if you find an unusual amount of resistance to doing anything that will cause people to focus their attention on you, you must ask yourself if there is a deeper reason for it. An unreasonable level of anxiety over doing something as simple as speaking up often signals that there are hidden catastrophic fears behind your reluctance. You will have to poke around and find out if those fears are rational or irrational. So ask yourself these questions to help deconstruct just what it is that you're afraid of: What is the absolute worst thing that could happen if I were to be seen by an auditorium full of people? Here are some possible worst-case scenarios: I'll die if I do it wrong. The world will end if I take this risk and I fail. I'll never get another chance if I blow this opportunity. I'll lose my job, the respect of my colleagues. I'll get fired, lose my paycheck. Then my spouse will slowly lose his respect for me. I'll lose him. Then I'll lose my house. Then I'll have to move and I'll lose all of my friends. My kids will lose their community and their quality of life. Life will never be the same. Why take the risk? It's just too big a price to pay if I get exposed as not really knowing what I'm doing.

Now who's the detractor? Take apart this argument. Is any of it true, or is it just a teeny, tiny bit exaggerated? And if it is true, if the worst happens, you will survive, and maybe even become stronger, tougher, and wiser as a result. Barbara Corcoran described her first public speaking experience many years ago during a Women's Business Alliance 60-Minute Expert Brief. Barbara told the story of how she found herself standing at the podium in front of an auditorium full of people. Her voice began shaking so badly that she couldn't speak and had to sit down. She was mortified and went home in shame. Barbara licked her wounds for about a day, but only for that long, before picking herself back up. As a pure show of personal strength, she called a university and told them she was an experienced speaker and would like to teach. She was hired as an adjunct instructor. Today she is one of the most charismatic speakers I've ever heard, a skill she learned from recovering with style and putting herself out there one more time.

Stand Up and Be Counted

At a large Women's Business Alliance meeting, I saw a woman who was a leader in her field attempt to talk to the group. I had asked people ahead of time to stand up when they spoke so that everyone could hear. However, she remained in her seat with her hands pressed into her knees. Her face turned bright red the longer she spoke, and her voice was tremulous. A half hour later, another woman, whom I knew to be an alumnus of a top graduate program and a successful physician, was so nervous to be the focus of attention that she actually overturned her chair when she rose. She confided to me later that before she came to a meeting like this, she had to talk herself into getting out of her car. These women were successful at what they did, but how many business opportunities had they missed out on because they were afraid to step forward in a group and put a face on their business or service?

Once I started looking for this theme, which I first spotted many years ago, I saw it recur with alarming regularity. I still witness it happening today all the time. This is true when I'm presenting at a top women's M.B.A. school annual conference, where not only students but alumni who are now leaders in their fields are in attendance. It's true if I'm giving a workshop at a Fortune 500 company meeting; and it doesn't matter if the group is all women—they are still reluctant to be visible. It's true whatever the group I'm working with, be it large or small, where accomplished women are asked to put themselves out there. So if you hate standing up in a meeting, you're in excellent company. Still, I do want you to begin counteracting this fear the very next time you find yourself in a meeting or other situation during which standing up once in a while would make your message more powerful.

Ambitchous Course Correction

"Oh, My God! I Could Never Do That!"

Right about now, you may be thinking: "It's easy for you to tell me to stand up when I talk, but I'm terrified of putting myself in the spotlight like that in a crowd. It's hard enough for me to open my mouth. There's no way I'm going to be able to stand up and get the courage to say what I want to say, and do it all coherently. No way." Correction: Yes, you can do this. The truth is that you'll feel more comfortable speaking on your feet once you get used to how much more power you feel standing up. Granted, I'm encouraging you to try this in situations where it's appropriate and not awkward. Obviously there's no need to stand up every time it's your turn to talk when it's just you and your boss sitting in her office kicking around some ideas. I mean, I am reasonable!

Below are eight easy behavioral tools that will help you overcome your fear of standing up before you speak up. These techniques will make it easier on you:

1. Formulate your thoughts in two or three bullet points before you stand. This way you're not facing an inner void. Promise yourself that you won't begin speaking until you are fully standing.
2. Plant both feet on the ground so you're not caught off balance. If you trip while standing up, just have a good, quick laugh, briefly say something to acknowledge that, hey, you're human and sometimes you stumble, and launch right into your bullet points.
3. Take at least one deep breath before you utter your first word. This will seem longer for you than it will for your audience.

4. Don't fold your arms across your chest in a protective gesture; keep your hands at your sides in a relaxed position so you can freely use them to emphasize a point. Raise your chest and keep your head upright. Feel free to move around a bit if doing so feels natural.

5. Speak from your diaphragm rather than from your throat to feel grounded; you will be able to feel and hear your voice resonate from deep in your chest. Speak slowly so that you don't sound rushed. This will seem longer for you than for your audience.

6. Don't sit down until you have completed your statement and until you have waited to ask if anyone has questions or responses to what you have said.

7. Keep breathing. You'd be surprised how often you start holding your breath when you're scared. Breathing is good.

8. Put your mind at ease if people start asking questions by remembering that you can always respond to feedback that stumps you with, "Great question. Don't have an answer for it at the moment, but I'll see what I can find out and e-mail you later."

Use your body to support your new confident attitude. Be relaxed, but straighten your backbone and lift the crown of your head. There is a certain majesty and dignity that accompanies this stance. When you are standing tall, it's harder to be self-effacing or speak like a churchmouse. A professional woman on her feet, calmly facing her listeners, using her full voice with her body at ease, visibly communicates: "Look at me. Listen to me. I have something valuable to contribute, and I know what I'm doing."

A bonus piece of advice I give clients is this: even when you're on the phone with a client, your boss, colleagues, or direct reports—stand up. Move around during the call. Doing this changes the way you project yourself, even when they can't see you.

Speak Up

Some women naturally speak in a voice that approaches a whisper. They are not using enough air, so the sound coming through their voice box is tiny and weak. If a woman is not speaking loudly enough for people to hear her, she is communicating that they should not listen to her.

A second group of women have voices that are high and tremulous. The best examples are young women in their twenties and thirties who have a habit of saying "Think you!" instead of "Thank you!"—and they say it in a saccharine-sweet, high soprano voice. A high-pitched voice sends the message that they are little girls and not yet fully developed.

Discipline yourself to not speak in a weak, quiet, timid tone by learning to speak from your diaphragm. Focus your attention on how your voice feels in your chest. Make sure you take in enough air to allow your words to cascade powerfully out of your diaphragm. You should actually feel the vibrations in your chest as you speak as well as hear the tone resonating.

Research has shown that if women at board meetings or senior-level meetings speak in a high register, someone else will take over their ideas. Women with high-pitched voices may speak clearly and articulately, but their viewpoint seems not to be heard. However, if a male colleague or even a woman with a deeper voice makes the identical suggestion, that statement manages to make it into the recorded minutes. Women whose natural voice is in a lower register find that, more often than not, all of their suggestions make it into the minutes. The lesson is simple: People pay more attention to low-register voices.

How well would it have come across if Marilyn Monroe had

reported on the invasion of Iraq? Maya Angelou, who has won three spoken-word Grammy awards, has a voice that commands attention. It is so resonant and impressive that people stop in their tracks to listen. The change in voice level boosts a woman's sense of competence. This, in turn, is enhanced by the fact that she is receiving positive feedback from her audience, whether that is one person or three hundred people.

Stop Apologizing

> *Men are taught to apologize for their weaknesses, women for their strengths.*
>
> —Lois Wyse, advertising executive

> *I've noticed that saying something authoritatively, instead of ending a statement she's just made with a question, like "What do you think?" or: "Does that make sense?" or: "Don't you think that sounds right?," is an important habit for professional women to adopt.*
>
> —Katrine Shelton, tax attorney, Internal Revenue Service, San Francisco

> *I've talked with a lot of younger women lawyers about women in meetings and their tendency to invariably start with, "I may be wrong, but . . ." "Correct me if I'm wrong, but . . ." etc. Something that I have never heard a guy use. So the easy advice is, "Don't do that! You may be fighting type, but just don't do it!"*
>
> —Judith Thoyer

Think about the different methods you have used to apologize for being a full human being. Check any behaviors that you recognize in your own style.

☐ You begin every other sentence with a disclaimer: "I may be out of my league, but it seems to me that . . ."

☐   You downplay your talents or accomplishments for fear of being perceived as conceited or arrogant: "I'm no expert, but . . ."

☐   You present a self-effacing demeanor by punctuating the end of your serious statements with a short laugh.

☐   In groups, you are reticent about rising to your feet when you speak. You feel a lot less conspicuous if you remain in your chair.

☐   You're afraid to charge for an initial consultation.

☐   You feel the need to explain or defend yourself when discussing fees or asking clients to sign a contract.

☐   Your knee-jerk reaction in a conflict is to back down: "Oh, you're probably right; let's just forget about it."

☐   When making a point or talking about your business, you speak quickly or foreshorten what you intended to say so as to take up less time.

☐   You minimize or forgive the time requirement for canceling an appointment, rather than making a client pay for the hour meeting he missed, even though he knows what your policy is.

☐   You delay asking for an overdue pay raise.

☐   After laying out money for a purchase for which you expect to be reimbursed, you obsessively explain to the client or boss why you had to buy it, how it was worth the cost, why anyone in your shoes would have done the same thing, and so on. Or you don't mention the purchase at all and decide to absorb the cost.

☐   Whenever you do something nice for yourself, or take care of your own basic needs, you feel the need to justify it: "I've put in seventy-hour weeks for months, so it's okay to take Friday off for my mother's funeral."

If the number of checks you made seems surprising or high to you, we've got some work to do, but don't worry. Soon you'll have erased the preemptive apology from your repertoire of workplace behaviors.

Strategies to Stop Yourself from Apologizing

Apologizing is only one of many ways that we limit ourselves, but it is one of the most pernicious and insidious of the manifestations. To counteract the pull to say you are sorry in professional situations, develop a No More Apologies! mentality. This is a two-phase process.

PHASE ONE: COUNT YOUR APOLOGIES

For one week, pay attention to the number of times you find yourself apologizing for anything at all. It may be explicit, or it may be built into the way you phrase a statement, or the fact that you don't say anything at all when you should be speaking up. Every time you do notice something, write it down in your Ambition Journal. At the end of the week, conduct a tally. You may be surprised at how quickly you were willing to place yourself in a contrite, weak position.

PHASE TWO: DON'T APOLOGIZE FOR ANYTHING

For the next week, no matter what happens, do not apologize either directly or indirectly for anything. For example, do not say to a client, "I can't get to your project until next week because you were late getting your paperwork to me. I'm so sorry. I hate to let you down." Or: "I realize that stop-and-go traffic caused you to miss your appointment . . . that seems to happen to you every other week . . . but I'm afraid I have to bill you for the time anyway."

Instead say, "Obviously I'll need an extra week to complete your project to make up for the week's delay you encountered getting the required materials to me." Or don't explain why you must bill someone for a missed appointment; just send the bill. If they challenge you, say, "As you know, I have a one-week cancellation policy. Otherwise all missed appointments are billed at full fee."

You don't have to do this for the rest of your life, just until you've purged the apology virus. If you do see that you made a mistake that resulted in adverse consequences for another person, simply correct the mistake without saying you're sorry. Do not say, "I'm sorry," explicitly or otherwise, no matter what happens—with the exception of something like if you smack someone by accident; of course you can say you're sorry then! I'm not saying to be heartless; I am saying don't apologize for how you go about doing your job. At the end of the week, you may find that the apologies you used to cling to are quite useless; they never did solve problems or serve much of a purpose.

Use Inner Doubt as a Motivator

Most accomplished people—men and women alike—experience a periodic lack of confidence. But professional uncertainty is especially problematic for women. We have spent a lifetime with the explicit and implicit bias that we aren't really as good as men. Internalizing the bias creates inner barriers that continue to trip us up, even as some of the external barriers are falling away. What they've done to us metamorphoses into what we are doing to ourselves.

Here's the good news: we can use being afraid of being found out to motivate ourselves. The fear actually energizes you to be at the top of your game because you are damn well not going to be caught with your pants down. You can be paralyzed by doubt and fear or you can outrun and outsmart it. Women tend to do the former. Here are some tips for turning that around:

1. Look in the mirror now. Look yourself in the eye and say, "I am an ambitchous woman—and I'm proud of it!" You can say this without cringing. You can say it without feeling like a fraud. And without feeling foolish. You can say it, mean it—and be flat-out proud of yourself for being ambitchous.

2. Declare your ambition. Assert your dreams and goals.

3. Figure out the first, smallest, and most achievable step you could take to realize your ambition and take it today.

4. Tell yourself that you can measure up to your biggest goals. Say it again, this time looking yourself in the eye, in the mirror. Or just think it as you look into your ambitchous eyes.

5. Acquire more objectivity about your accomplishments, expertise, and ambitchous potential by trying a little trick: Look at the skills, talents, accomplishments, and credentials you have amassed as if you were looking at another person. Now what does your résumé look like? Try actually typing a different name on your résumé, and then review it. Are you impressed? Does it shut up the inner critic?

Instead of worrying that the fraud police are going to break your door down and place you in handcuffs, focus on your own internal gold standard. Buddha told his followers to be a "lantern unto yourself." Know who you are from the inside.

Adopt the Attitude: Take All the Time You Need— Even If You Have Only Three Minutes

Once I was at an awards dinner in San Francisco where I was waiting my turn to go onstage and accept an award before an audience of around a thousand people. This was a celebratory event jointly sponsored by the U.S. Small Business Administration and the National Association of Women Business Owners. Part of the award recipients' role was to rally the troops, and we had been told that we had something like three minutes to give an acceptance speech. We were also asked to make what we had to say inspiring and meaningful.

I'd watched an hour of acceptance speeches made during dinner and had observed many women talking with people at their tables rather than paying attention to what the folks at the podium had to say. I began to sweat. Just before it was my turn to go up, I whispered to my brother, Alan, who was at my table along with my son, Devin, and some of my friends: "I think my speech is five minutes rather than three minutes. No one is listening anyway. I should probably just say a quick thank-you to the SBA, plus my mentoring group and the Women's Business Alliance participants, and then sit down." Alan said, "No. This is your time to shine and to communicate your message. You've earned this award. You're here at this amazing event. Say what you took the time to prepare. Take all the time you need."

The "take all the time you need" part of my brother's message was what got me, and when I found myself up on the stage, that was the mind-set from which I began to speak. And the most amazing thing happened. The entire hotel banquet room went silent as I began. No forks clanging; no people talking. And I think I would have been able to keep my speech to the three-minute limit had I not been interrupted twice by women on their feet cheering and applauding—not for me, but for my message: why and how they should be more ambitchous, and why and how they should fight to earn their worth. I always remember that night, but not in terms of my ego getting stroked. I remember it as a lesson, as a moment when I took as much time as I needed—and, in doing so, a message came out of my mouth that inspired a roomful of ambitchous women. What would the cost have been had I caved in to my fear of taking up too much space and too much time, or to my fear of feeling embarrassed if people talked among themselves rather than listened to me? The cost would have been a missed opportunity to communicate a message of empowerment to a large gathering of motivated women in business. It would have been a wasted precious chance to inspire women and to make a contribution to what was, by that time, my career mission.

Our self-doubt can be turned around and used as a powerful tool for success and mastery. Uncertainty can be leveraged into power. We women are setting our sights higher every day. We can step into the spotlight if we just step out of the shadows and realize that we belong there.

Remove the gag from your own voice. Feel, inside of yourself, your own professional power that is just waiting to be unleashed. That power is made up of your passion for your work, your sweat, stamina, and accomplishments, your integrity and respect for yourself, and your belief in your right to earn your worth. All of these qualities shore up your courage to stay true to yourself and your personally defined ambitchous dream. The power radiates outward and fuels your ability to actualize your potential and become a leader and mentor to others. You are the real deal. Believe it. Dare to be ambitchous. Dare to be it now.

Part III

You Have Only One Precious Life— Dare to Be Great

fourteen

Lifelong amBITCHous Maintenance

Your work is to discover your work and then with all your heart to give yourself to it.

—Buddha

My work has just grown into something that is so much bigger than a job—or even a career. There is so much psychic benefit from doing something that I'm good at professionally, and from doing something that I love doing. It's something that is personally rewarding. There's a tremendous sense of satisfaction and feeling of accomplishment when I finish negotiating a deal or when I make the client happy. There's a matchless feeling you get from doing something well. And it's not just for money or about ambition for commercial success, it's beyond that—it's the whole package. It's about my relationships with my partners, colleagues, and clients. It's about loving my work. It's about making a contribution. And it's about being a great role model to my children as someone who is working hard to be the best she can be—and who benefits on so many fronts from staying true to my ambition over a lifetime.

—Rebecca F. Silberstein, thirty-eight, corporate
partner and member of the Investment
Management Practice Group, Debevoise &
Plimpton LLP, New York

EACH ambitchous woman has within her unique contributions to make. Your challenge for lifelong ambition maintenance is to have the courage to stay your ambitchous course. This is a twofold challenge: One, protecting your passion by checking in with yourself periodically throughout your career to see if you're heading in the direction you want. Two, asking yourself if you are making the unique contributions you are capable of. Remember—the world deserves to hear from you.

The prize itself stirs that fire in the belly, which cannot burn at full tilt all of the time—we'd burn up and out if it did. But if we fall out of touch with our specific goals, we'll find that it's all too easy for the details of daily life to sever the connection to the source of heat. We need a conscious connection to stay in the forefront of our awareness so we can keep the forward momentum. Having a strategic plan and checking in with it—and with yourself—on a regular basis allows you to trust in your self-directed wisdom and your sense of what your real, current ambition is. Ambitchous women must continually refine their plan, decide what to retain, what to dump, which part of the dream we wish to modify, what new shape our ambitions are taking.

Protect Your Passion

> I got really serious about deciding what does make me feel alive. What makes me feel like I can face myself every morning? And to me that was living my dream. You know everybody has them. I decided it's all that mattered in the world, and I'd rather die than not live my dream— it just wasn't worth it to be alive otherwise. And this [her singing career] came along, and since then I've had no problem getting up, working twenty-hour days, and touring forty cities every thirty days because I feel a lot less alone and I also feel like I get to help other people too, and that gives me great fulfillment.
>
> —Jewel, recording artist, interviewed by
> Sarah McLachlan

You can protect your passion and follow your aspirations through any number of options or courses of action, and you can set whatever time frame works for you. Your only limits are the breadth and depth of your imagination and the strength of your ambition. Oh, and let's not forget about self-confidence. Above all, remember that you are the kind of woman for whom the sky is the limit.

As an ambitchous woman, always be mindful to protect your passion by focusing on inspiration in your career. You have to train yourself continually, over the life of your ambitchous career, to drill down to what really inspires you. What inspires you will change shape or deepen or may even shift directions. That's normal and just fine; it's common that professional women will switch companies or career directions or even industries between five and seven times over the course of their ambitchous careers.

No matter where you find yourself in your career, stay in tune with whether or not you're on track. Staying on track means that you are doing ambitchous work that you love, work that gives you increasing power, recognition, and money and that fuels your determination to pursue meaningful, challenging work. Check in with yourself at least once a quarter, and then at the end of each year, to look over your ambitchous goals, progress, roadblocks, obstacles, and opportunities you've pursued or haven't yet tackled, to measure where you are against where you want to be.

Writing down your ambitchous goals and periodically assessing how you are progressing is one way to bring greater intention and volition to the whole process of protecting your career passion. Answer the following seven questions to take stock of where you're at in your career and with your ambitchous goals. You can circle back to this exercise each time you are checking in with yourself. Go back to your Ambition Journal and read what you wrote last time you did an ambitchous goal assessment. Be honest with yourself. Record the answers in your Ambition Journal.

1. How satisfied are you with your career, your earnings, the level of challenge, and your future opportunities to grow and stretch yourself?
2. What are your short-term, intermediate, and long-term professional goals? List at least five goals.
3. In what ways are you moving forward? List five ways.
4. In what ways are you stuck or unclear? List five of these now.
5. How do you maintain your edge? What works to keep your ambitchous dreams fired up? List five ways.
6. In what ways have you gone soft? List those.
7. What is your definition—right now—of what it means, for you personally, to be an ambitchous woman? List seven qualities. Put a check by each of these qualities that you're happy with in your own life. Put an X by those that need some work.

Refocus and Check In to Keep Your Determination Fired Up

Learning to refocus your attention on your ambition and on your career passions, and doing this on a regular basis will keep you determined and on track. It will help you to avoid putting your goals on hold for long periods and losing sight of them. You can hold on to them internally, even if externally they seem miles away. Keep them in your heart and mind, no matter what is going on in your daily life. Just keep your career front and center and refuse to squelch the insistent yearnings to be as ambitchous as you really want to be, in the way you want to be, that evolve as you move forward.

And keep in mind that protecting your passion doesn't mean setting your cap to reach the top of your field, or to stay there if you decide to switch ambition directions. Many successful women decided, with intention, that the top of the pecking order is precisely where they don't want to land. They're much happier not being the alpha dog. Christine Comaford-Lynch landed the brass ring—several times over. Christine created and sold five businesses. She has twenty-plus years in high-tech, consulting to Microsoft, Apple, Oracle, Symantec, and many other major players, and served as an adviser to the Clinton and Bush administrations. Christine ultimately decided that she'd been sated by her stint at the top of one heap, so she jumped off to see what other opportunities were calling to her at this point in her career and life:

I am not Jack Welch or Oprah or some major business mogul. I'm an ordinary person who is somewhat geeky and who's had extraordinary experiences. By age seventeen, I was world-weary. I'd already run away to New York City, had had a career there; I'd experienced the good life and it had left me feeling empty. I became a celibate Buddhist monk. At twenty-four I realized it was time to stop trying to transcend the human condition. Diving right into it and still maintaining one's spirituality was the path for me, so I broke my vows, got a burger, a boyfriend, and within a few years I started building companies. At twenty-eight I decided to become a millionaire. Twelve years later at age forty I retired, having earned over ten million dollars (without a high school diploma or college degree) and giving three million dollars to assorted nonprofits. In the process I consulted to seven hundred of the Fortune 1000, over one hundred small businesses, created over five thousand jobs, passed a bill in Congress, found the man of my dreams, and got married. I did not follow a straight path; I had many dead-end detours trying my hand as a geisha, having two cancer scares, hitting and missing on a number of different businesses, and disastrous attempts at love relationships.

Ultimately Christine decided she would be happier in a different heap, one that she felt matched her ambition values. Today a sought-after entrepreneurship expert, she is writing her first book. She can, in her words, "focus solely on pursuing my ambition and professional passion in the shape it's morphed into at this particular point in my life."

Career passion ebbs and flows. Hitting periods of being less than inspired does happen. What can you do about it? Two things:

1. Articulate the underlying cause of your frustration.
2. Pinpoint what you have always been passionate about in your career.

Consider these examples.

Beth was a successful interior designer who catered to wealthy clients. By all outward standards she was a success. But one day she realized that she wasn't genuinely fulfilled in her work anymore, which was hard to understand since she was using her artistic talents. Over the course of our work together it emerged that as much as she enjoyed interior design, her true passion was painting, and she had been afraid to acknowledge it because she had convinced herself that painting could never bring in the same salary as interior design.

Beth and I worked out a multipronged plan to free up some space, time, and energy to refocus her passion on painting while continuing to pay the bills with interior design. I helped her curtail her desire to be a people-pleaser, which had allowed clients to take advantage of her and caused her to lose income. We also mapped out business and client-development strategies, along with marketing and public relations tactics. Specifically, she eliminated all hourly based consulting and raised her project fees. This, of course, left her more time to paint.

It turned out that she also loved writing. In the end, she was able to write and illustrate a highly original work of fiction and procure a top literary agent. None of this would have been possible if Beth hadn't articulated her real passion and been willing to pursue it vigorously.

Sometimes ambitchous women make dramatic ambition career changes. Elana was twenty-nine when she decided to assess where she was in her career and see if her ambition was being fulfilled. She made the courageous decision to leave an almost completed Ph.D. program in physics at Stanford University in order to chase her dream of becoming an intellectual property and patent attorney. She went to a top law school and is today on partner track with a top New York City firm. When last I spoke with her a few months ago, she said, "I absolutely love my work. It inspires me each and every day. I've finally found what I was meant to do with my ambition and talents."

Some women stay in their originally chosen field but expand their vision and goals. Anita is a thirty-nine-year-old organizational psychologist and executive coach based in the San Francisco Bay Area. She's always loved her work, but five years ago she wanted to kick it up a notch. It took her a while to pinpoint what else she could do that would feed that hunger. She finally figured it out:

> I dicked around on my book proposal for four years. When I finally sent it off, it went into a bidding war and sold immediately for a two-hundred-and-fifty-thousand-dollar advance. Did all that extra time make it better? No, it did not. I didn't change that much during that time. I was just putting off putting it out there, which meant that I needlessly delayed personal and financial gratification, I unnecessarily postponed getting professional recognition and increased consulting opportunities, and I slowed

myself down from moving on and working on other projects I knew I wanted to do next.

Anita is currently consulting all over the world. And she's working on her second book. She says that learning to check in with herself more regularly about what inspires her and feeds her ambition and her sense of accomplishment keeps her moving forward and happy. She says she no longer procrastinates where her ambitchous life maintenance is concerned: "I check in regularly and aggressively with myself about my goals, what I'd like to be doing that I'm not yet pursuing—and then I plan and map out options for making it happen, strategies for getting to my next goal. It makes for an exciting and thrilling career."

Take a One-Woman Sabbatical

Many women I've worked with have protected their ambition over many years by taking a solo sabbatical periodically. I'm not talking about spa treatments or having a pedicure—not that there's anything wrong with that! I'm talking about taking time away from the daily grind and concentrating on your professional future. Ambitchous women tend to be busy women. Every day they juggle the relentless demands of life. To reflect and reconnect with their inner fire and their dreams, they need periodic solitude and the space to be silent.

Try to schedule a solo sabbatical once every three months, at a minimum. Yes, yes, I know: you can't possibly manage this. But read on. Going away overnight is ideal, and a weekend or a whole week is even better. If you really can't get away, take a daylong retreat. However, don't jump to the conclusion too quickly that that's the best you can do. After all, this is why the Great Goddess made babysitters and daddies and sick days. Pack a lunch, go to your favorite spot, or rent a hotel room for the day. Whatever spot you pick, seclusion must be its most prized characteristic. No phones, no TV, no e-mail. This is a time that you commit to strong cerebral focus on where you are in your career.

You need the alone time and self-sovereignty to get a clear read on whether your career course of action is still working for you. It's the room-of-one's-own idea that Virginia Woolf concluded was half of the required equation for achieving full greatness as a writer (the other half being a solid income).

Even if you're taking time off from your career right now, you still need reflective time alone. Countless women have found the solo sabbatical to be one of the most powerful and surest ways to break out of a dead zone. Consider this a board meeting of one, to quote sales and marketing exec Susan Donegan. It is a time and place to use your intellect and imagination fully. It's impossible to be mindful of your own passions and aspirations when clients want you to take their calls, bosses want you to meet their deadlines, colleagues want you to proofread their reports, your kids want you to drive them all over the place, and your husband wants you to cook because he's working late.

Go back to your Ambition Journal. Assess the following questions during each of your board meetings of one.

- Which companies or firms or industries would you most love to end up in?
- What is your dream job, no matter how far-fetched?
- What specific responsibilities would you want to take on in a new position?
- Do you want to be a professional adviser working one-on-one with clients, or do you enjoy the communal hum of a team?
- Do you want to do research, write, or teach? And if you want to teach, do you want to work with adults or children, or do you dream of doing corporate training?

- Which careers fire you up when you read about them?
- What is your dream career configuration? Think big. No self-censoring.

Half my clients balk at this idea. "I can't afford the time off." "I don't have anyone to take care of my kids." "I can't take time off from work; they need me." "I'd feel guilty—if I were going to do something like this, it should be with my husband." It's really interesting how enthusiastic they become when they have to do it because I threaten to quit coaching them if they don't. I've also given physicians, psychologists, and other executive coaches the same prescription. Afterward they tell me, "This is exactly the sort of advice I give my female clients—but I would never have thought of it for myself!"

If you're really afraid the world will fall apart without you, try going away no longer than overnight for your first sabbatical. Trust me: you won't miss anything. Take plenty of pens and notebooks—one for each room, one next to your bed, one for your car, one in the bathroom, one small steno pad to take on walks. You will encounter a proliferation of ideas during this sabbatical, and you should be ready to write them down so you don't lose any thoughts during this mental flow. Take your laptop, but don't check e-mail. Pack a range of stimulating reading material that you've stockpiled over the last few months to feed your mind and imagination. Arrange your schedule intuitively—eat, sleep, take walks, write anything and everything that comes to mind about where you are at this point in your career, what goals you are on track with, and which ones need refocusing. This time can be incredibly productive in terms of fresh ideas, strategic planning, and contemplating the unforeseen. In the midst of reflective time, many otherwise invisible events can seem so obvious.

Jill, a forty-nine-year-old San Francisco physician, couldn't decide whether to leave her practice altogether, move into a different area of medicine, or accept a publisher's offer to update her book. She was burned out from endless insurance billing quagmires. She was feeling removed from her craft. Despite all this, she hadn't taken time off in over a year.

I prescribed a solo sabbatical. She took along coaching session notes, questions recorded in her notebook, the textbook she'd written that she was thinking of revising, the career assessment and interest testing reports I had given her, as well as my analysis and summary recommendations of six possible directions that best suited her current professional, personal, and financial objectives. She also toted a bag of fresh fruit and vegetables and ingredients for a couple of delicious, simple meals so she could spend minimal time cooking.

For four days at a friend's house in Lake Tahoe, Jill hiked in silence, went horseback riding alone, kayaked, and spent quiet evenings in front of a fireplace eating and thinking and working on her options list. Away from the distractions of the everyday, Jill's mind quickly unwound, allowing her to focus on how she really felt about her options. By the time she returned from her sabbatical, she'd made her decision to sell her practice, accept a position with Hewlett-Packard's medical device division, and create an updated edition of her health book.

Try this. You will return from your sabbatical with a renewed vigor and passion—either for the work you already do or for preparing to change directions. I promise you that you'll find in your solo retreat a new and necessary part of your life; you have my enthusiastic permission to repeat it next quarter.

You Don't Have to Decide Today

You have to live your life in a way that you're comfortable with and that will make you happy. But always protect your long-term ambition goals. How? Don't make hasty decisions under pressure, don't let peo-

ple pressure you, and don't pressure yourself; these influences can
cause you to fumble. If you're that close to the end zone, for heaven's
sake, figure out how to finish the play. Hang tough and don't rush your
game plan.

—Margaret (Peggy) Andrews Davenport, partner
and cochair of Debevoise & Plimpton LLP's
private equity group

Years ago I knew a woman who was in a therapy group. She was famous among her crowd for always saying she would do something, and then backpedaling later and not keeping her word. She meant well, but ended up inconveniencing a lot of people. One day the group leader gave her a stiff assignment. He told her that for one week, she had to say no every time she meant to say yes, and she had to say yes every time she wanted to say no. She had to do this in every instance; there were no exceptions. All the group members expected her to return a week later and declare how difficult the assignment had been. And indeed she did. But then she added something interesting. She said that after five days, she realized that this was actually what she did all the time anyway: say yes when she meant no, and vice versa. The only difference this week was that she made it conscious. Learn to say no when you have to and free up your time to pursue your real goals.

Many choices have far-reaching consequences and costs, so don't make them precipitously. Make sure you set limits with people who want to push you into a quick decision by saying, "I'll get back to you on this when I've had time to absorb all the factors and information." If you are a yes person, you'll have to retrain yourself to say, "I'll think about it," instead of offering an immediate answer. "I'll think about it" gives you enough breathing room to consider what you really want and make an authentic decision, not just one that is meant to please. This assures you that later on, you won't have to go back on your word.

Before making any big decisions, consult with your trusted

steering committee advisers—not with your biased (though well-meaning) friends and family. Also, fully scope out your options—don't just assume you know what they are. What's the worst that can happen if you head in a new direction? What's the best that can happen? Check in with your gut about making a certain compromise, such as pledging a sum of money to reeducation, or quitting a company that's been good to you.

When you're feeling confused or overtired, don't act. Concentrate on laying the groundwork for the next steps to take in your career. Believe me, you aren't wasting time. You are waiting until the time is right to jump. This preparation buys you peace of mind and helps you avoid the panic attacks that lead to short-sighted decisions. I asked one of my clients, a thirty-nine-year-old executive with two small children, who's currently consulting from home, how she reconciles her ambition and those other competing values and how she keeps her goals fresh in her mind. Here's her wise response to me:

> I always tell myself I will do everything I want to do later, and I fully expect to. It's not that I won't ever do the things that I want to do career-wise; I'm just not doing everything at the same time. I have absolutely no doubt in my mind about whether or not I'll reach my goals eventually. I've never had any problem with not getting things done, so I have a calm certainty about all this. It's a matter of timing. I will know when it's time, when I'm ready, to make those goals a priority, and what my priorities are for right now. In the future, I will most certainly be taking on larger consulting engagements, but right now I'm actually turning things down that would be quite fun to do. At some point, though, it will again be the right thing to do.

I also often tell my nieces and my son and stepson to adopt this mantra. It's worth repeating regularly.

YOU DON'T HAVE TO DECIDE TODAY. AND
YOU DON'T HAVE TO DO ANYTHING YOU
DON'T WANT TO DO.

You don't have to make important career decisions when you're at your most vulnerable, confused, or stressed out. One of my clients told me about attending a new-mothers group for working professionals. At the first meeting, one of the women who'd decided to quit her job took up a great deal of time excoriating the other women for continuing to work, and leaving their babies in the care of others. The next morning, one of the attendees sent an angst-filled e-mail to the other members of the group describing how she'd had a very bad night with a baby who didn't sleep more than two hours. Overnight, she too had decided to quit her job—and weren't the other moms worried about whether they should do the same? In a moment of extreme sleep deprivation and vulnerability, this woman had mistakenly believed she had only an extreme either/or choice, and she acted impulsively.

You need a clear mind to make a sound decision. While you do not need to be free from worries, you cannot be so weighed down by them that you can't see straight. You especially don't want to make any decisions when you are sleep deprived—and I don't just mean new mothers. We can all lose sleep for a lot of reasons. Always sleep on a decision, sometimes for a week. Hey, go into a coma if you have to.

Remember Your Expertise—And Use Your Marketplace Value

Too many ambitchous women get stuck in dead-end jobs because they don't recognize their own value and see how many options it can make available to them. They've lost sight of their own fabulous track record and expertise; they have put blinders on. Gone is the peripheral vision that would allow them to glimpse other professional possibilities based on past performance.

I give my clients a very simple exercise to remind them of their marketplace value: Go through your résumé and take in the sheer volume of experience and knowledge you have accumulated. In your Ambition Journal, write down everything you did and learned at a particular job. Then update the résumé. If you're like many of my clients, it's been years since you've pulled your résumé out of mothballs and used it to boost your self-image. If you've never created a résumé because you got your position through networking, it's time to write one up. Go through your files to refresh your memory about your educational and professional accomplishments. Maybe you haven't recorded your recent wins on the job, awards you've received, raises, formal feedback—evidence of greatness you have. Get your KaChing! File out and in order.

I've worked with many women who almost didn't recognize themselves on paper after they completed this exercise. One client collected all her accomplishments down on paper and then marveled, "That just doesn't seem like me." She was now an external observer to her own professional achievements, and it helped her see just how impressive her body of work was. This boost freed her mind to consider career directions she hadn't thought of before. Many people awaken to the realization that their quantifiable marketplace value is higher than they'd initially supposed.

Think of your own career the way you would view a portfolio of stocks: the best predictor of future behavior is past behavior. Everything you've accomplished so far is an indicator of how far you can go. The simple act of updating your résumé and reviewing your files will instantly motivate you to reach out for a new opportunity, because you can see that you're ready for it.

Once you make your first move and put yourself out there,

you may find that a little bit of positive feedback takes you even further. Ella, a thirty-five-year-old senior editor at a major New York publishing house, found just that:

> I was really dissatisfied with my last company, yet didn't look for a new job for a long time. I'm one of those people whose work ethic is that if the company is doing the right thing for you, then you have to stay with it. But I reached a point where I really wanted to go somewhere else. I made a few calls, and then sent my résumé off to this one place. I got back an ecstatically positive response, which I so wasn't expecting. It hit me so hard, like, "Oh, my God! I have value!"

Women do tend to undervalue how proficient they are and how readily people will recognize that. The encouraging news is that there are clear signs of a historical shift of this gender trend. We can teach ourselves to believe in ourselves and admit that our success is a result of our own talent, hard work, and volition. Many ambitchous women I've worked with get to the place where they can say with clarion self-assuredness: "My success is because I made the thing happen." This is precisely where you want to be with your own ambitchous life.

Cultivate the Contribution You Were Born to Make

Ambition is a good thing. What's the opposite? Having no drive? No social consciousness? We can't take things for granted. We can't take the progressive society we live in for granted. I think we all have a larger obligation than just to ourselves, whether it's being a responsible corporate leader—which is a good thing, because you're employing people, creating jobs, and respecting and enhancing the community in which you operate—or getting involved in public life and government. If you're a single mother working three jobs and struggling to meet your family's basic needs, you're doing all you can do; you're fighting to survive. But when you have good fortune, a good education, a platform to effect change, that's when I think you have a greater responsibility to make a contribution, to make an impact. To sit on the sidelines when you have talent and resources—that's an injustice.

—Belinda Stronach, leading member of the
Liberal Party of Canada and chair of the
national caucus of women Liberal MPs;
former president and CEO of Magna
International Inc.; ranked in 2004 by *Time*
magazine as one of the world's 100 most
influential people

The woman with ambition at her core defines herself by the contributions she makes. I have heard many ambitious women say that leading and inspiring others is another way of giving back. It's just done on a much larger scale than giving to their spouse or kids or community.

Going after our ambitchous goals is not just a way to greedily take for ourselves, like the old definition of *ambition* says. It is a chance to give back. Always cultivate your ambitchous contribution. You'll be happy and inspired during your days, and you'll sleep peacefully at night knowing that you are contributing to yourself and you are letting the world benefit from the contributions you are here on the planet to make.

fifteen

Ambition Integration
Imbalance, Not Balance, Makes for a Great, AmBITCHous Life

Every woman is different; not every woman has the potential, desire, or ambition to do it all. But I think women should feel that they can do anything and everything they want to do and that it's just a matter of prioritizing. I am an extremely focused and motivated individual, and I work very hard. In my industry, I have set an example that you can be a mother and an executive—that you can do all of it. You know, they always say women can't do all of it—you have to give something up. But it isn't true. You have to broaden the plate or change how you do things to get everything done. Women are great multitaskers and can be extremely career-focused, while also doing charitable work, raising a family, playing the violin, or whatever other passions they have. I believe you can have all of it, and I sure am trying.

> —Judy Johnson, forty-three, executive vice
> president and managing director of the
> western region of GolinHarris, Los Angeles

What's her secret? She doesn't treat it like a job—it's a career for her. She's totally into it. And her fears propel her to be excellent.

> —Deborah Saweuyer-Parks, on her talented
> protégée, Lisa Taylor, twenty-eight

Imagine yourself at the end of your life. What do you want your legacy to be? Yes, I was completely equitable in how I spent my time. Yes, I missed out on some great opportunities. I could have been a contender, and I lost my chance to make my mark on the world because I wanted to balance work and family life. But that's okay. After all, I did balance my time. Great, you balanced your time, but did you balance your needs? If you have the need to make a genuine contribution in the world and you settle for less to spend more time at home, you may not realize it, but that's not balance; that's sacrifice. Some souls have greatness inside them, and they owe it to themselves to put in the time, energy, and money to actualize their potential. If you are one of those souls, and you cheat an important part of yourself to appease society's need for you to give equally to everyone all the time, you commit what I call soul murder.

The idea that we should make balancing our lives our top priority is bunk. Balance is bunk.

Nature abhors a vacuum. If you want to abandon the tired old work/life balance myth and free yourself from its tyranny, you have to construct a new paradigm. The old model leaves you with a King Solomon solution: a baby that is torn in two. What good is tearing yourself in two? To be ambitchous, you don't want to choose work instead of a full life of family, friends, and outside interests. You don't want to divide your loyalties between being a good executive and a good lover, partner, friend, or mom.

Sounds great, you're probably saying. But how do we get there? How can I make life work? If the work/life balance model is really an incorrect, unfeasible paradigm, how do I identify and implement the actual nuts and bolts of a happier solution so that my ambition becomes a necessary, indispensable component of a fulfilling life? How do I actually make both my ambition and my other nonnegotiable priorities work? How do I integrate it all and feel good about myself and all of my choices, be it at work or at home?

A New Paradigm for Ambitchous Women

Our new model integrates, meaning it allows you to view your life, in all of its contradictions and layers, as a unified, workable whole, somehow, some way. Below are lifelong maintenance instructions for how to maintain an ambitchous life without driving yourself crazy going after the wrong goal, i.e., balance.

Find Your Own Comfort Zone, Work Your Own Plan

What's feasible in your life is a very personal issue. Every ambitchous woman has her own unique set of responsibilities, stressors, resources, support systems, choices, levels of coping, and schedule predictability. What works for one person might be intolerable for the next. Each woman must evaluate her own life and listen to her own instincts when making choices about how to divvy up her time, energy, and attention. The only person who is an expert on your life and how the balance sheet should read is you.

"Should I reschedule my clients to drive my son around to look at colleges, or leave that job to his father?" "Should I go clubbing tonight even though I'll be tired tomorrow, just because I'm ready to have some fun?" "Should I use some of my savings to go after an M.B.A. or spend it on a better pre-school for my three-year-old?" These are all very personal questions that only you can answer. The pundits tell you that one rule fits all, but they are wrong. They are on the outside looking in; you're on the inside trying to make it all work, and this is why you and so many others feel misunderstood when you read these articles in magazines telling you what rules to follow. Just find the comfort zone that is right for you and damn the torpedoes.

Another consideration: decisions that are appropriate during one period or phase in your life will be all wrong during others. Today's woman has a lot of balls in the air pretty much all of the time. One year she's still taking classes at night, the next she's having her first child, and the next she's offered a job that will force her to work evenings and weekends. Each year she may be facing a whole different set of responsibilities, stressors, choices, scheduling nightmares, and on and on. Add to this the fact that there is always a certain degree of unpredictability in life because of unexpected events. An elderly parent falls ill, a child is diagnosed with autism, a best friend is going through a nasty divorce, your company files for bankruptcy. We may sail along for a while thinking we've got it all handled, yet the bottom can still fall out. There is no one comfort zone for life. You have to keep seeking it all the time.

If you think any one rule fits everyone, consider these scenarios:

• One woman faces an hour commute each way to work, one telecommutes from her home-based office, and one flies out of town three times a week. How should they allocate their free time?

• One working mom has on-site child care, while another has to fork over a quarter of her salary for the service. Which one should spend her hard-earned year-end bonus on her children instead of herself?

• A solo practitioner has just hit the five-year cancer-free milestone. Another is cancer-free, but multiple sclerosis runs in her family and she has a good chance of getting it. Both have two children. Should they change jobs to get better health care coverage, even though they love the jobs they have?

These are only a few of the tough choices women make about resources, time, and energy. To make your life easier, give yourself permission to create a flexible blueprint that will work better than the outdated work/life balance idea. Trust yourself enough to be the author of your own rules and establish the right balance for your life. My feasibility strategies below will help you work out your own plan according to your own sensibilities.

Imbalance Is Normal. Go for Acceptance— Expect and Accept Imbalance

Here's the truth that no one tells us, especially those glib work/life balance evangelists: Once you get out into the world of work (and even before that—in college, for example), you should just expect that your day-to-day life simply isn't always going to flow smoothly. You have to cede a certain amount of control in your life—particularly if and when you have kids. And the older we get, the more evident it becomes that you have to accept that things are not going to be even all the time. Things are going to be lopsided and messy—and that's normal. Lesley Alderman, a magazine editor, author, and full-time working mom of a toddler and a teenage stepson, described to me her own journey of discovering how this model works better in her life:

> For instance, this week, I have a couple of [work] things I have to do during the night, and I'd really prefer to be home in the evenings to see my son, because I don't see him during the day, and so I know it's going to bother him those nights when I'm working late. But you know what? Two nights every once in a while is okay. So I just have to say to myself, "Okay, that's what this week is going to be like—it's not going to be a balanced week."

Some days you're going to feel like, "Shit! I'm so overextended." That feeling can be extremely frustrating—until you say to yourself, "You know, things are just always going to be kind of out of balance." And once you do that—once you expect at least a little normal life chaos—acceptance takes over. And here's the irony: once we begin expecting and accepting imbalance, that mind-set paradoxically guides us to periods of—guess what?—balance.

IMBALANCE IS NORMAL; BALANCE IS NOT NORMAL.

Now you can begin deploying comforting self-talk like, "You know what, self? I'll put that in order later, when I get to it." Or: "Things are too crazy this week; I'll delegate more until they slow down." Or: "So we're ordering in again tonight. You know what? I made my own organic baby food with a hand grinder for those first couple of years. I haven't even started that presentation. So to hell with it—I'm a good enough mother; let's have pizza tonight!" With this new sensibility, you'll be amazed at the refreshing and enjoyable sense of relief you'll experience—relief from internal pressures, including pointless, nonproductive, and self-destructive worry, emotional angst, and guilt. You will also dramatically reduce the wear and tear on your body and mind that come from running faster than you need to (and faster than you can healthily handle) in order to reach an unattainable ever-balanced state.

Too type-A just to let go? Try designating little balance pockets in your life that you can—for the most part—have control over, and (here's that concept again) accept that you'll limit yourself to expecting steadiness, i.e., at least most of the time in those areas.

Examples: Set up autopay on most of your bills so that you know you're not going to be knocked off balance by a late fee (or eviction notice!). Can't keep your plants alive at home because you're too tired to remember when to water them? Feed your green thumb need with orchids and bamboo in your office—they hardly need water. Is the first thing you're hit with when you walk in your front door after seeing clients the smell of kitty poop? Invest the three hundred dollars in the amazing new automatic cat-poop scooper; you have to empty out the receptacle only three times a week, and you can spend more quality time with your cats instead of scooping poop. Tell yourself you're going to leave your chaos on your desk, behind closed doors in your home-based office or in your corporate workplace confines. You can always come back to it the next day, after a restful night's sleep. Or does having a messy house drive you crazy? Keep your office scrupulously neat to offset the home-based clutter. Or delegate more to your family or roommates, or hire a cleaning service on a regular basis. Follow Lesley Alderman's example and take a load off of your mind:

> Of course it's great to have a neat house. I feel better when things are in order. But then I come home and everything is chaotic and I think, "Oy! The kids' things are everywhere . . . and people are playing and in and out." So I just have to say to myself, "Okay, I'll deal with it later," or "I'm going to try to get people to pick up and do more." There is one room—the living room—that I try to keep clutter-free and then people sort of seem to follow that, so I have a sacrosanct, orderly room. But then our kitchen and the living area off of that are often chaotic. I just try to take a deep breath and accept it and say to myself, "Okay, fine." Because otherwise, I think if I had this ideal of how my life should be and it wasn't getting there, I'd be really kind of bitchy and stressed out.

Buddha said, "Life is a struggle." *Struggle* is code for *imbalance*. Struggle and imbalance are a normal part of life; balance is not normal. This realization is freeing.

Measure Your Success at Work and Home over the Long-Term

Don't twist yourself into a pretzel to have a prize career and a perfect home life all at the same time, each and every moment of each and every day. Remember:

LIFE IS LONG.

Write this down on a note card and put it next to your phone to shore up your inner strength during especially challenging moments. Hell, write it on seven note cards and put duplicates everywhere—in your car, at your office, in your wallet, inside of your suitcase, on your refrigerator. In other words, remind yourself that you've got a long time to get it right. And as long as you are trying and honing and doing your best every day, that's what counts.

You simply cannot measure your success, or whether you're getting it right, each and every moment of each and every day or week. It's not like every day is going to be balanced or every month is going to be balanced or even every year is going to be balanced. The reality is that the women (and men) I've known who are successful and satisfied with their work and personal lives don't think about balance in that way; they think about it much more in terms of the big picture over the long term. Because of that viewpoint, they are able to be comfortable being very lopsided at times. They can focus all or most of their energies on the priority of the moment—be it work or personal life—in a way that would appear imbalanced to the work/life balance evangelists.

But this is as it should be, because, to some degree, in order to be the best you can be and to achieve greatness, you need to be myopic. Why? Because sometimes you have to make it okay for yourself to have a laser-beam focus on your work. In her book

Bird by Bird: Some Instructions on Writing and Life. Anne Lamott promoted the virtues of learning to write while ignoring the contextual backdrop of the messiness of life: "Perfectionism means that you try desperately not to leave so much mess to clean up. But clutter and mess show us that life is being lived." I know she walked her talk, too. Our sons went to public elementary school together and, though I didn't know her personally, I saw her as a real-life model and partner in crime; she dropped her son off each day when I took my son to school (both of us were possibly wearing pajama bottoms and toting coffee in the car; she always had a notepad hanging from her rearview mirror, presumably to capture thoughts while living day by day). We worked out at the same tiny women's gym in our town. We plodded along and made it happen, bit by bit, bird by bird.

Freedom from the Formulaic

One size doesn't fit all.

> I've had talks with young women who are just coming out of school and they ask "What are your tips?" questions. One of my tips relates to the fact that some women have too much of a tendency to be incredible planners. I've spoken, for example, with young women who just graduated from their M.B.A. programs, and they'll say, "Okay, I'm going to go take a job in this industry at company X. And then in three years or five years I will have my first child." And they're making this whole plan yet haven't even met the man they're going to marry. They haven't even started the new career to see whether they like it. I look at this and my advice is, if you are so focused on implementing a rigid plan, you're likely to miss opportunities that are right in front of your face because they weren't a part of your plan.
>
> —Tanya Styblo Beder, CEO of Citigroup
> Alternative Investments' multi-strategy,
> proprietary hedge fund unit, Tribeca Global
> Management LLC

*A plan is now, not in the future. A zillion things can change. Your mar-
riage doesn't work out. You decide to take a different ambition path
than you originally expected. And so you just need to be open-minded.
Also be circumspect about your career plans. Don't let people know
everything you're thinking; if you're planning on just trying something,
you don't have to tell everybody, because that limits your options.
Women are absolutely prone to tell people too much. And you know
what? We don't always know how our life will play out; we don't know
how life works. By revealing too much about what's going on in their
heads, women can articulate a shorter career path than would make it
sensible for someone who is investing in your career. For example, if I
know you're here for two years I'm going to treat you a little differently
than if I think you want to do this forever—because I don't want to invest time in someone who's a disappearing asset. So know when it's
wise to keep your ambition plans to yourself as you're figuring out
what you want to do with your life.*

—Franci Blassberg

Freedom from the formulaic frees you up to give yourself permission to do what you need to do to maximize your skills, talents, and vision without guilt, and without beating yourself up
because others—or even you, yourself—may be judging you as
being disproportionately focused on your ambition. Go for it. You
are free to pursue your ambition.

Yet even during periods of intense work pressure, it doesn't
mean ignoring other parts of life. This leads us to the next way to
integrate ambition into a harmonious life.

Learn to Switch Focus on a Dime

True, the women I've worked with who are ambitious and successful do have periods of intense imbalance in their lives. I can
also say that many of these same women have the ability—or have
consciously learned to cultivate the skill of being able—to switch

settings with a concurrent and rapid shift of their attention, focus, and energy. This means that they are able to move in and out of environments while being present and productive and capable of interacting effectively with a range of people, from boss to baby, from husband to client, from boyfriend to colleague. And switching focus allows them to engage fully with others, or permits them to spend some mindful solo time alone, as the case may be. Here's an extreme and exemplary example. Barbara Corcoran had just walked up to the podium in a thousand-or-so-seat, filled-to-capacity auditorium to deliver a keynote talk when her cell phone rang. As it was told to me by a member of the audience, Barbara, in her inimitably authentic-no-matter-what style, pulled out the phone, looked at the number, looked the audience in the eyes (a daunting, but possible task, no matter the size of the crowd!), and said, "Please excuse me for just a moment; this is my seven-year-old son and I need to make sure he's okay," which she did in under five seconds, and then returned to what she was saying without missing a beat. That keynote, like most of those she delivers, received a standing ovation. Had she not picked up that call, she wouldn't have been able to focus on delivering a moving, inspirational talk because she would have been thinking, "Is my son okay?" She modeled something important: Authenticity has an irresistible integrity, and it's easier—and more compelling—just to be you, whatever situation you find yourself in.

Like Barbara, the happily ambitious women (and men) I know learn that if they are able to switch mind-sets quickly, then even if there is imbalance, they're completely in the moment. Whatever they're doing, it's still imbalanced in the sense of one thing being prioritized greatly over the other thing (at that point in time), but at least at the moment in time when they are focusing on what is a lesser priority, they're really focused on it. Part of being able to build this more feasible and satisfying model requires you to understand the range of priorities in your life without the illusion that you're always going to be able to balance them or allocate some preset amount of time to them.

Remember, it's okay to have simultaneous desires and priorities. Once you get comfortable with that, then you can learn to implement your newly honed ability to switch back and forth very deliberately and consciously between things that matter to you.

Finally, you can sharpen your instincts when it comes to deciding when you should set and hold boundaries versus when those boundaries are more flexible. Barbara Corcoran demonstrated when to fold in the story above. Forty-six-year-old Stephanie, a litigator in a top New York City law firm, explained when to hold:

> I talk to people all day long and frequently on the phone. So one of the reasons I don't like talking on the phone at home, away from work, is because that's just not anywhere in the priority scheme for me. I hate talking on the phone at home. Plus I'd much rather try to be focused and fully present with my husband and kids. That's hard enough to do—it takes some time and conscious effort to unwind and let down and switch gears once I get home so that I can at least be there in a real and focused way with them, even if I haven't been there very often that week or that month because of competing priorities and work demands. And it just doesn't work for me if I'm spending a lot of time talking on the phone at home. So I just don't do it. I make dates and see my friends and extended family, and we e-mail, and we're very connected and close, but they understand that I'm not a phone person.

Another corporate law partner I know holds her priority of going home at sundown every Friday night, no matter what corporate deal is threatening to close or implode, in order to be with her husband and children for the Sabbath. So figure out what and where your priorities are, at any given point in time, and learn to switch adroitly between them.

There Is More Than One Way to Fill a Need

If you cannot give your family as much attention as they need, give them relevant attention, the kind that is pertinent to their immediate needs. If you aren't spending a lot of time with your kids—probably the most common lament from working mothers—then find other ways to keep them from feeling neglected. If you are afraid that your children feel unloved or uncared for, find other ways to make them feel loved and cared for. Look carefully at what they feel they're being deprived of and then be creative about filling that need.

One of the things that many mothers with careers worry about as their children grow up is that they, as parents, weren't a strong enough influence in their children's lives because they weren't there all the time. Out of sight, out of mind, as the saying goes. If it is influence you are worried about, what else can you do to be influential in their lives? The type of influence you most want to have is on their values, their goals, their friends, their self-esteem, their ability to handle challenges and face danger, and so on. Pay attention to how your child learns, how she takes in information, how he is impacted by others, and use that to your advantage. Pay attention to slices of time in their lives that offer you maximum ability to show your love and make them feel grounded. Here are some examples.

- Many kids, particularly preteens and adolescents, feel more talkative in the car. There, many a quality conversation is jump-started, when parent and child are somehow magically freed up to talk more easily because by looking ahead eye contact is avoided (this especially works with middle schoolers and teens). Can you drive your kid to and/or from school several days a week? Use those driving times to practice active, focused listening to them, with much less talking on your part. This should not turn into Advice Hour from Mom. The deficit you are addressing during this time is the lack of attention from you. So give them a rich, genuine form of attention. Kids love to be listened to and taken seriously—and rarely are. Don't make conversations obvious or forced; just let them happen. Establish a predictable pattern for car time; your kids will look forward to getting your full attention in a relaxed, comfortable, predictable setting. This is when they can be themselves and be appreciated for it. My son, Devin, and I always listened to *Morning Edition* on National Public Radio during the ride to school, which primed the conversation to cover just about everything. It also assured me that he was keeping in touch with the world outside high school. And the program's subject matter would often trigger personal conversations that had been lurking in the background, such as when I embarrassed him in front of his friends, sex, drugs, music, politics, and even new lunch preferences.

• Look for any opportunity when you have your child alone to discuss small but impactful subjects. Remember, it is the quality of your attention that makes it meaningful, not necessarily the subject itself. I know women who have learned lots about their daughters' social interactions by letting them talk about cheerleading practice. When you offer genuine empathy, interest, and respect, you ensure that these little exchanges will build over time to secure a strong sense of self-esteem in the child and a strong sense of connectedness with you. They will come to see you as a valued guide and confidante. This is the kind of secure parental base you have been looking for. As difficult as it is to make it happen in the beginning, carving out these slices in your day will reap huge rewards in the future.

- Valuable time can be shared time. Do your share of carpool driving to school, dance lessons, baseball practice, or to the movies. Kids packed into your car, at whatever age, carry on conversations as if you're not there. This gives you an opening into your child's way of relating to friends and peers (his or her emotional intelligence style) and a glimpse of what's going on in his or her social circle. Here's how I've done it over the years. When my son was in preschool I made it a point to phone his classmates' parents (complete strangers to me at the time) and to coordinate a carpool schedule. This immediately helped my three-year-old and me get to know four other kids and their parents, gave my son a sense of security and connectedness, and rewarded me with the opportunity to be present and privy to their post-toddler transition into nursery school.

- Volunteer in the classroom at regular intervals. Most businesses will let you work this into your schedule. I accomplished this while completing a master's and Ph.D. and while holding down jobs and internships and studying for the state boards, so I know it can be managed if you massage your schedule a little. For your child's sake, try to make it predictable when you will show up. You get to know classmates, the environment, the teachers, and the administration. This makes you a better advocate for your child when needed. Once, after I battled to pull my son from a classroom where the teacher was verbally abusive and put him in a different class with a nurturing and inspiring teacher, he said, "Mom, you're like my attorney."

- Show up. Just get yourself into his or her life somehow. Even if it meant dragging myself in looking like hell after chugging a triple espresso, I always managed to make it to parent/teacher meetings. This may seem like obvious advice, but I have seen many kids whose parents don't make it happen. Showing up means everything. It buys you emotional security. It tells your child that having a job doesn't mean you're not a good mother. It lets him know you're plugged in. Whenever you can, be in the audience, go over his homework, make sure you're the loudest one cheering at practice, throw him birthday parties, listen to his speeches. Make sure he knows you're there, because that's how he knows you care. Even if the outfit you've shown up in embarrasses him, or your comments annoy him, he'll store in his memory banks the fact that you showed up (and kids have a long memory).

- If you can't always show up in person, call on your child's cell phone. Isn't technology wonderful? And nowadays, if you choose to spend time with your kid, you don't have to worry about being out of touch with clients. You can be on a hike in the woods and still answer the phone.

- Pick out special books and films that you sense will resonate with your child's sensibilities. Don't just park her in front of the video or stick a book in her hands and disappear. Afterward, spend time talking about points of interest. Limit her access to TV to expand her access to you.

- When you do let your kids watch television, there can be a big payoff to watching with them. Virginia Beane Rutter, an analyst member on the faculty of the C. G. Jung Institute and author of *Celebrating Girls* and *Embracing Persephone,* advises women to do this, even if some of the subject matter makes them uneasy. She also suggests accepting your teen's invitation to check out her online Facebook or My Space information; you'll learn a great deal about the friends she gravitates to, how she sees herself in the world of her peers, and what advice or feedback she explicitly or implicitly seeks from you. The movies, media images, and music our kids are paying attention to are mirrors into their minds—by noticing what interests them, we gain glimpses into their sensibilities, societal perspectives, blind spots, and areas where our wisdom and life experiences might add a meaningful contrasting perspective. If you really want to understand them, learn what interests them—then talk about it when they invite you to do so. They are receiving a great deal of input from the culture. Be there to interpret it for them.

Let Them See You Try

If you're concerned about your emotional connection with your spouse, child, or friends, find other avenues for showing your unconditional love. Don't underestimate the power of letting them see how hard you are trying. This sends them a very strong message that you truly care and that you're putting a great deal of thought into being a good parent (even if you can't be perfect) because you love them. Try saying, "I wish I could be at basketball practice on Thursday, but I can't. However, come hell or high water, I will make it to the game on Saturday." The message is that you can't do everything for them, but you will make a huge effort to do whatever you can. Just making the effort communicates a lot of love and the sense that you value them.

When preparing to enter high school, my son wanted to live full-time with his father for the first time rather than move to New York with me. At first I pushed for him to relocate with me before eventually seeing the benefits of his wish to do something other than what I wanted. To support his desire, and admittedly to keep myself from going crazy with loss and separation anxiety, I made sure to maintain our connection—which I also understood that he needed, even if he didn't consciously recognize it at the time—by putting myself through the monumental grind of commuting from East Coast to West Coast for a week out of every month to be with him. It wasn't heroic—it was simply what had to be done; my husband, Stephen, and I figured out a way to absorb the cost of airfares and keeping an apartment on the West Coast for four-plus years. And even though I was away from my

son for the three other weeks of the month, he knew (and he recognizes it even more, now that he is older) that I was moving
heaven and earth to be there when I was. That let him know that
my commitment to him was unshakable.

This point is worth making twice: there's more than one way to
fill a need. It's not just time—and that's exactly what you can be
creative about.

Here is a high-profile example. My friend editor Amanita Rosenbush told me about a television interview in which Barbara
Walters's daughter said that her mother was gone a lot when she
was young, yet she knew she was loved. Whenever her mother
came home from a trip in the middle of the night, she set her bags
down and headed straight for her bedroom. No glass of water
first; no other stops. The fact that her mother made a beeline for
her door told her volumes about how much she was missed. Even
if she was asleep, Barbara would pick her up and hold her. No
matter how much Mom had to work, her daughter was the most
important thing in her life. This knowledge was enough to sustain
the girl when her mother was gone.

Comedienne Whoopi Goldberg talks about how she would
have ended up abandoning her daughter more if she had not followed her ambition. Her career was beginning to take off and it
was demanding a great deal of her time. Whoopi was having trouble explaining this change to her daughter. "They have no computer to process it," she pointed out. "I made a conscious decision
to go ahead and pursue a career that had been handed to me at, I
think, the expense of my child. Had I not done what I did, I think
I would have been a much worse parent. I might have been there
more, but I wouldn't have made myself happy."

Many people will probably disagree with this, but I believe
that it is worse to abandon yourself than to be away from your

children. You are a better mother if you are fulfilled and happy than if you are bitter and unfulfilled. Who wants an unhappy mother? And as kids get older, they are better able to appreciate your choices. They simply can't compute them when they're very young.

Women who are driven by a passion for what they do cannot be expected to give that up. Actress Alfre Woodard told this story about learning to make choices. Her daughter Mavis was a year old when Woodard was offered a movie role. Because of her child's age, she was hesitant to accept it and go on location to South Africa. She recalled discussing her concerns with her father: "He said, 'Babe . . . that sounds right up your alley.' And I said [in a teary voice], 'Yeah, but I can't leave my baby.' He said, 'You know, it sounds like it's your problem. That baby will be fine.' He said, 'I think sometimes you have to do what you have to do . . . working women have to work; it's nothing about being an actress . . . working women have always had to make arrangements.' "

Instead of sacrificing your ambitchous self, you can strategize to avoid damage when life is out of control. Not only do you have to be creative about how to spend time with loved ones, but you have to do the same with taking time away from work. When you do spend time outside work, make sure you do it in a way that doesn't damage your career. If you want to have a baby, make arrangements at work so that you don't lose your position. I worked with one woman physician and radio program host who was up for a tenure-track position against two male colleagues. She chose not to reveal the fact that she was pregnant until after she'd won the promotion, much to the vocal chagrin of at least one of her supervisors (a woman, as it turned out). But by strategizing to keep her competitive edge, she was able to ignore the anticipated criticism and rejection and fight for what was due her. Of course, she felt a great deal of internal pressure, as women so often do, to lay all of her cards on the table. At the end of the day, though, she got the position she deserved and managed to have her baby without derailing her career.

Abandonment isn't just leaving someone—if you're in the same room as your kids, but you want to be somewhere else, they sense it and they feel abandoned. In a way, that's worse than if you just go. Not wanting to be with someone is a form of abandonment. So while the work/life balance evangelists treat it as such a simplistic choice, it's *not* as simple as, "Oh, I'll just stay home and then my kids won't feel abandoned." Honey, if you're ambitious and you want a career and you give that up to stay at home with the kids, guess what? They're going to feel abandoned anyway; do you think they don't know? So go for integration; go for expecting and accepting imbalance. It's a much happier solution.

Childlessness Is a Viable Choice

The need to have a child often comes from a deep and powerful biological urge. The urge itself is legitimate, but does it always have to be acted upon? Does biology have to be obeyed? What you need to ask yourself are these three questions: One, is my life going to be better if I heed the call? Two, given the extraordinary task it is to raise a child, can I do a good job if I'm hardly ever home? Three, is this an impulse I will outgrow?

The biological pull leads a woman to think she is cut out to be a mother just because she is physically equipped to give birth. However, not all women are emotionally built to be nurturing, patient, and attentive for eighteen years, the approximate time for which she is totally responsible for her offspring's well-being. While her body is longing to be pregnant, she thinks fondly of this adorable baby she will hold in her arms. You hear women say all the time, "I really, really, *really* want to have a baby." The problem is, you aren't actually having a baby; you are having a human being. They're babies for only the blink of an eye. They grow up very fast, and you soon realize that your choice of a cute, cuddly baby will have consequences for you that last a lifetime. If you are not unconditionally prepared to host that person for a lifetime, don't do it.

You need to evaluate whether you should do it just because you can do it. If you know that your career, which is of critical importance to you, is going to demand fifty- to seventy-hour weeks until you are old and toothless, should you really have a child and leave its care in someone else's hands for most of its waking life? Louise Nevelson, the acclaimed sculptor, had a son and didn't realize until after he was born that she wasn't cut out for motherhood at all. She wanted to be in the studio all hours working; it's what she had always wanted, and she wasn't about to change her ways. By her own admission, she paid little attention to her child, because her art was more important. "I'm an artist," she said. "It's my soul." The problem, of course, was that her son needed a mother and he had one for only a few minutes a week. In interviews with him, his bitterness is quite plain, and one can hardly blame him.

It is possible to be a good mother and have a good career, but not always. If you really are geared to be in business, academics, medicine, and so on, and the career you seek demands all your time, you need to do some serious soul searching about whether you really have enough of your time and of yourself left over to do justice to motherhood. Must you procreate to be fulfilled? Oprah Winfrey once said that she loved children. However, she recognized how much it took out of a person to be good at it and realized that she couldn't sacrifice that much. If she couldn't do a great job, she would choose not to do it at all. Oprah thought about all the nuances and consequences of the choice and came to the conclusion that it wasn't right for her and it wouldn't be right for the child. Actress Katharine Hepburn said, "I was ambitious and knew I would not have children. I wanted total freedom." Comedian Ellen DeGeneres said, "Listen, I love kids. But I also like being able to do whatever I want when I want." Other women see a sort of moral imperative in not choosing motherhood. Author Marguerite Yourcenar said, "Leaving behind books is even more beautiful. There are far too many children." And actress Helen Mirren's point was, "I think of it as a contribution to the ecology of the world."

Consider this, even if you have a strong mothering instinct: there may be other ways to satisfy it than bearing your own offspring. Oprah, for instance, focuses her resources on helping the world's children, donating $40 million to establish the Oprah Winfrey Leadership Academy for Girls—South Africa. Some female authors see their children's books as their kids and as a gift to the world's children. I have friends who happily donate their time to the Humane Society nursing small kittens and puppies, or who do charitable work at a children's hospital, standing in when the mothers cannot be there. Experienced businesswomen find a lot of satisfaction mentoring young people who are just coming up in the world, including nieces, nephews, or other protégées. The need to nurture and be of service and pass down something of yourself to others does not have to be filled through mothering a child. There are many ways to be a mother.

Actress Janeane Garafalo has spoken out frankly in the press about her observation that "people think that you are a nasty, selfish person if you don't want to have children." Many women I interviewed who chose not to have children told me that they received little support for their decision. Most people don't realize that choosing to be childless can be the most responsible decision you ever made—depending on who you are, what you want, and what you feel is right for you.

Life happens, and it's rarely smooth, clean, and easy. The problem with believing that life balance is the Holy Grail is that when periods in life are particularly messy and you're pulled in different directions, your default thought is, "I must be spending too much time at the office." Rarely do we say the reverse. The truth is, balance graces us once in a while, but the majority of the time, we can't keep all of the balls in the air. We drop the ball sometimes—we just do. The secret is that this doesn't mean we're failing, or that our lives are hopelessly out of control, or that we're inept and others juggle better. It just means some days we get it more right than others.

Being a career woman in our society and sustaining your ambitchous goals takes nothing less than a heroic effort. If you feel fear or anxiety or self-doubt as you strive to define for yourself just what ambition goals you want to pursue and how to get there, don't worry. Instead of holding yourself to an impossible standard, know two things: First, you are not alone; and second, it is indeed possible to let go of the life-balance myth.

No one can maintain the version of balance that the culture and the media sell us. It's a fallacy, so cut yourself some slack. Stop feeling like you're failing at the balance equation and start realizing that what you can get right is acceptance and strategy. You can ease your own mind by accepting the messiness of being an ambitchous woman with kids—or just an ambitchous woman period.

sixteen

■ ■ ■ ■ ■ ■ ■ ■ ■ ■ ■ ■ ■ ■ ■ ■ ■ ■

Dare to Be Great

■ ■ ■ ■ ■ ■ ■ ■ ■ ■ ■ ■ ■ ■ ■ ■ ■ ■

PUTTING top priority on doing ambitchous work that you love—and maintaining that ambitchous vision over the entirety of your life—means that you will always have a sanctuary to come home to. It means you'll know that your ambitchous core and sense of competence can take hits and never be completely shattered. Staying determined to live an ambitchous life doesn't mean that your confidence isn't shaken at times. It doesn't mean that you won't have clashing priorities. But your ambitchous passion will sustain and nourish you even when you can't fix other things in your life.

I make my living teaching women how to own their ambition. I walk my talk. But just like you, I take hits; I get shaken. In a moment of trauma, I too succumbed to those deeply ingrained cultural beliefs about how women are supposed to behave. It happened to me when my son almost died.

On July 14, 2005, two weeks before this book was due to my publisher, I was awakened at four thirty a.m. by a phone call. My seventeen-year-old son, Devin, had been hit by a car and was lying in the trauma unit of a hospital twenty-five hundred miles away from my New York City home. His condition was unknown.

I was supposed to have been with him, but I'd stayed behind from a family vacation to write this book. I numbly threw some clothes into suitcases and barely managed to catch a seven a.m. flight to the San Francisco Bay Area to get to him.

As I sat on the plane, the first thought that popped into my mind was, "Is my son being punished for my ambition?" After all, I'd been pouring most of my time lately into my book and business. If I hadn't bailed on the family vacation, would Devin have been spared? The guilt went deeper than that. Several years earlier, as you now know, I'd chosen to expand my business into New York and spend countless hours commuting between San Francisco, where Devin lived with his father, and my new East Coast office. That meant less time with Devin. A few years before *that,* I'd struggled as a single working mother, often having to deny him the finer things while I scrimped and saved. When I remarried, I spent lots of time with my new husband and stepson who, in truth, also sometimes took a backseat while I continued to grow my business, my life's passion.

In between hourly calls from the airplane phone to Devin's father at the hospital, I ticked off the items on the guilty-mother's checklist. Dumped my child in day care more than I'd have liked? Check. Dragged him through a difficult divorce? Check. Denied him the fancy bicycle and fancier private school while I earned my degree? Check. Remarried? Check. Moved away from my own son? Check. But all that paled next to my biggest sin: for the last several months, I'd consistently put work ahead of family. Who cared that I'd logged a lifetime of being a good, sometimes great, mom? Who cared that I loved my work with a passion, that I'd helped thousands of women realize their lifelong dreams? Clearly, the gods were punishing me for being too ambitious, and Devin was paying the ultimate price. Of course, this was crazy, irrational thinking—but that's what we women do, isn't it? Isn't a good

mother one who has the grace to feel guilty about any choice beyond putting family first?

I'd survived career derailments, money struggles, and lack of
support as a single mom. I'd worked hard to regain professional
traction, passion for my career, and financial stability, and I'd
built what I thought was a solid infrastructure for my son and myself. This false notion of security took seventeen years to build,
but it was shattered in the moment of that phone call. And my
first thought was that I—specifically, my ambition—was somehow to blame for a mother's worst nightmare.

I end the book with this story because I want you to know that,
like you, I understand on a deep, visceral level—one that can't be
duplicated by intellectual reasoning or academic polemics—what
it means to try to balance love and ambition with guilt, financial
hardship, and questions about the meaning of life. On a less dramatic level, I understand what it means to live daily with the di-
alectical tension of loving your work every bit as much as your
children and family, of trying to nurture mutually exclusive yet
equally sacrosanct priorities. I've lived a complex and nonformu-
laic life as a deeply devoted (and deeply flawed) divorced single
mother, as well as a determined, ambitious professional woman.
Your story is doubtless no less complex. What we share as high-
achieving women—consciously or unconsciously—is the challenge of valuing our pure ambition in a culture that tells us that
doing so is going to bring us down hard, sometime, somehow. We
absorb the message that there will be hell to pay for loving our
work with a grand passion. As my own story shows, I know how
simplistic the formulaic how-to plans, advice, and strategies for
the working woman often completely and utterly miss the point.

For the first month after Devin's accident, I did little but re-
play in my mind the details of his accident. He'd been standing on
a quiet neighborhood sidewalk when a speeding, out-of-control

truck hit him, throwing him twenty-five feet. His friends looked for him under the vehicle and then between it and the metal pole that it crashed into. Upon awakening after being knocked unconscious, his first thought was, "I'm going to die." He'd suffered a concussion, multiple pelvic fractures, and a separated sacroiliac joint. We didn't know initially whether he'd be brain-injured or paralyzed. I stayed by his side almost constantly in that initial recuperative phase. A constant stream of friends and family visited regularly. At last the doctors offered a guardedly optimistic prognosis—Devin faced an uphill climb through healing and long-term rehabilitation, but they believed that he'd come through fine. I forced myself to get back to my writing (obviously my editor had extended my deadline and advised me to take my time getting back to the book). As soon as I sat myself down, booted up my computer, and began to work, I felt myself take a deep, refreshing breath. I was going back into my body, into my mind. I felt myself truly relax for the first time since Devin's accident. Relaxing in both mind and body, I felt myself letting go by focusing on my work.

Getting back in touch with my ambition gave me a sense of normalcy, a sense that our lives could get back on track. My ambition was what soothed me at a time when I was deeply traumatized. Of course, I welcomed the love and support of my husband, Stephen, and my stepson, Jake. But I had needed something more. Something more than the affection of my caring friends and family—though I'd never needed that love and support so much in my life as then. Something more than any prescription drug. Something more than running or yoga. Something even more than being with and caring for my son for six weeks during his acute healing process—although being there for him was non-negotiable and critical to me. I needed something else to find my way back to myself, and to heal. And what I needed was to return to my ambitchous work, even at the same time that I was sitting in the same room with my son and his friends, on my computer, doing my own thing while they did theirs.

The subliminal cultural influences that come with being an ambitchous woman hit me again a few days later. Still feeling traumatized and guilty, I confessed to my friends Nancy and Sheryl that I was feeling good about getting back to work. "Still," I rushed to assure them, lest the gods punish me again for daring to think about my career, "I'd chuck it all—my work, my business, everything—to have prevented this from happening to my son." But then it hit me, and I said to them, "But you know what? That's a false choice; I don't have to choose between my child's well-being and my ambition. And that's precisely what I'm writing about!"

Even though I occasionally do battle with myself, just as many of us do, I believe deep in my soul that returning to our sacrosanct ambition—that which inspires us to get back to work more days than not—is what grounds us and stabilizes us when we're rocked, personally or professionally. And we should feel unapologetic about having that guidepost and touchstone in our lives; we should resist feelings of guilt, self-recrimination, and blame, and instead feel strengthened and sustained by our inner professional passion and drive to do the work and make the contribution we were born to make.

I want to be clear here: my work wasn't merely a soothing routine to which I could return, a distraction or escape that would take my mind off my worries about my son, or a task that could restore my shaky illusion of control. It did serve those roles, but my work—and, more specifically, my love and passion for my work—did and does so much more. It brings me back home to myself. It is my anchor, my nourishment. Nancy Lafferty-Wellott, CEO and founder of Habits & Habitats, described it this way: "My ambition is always a soothing ointment for my soul, no matter what's going on in my life."

Putting top priority on doing work that you love means that you will always have a steady internal foundation upon which to stand and from which to launch and live your ambitchous life. Through the ups and downs you encounter, your ambitchous passion will sustain you even when you can't fix other things in your life.

Your life, like mine, will throw you an infinite number of curveballs. Your child gets hurt—you can't fix it, or you can't fix it immediately. You get promoted to a dream job that brings with it a steep learning curve, plus a new team of high-maintenance talent to manage—it takes time to figure out how to make that dynamic work. Your husband has an affair—you can't fix that; your child can't fix that. You get married, you're in love—you can't always spend as much time together as you'd like. You get sick—you can't immediately fix it, and neither, necessarily, can anyone else. Things outside of your control may let you down and frighten you, but your ambition anchor will help reground and center you. You will always have access to your inner belief in your business smarts and brainpower and creativity and professional problem solving; you will always have that to come home to.

When things in my life are going my way, my ambition keeps me happy, fired up, and feeling young, vibrant, and fully engaged in every part of my life. Perhaps even more important, it is also the one thing that I can count on and come back to when I'm in over my head, when life disappoints or scares me or dares me to be stronger than I thought myself capable of.

Ambition is my anchor because it comes from within me, rather than from some external source—be it colleagues, promotion, friends, partner, boss, fat paycheck, mentor, or some mercurial other. As supportive and caring as others can be, I know I can't necessarily count on them; I have only myself at the end of the day.

Life delights us, and things seem relatively easy. But life also disappoints. We don't get the job, the relationship, the other brass ring. Others disappoint—sometimes they can't help it, sometimes they're unable or unwilling or just don't know what we need, or sometimes we don't know how to spell out what we need. We look to our children to fulfill us, but they cannot be our anchor—they have their own lives. More important, it's simply too much to expect that they can fulfill everything we long for or that they will replace our ambition and become the organizing principle in our lives. We cannot pressure our children to embody our ambition; we must find it in ourselves.

We cannot look to others to live out our dreams for us. We have to nurture the ambition in our own guts. If we can't find it in ourselves, we'll have to pile up some kindling and nurture the first tiny flickers into a consuming fire in our bellies. Sustaining our sacrosanct ambition is what will bring us back to ourselves, time after time, through life's inevitable struggles, through the highs and lows. It is with this immutable belief that I've offered you this book on sustaining your own inviolable ambition.

I now want to leave you with a final ambitchous mantra:

DARE TO BE GREAT.

From this day forward, let's make a pact as ambitchous women. Let's imagine that we live in a parallel universe. In this parallel universe, women have no more problem acknowledging that they are ambitious than admitting that they like chocolate. How do we define ambition in that realm? As that which drives our creative existence, provides an outlet for our talents and passions, defines who we are, and allows us to earn our full worth without apology.

Imagine this is a world where you treat and protect your ambition as you would a lover or beloved. In this universe, you can be a loyal friend and a great coworker. Without guilt from within or judgment from without, you could be a good mother, a caring partner, *and* a woman with big goals, nurturing all your relationships, your child, and your ambition dreams.

In this universe, a woman's ambition is not just a job. It embodies a conscious, deliberate, and mindful search for truth and meaning in her life, a return to her natural wellspring of passion and purpose—even when she is lost or off course, a letting go of the fears and doubts that block her path. In this universe she sees clearly for the first time how to free herself from the shackles that have, in the past, hobbled her ambition.

Visualize yourself in that world now. You are there—you are ambitchous. Believe it: your ambition is a virtue. Hold the choices you make to fulfill your ambition precious, sacrosanct. Sometimes you'll have to make tough sacrifices or compromises. Each of those decisions represents an acceptance and honoring of the fire within you. Regard them as gifts you give to yourself to protect and cherish your dreams—for your career, for your one precious life.

Dare to be great. You have a responsibility to yourself to actualize the talents you were born with and to make the contribution you were put here to make. You've gotten the message that you can be good, even very good. But I don't want you to stop at good enough, good, or very good. Take the leap; elevate your aspirations to greatness. Strive to be the best in your field, your industry, your niche. Promise yourself you will always earn your worth.

The life I dare you to lead is a life filled with hope, dreams, aspirations—and the expectation of having them fulfilled. When you make the choice to lead that kind of life, who knows how many others you'll inspire? It never occurred to me that my son, Devin, paid a whole lot of attention to my career decisions, but one day when he was fifteen he said, "I don't want to be one of those people who get up every day and go to a boring job they hate just to get a paycheck. I think that's sad. I want to be like you, Mom. You have an interesting life. You work for yourself, you travel, you decide what you want to do and how you want to work." It was deeply validating to realize that however much I might have messed up as a parent, I'd given my son a powerful role model for prizing ambition and intention, for creating a life based on passion.

You deserve to love your work, to be as ambitious as you wish, to earn your worth, and to find fulfillment. Give yourself permission to be true to your ambition, to make the choices you deem appropriate without pause, without second-guessing yourself. This means you'll need to check in with yourself daily, tuning in to what you want in your heart of hearts, staying true to your ambition as you define it. When you build your life's work from that place of sanctuary, you'll be richly rewarded with lifelong intellectual and creative curiosity, evolving opportunities, and healthier, happier relationships with loved ones. And you will earn your worth.

What we don't hear from the cultural messages telling us what we *ought* to value as women in this society is that ambition *is* a part of living our best and greatest life. There is no societal clarion call ringing with the message that our ambition is a vital, irreplaceable component of our lives. Our pact is to change that. Let's each of us agree to be an ambitchous woman—and to be her now.

As the ambitchous woman you now know you are—and now know you are entitled to be—I encourage you to answer for yourself, every day, a question posed in Mary Oliver's poem "The Summer Day":

Tell me,
What is it you plan to do with your one
wild and precious life?

Acknowledgments

I am deeply indebted to the amBITCHous women who have shared their stories with me over the years, including those who helped build the Women's Business Alliance, and the women of PowerShare International who generously mentored me. Dr. Lucy Scott, your guidance as my doctoral dissertation chair and inspiring dedication to research that makes a difference in women's lives launched my belief that I, too, could make a difference.

It has been thrilling to work with the entire Morgan Road Books team. My deepest thanks to my editor and publisher extraordinaire, Amy Hertz. Your ability to see this book in full relief when it was but a roughly hewn piece of stone; your overall vision, faith, and commitment to excellence throughout our collaboration; your unerring ability to know when to wait, when to push; and your ability to manage, motivate, and move me throughout our creative journey embody the very ideal of the ambitchous woman. Julie Miesionczek, editorial assistant prodigy, you dazzle me with your command of the English language, your creativity, and your stamina. I am fortunate that Amy brought us together for our mutual first line-editing experience. And thanks for the un-split infinitives and the baby seals. KaChing! Jean Traina, thank you for designing the perfect book cover.

Elizabeth "Betsy" Rapoport, you expertly got me to the first finish line of a golden proposal with your master's-hand edits. Thank you for sharing your humorous take on the world and those of us who inhabit it. I appreciate your brilliant mind, your honest, direct feedback, and your warm and generous friendship. I am especially grateful for your wolf-in-sheep's-clothing brainstorm, and for introducing me to my agent, James Levine. Jim, you are a consummate pro. You intuited from the beginning who my soul mate editor was, but didn't bias me; everything plays out as it should. I am grateful for your wise and steady guidance. Thank you, Lindsay Edgecombe, also of the Levine Greenberg Literary Agency and my talented twenty-something representative, for your unerring support and enthusiasm, and for showing up for me.

Book Mother, Amanita Rosenbush, my early editor, you guided me through the uncharted territory of building a proposal and sample chapters when I first had the idea for this book. What you taught me about writing and staying the course, with your sharp, intelligent eye and tough yet compassionate advice, is incalculable and I am deeply grateful for your support and friendship.

I so appreciate my mother for enthusiastically driving some 525,600 miles to provide art, piano, and other lessons that fed my ambitions. I thank my dad for modeling the entrepreneurial spirit and for a lifetime of fatherly acts, like framing my just-finished painting at 4:30 a.m. for the high school state art contest where I took first place a few hours later—see, Dad, I told you it pays to procrastinate. Thanks to my brother, Alan Condren, for not billing me for whine-time conversations when I hit writing bumps, and for offering me a choice, each time I called, of touchy-feely-granola-snowflake support or the suck-it-up-get-back-in-the-game version. Thanks to my favorite aunt and uncle, Doris

Marie Mabray and Bill Ed Mabray, for celebrating my ambitchous antics from the time I was small. Thank you to my cousins Bill Sam Mabray, Lea Ann Mabray, and Sue Vest McKay for cheering me on.

I am grateful to Sister Mildred Dunn, who taught me classical piano for eleven years and threw in lectures about always putting my ambitious studies first. Thank you, Keith Mahaffey, my honors high school world history teacher; your encouragement switched on a lightbulb that illuminated my interest in the psychological study of social issues. Thanks to Diana Josenberger and Connie Stringer for early race, gender, and ambition lessons at the Sunnymeade tetherball courts. Jennifer Jeffries, Gail Davis, and Liz Beckman: our Team-Ambitious taught me girl power!

Rusti "Dude-isn't-that-the-Washington-monument?" Green, I love you for your sweet support, your irrepressible humor, and your dedication to your ambitchous dreams. Randi Cruz-Green, thank you for lovingly supporting me during this final year of writing, while sharing with us your gutsy freshman year of college in New York City and the BX. You will have many more ambitchous adventures in your life, I promise. Thanks to Trey chain-chain-chain Mabray for constant writing encouragement and much-needed laughs.

I am fortunate to have ongoing love and support from the three other members of The Core Four: Sheryl Menefee Cahill, Nancy C. Compton, and Kathryn Orfirer. We've been friends in various incarnations for almost two decades. You are my three sisters sitting on rocks of black obsidian, to invoke Adrienne Rich. I thank my friend, journalist, musicologist, and father extraordinaire, Greg Cahill, for answering countless grammar and writing questions, and for all the other life support you've offered over the years. Tammy Brasuell Gattis Owings, thank you for always saying to me, since middle school, "I'm so proud of you." I'm so proud of you, too. Liz Conn, I love you for being my first New

York City friend, constant supporter, and confidant, and for being fabulous in every way possible. Dr. Ann Demarais, my first independently made New York City friend, thank you for being my experienced guide through the process of writing a book; your affirmations were, well, affirming! Meredith Lindsey, thank you for being my ever-supportive friend, surrogate daughter, surrogate sister, surrogate mom . . . I mean, there just isn't a label, but you're always there for me. Susan Lindsey, thank you for your sage advice over the years and for sharing Mere. I so appreciate Mildred Barecca (a.k.a. Mrs. Laningham) for helping with the story of you-know-who, and for always keeping us in your prayers. Christina Champagne, thank you for your loving support in the summer of 2005, when we so needed it (sorry about that first house); I expect ambitchous things from you. Thank you, Luis Hincapie and Marvin Miguel, for organizing my life. Jane Curtis Land, I so appreciate your rapid-fire, spot-on research efforts. Austin Cahill, thank you for crashed-computer troubleshooting; Miles Cahill, kudos for finding the chartreuse Petaluma writing table.

I am deeply indebted to Virginia Beane Rutter. You have been a trusted and cherished adviser since I phoned you in 2000 saying that I wanted to get it right.

Thank you, Patty Hertz and Meshulam "Shuly" Plaves, for being there for me all those years; Devin and Lev brought us together in more ways than we could have imagined. P, thanks so much for saying, "Okay, but you're a dope." That made all the difference. I am deeply indebted to Sy and Elaine Hertz for shoring me, and us, up; for always being there. Sandy Hertz and Bob Dorian, thank you for your encouraging notes and words throughout this process. Joan Gelfand and Adam Hertz, thanks for networking and Cardboard J. Consults. Aunt Ruth Hertz, thanks for your supportive cards and for being a fellow outlaw.

Judy, Judy, Judy Soloman, I appreciated your kind support and the books you sent. Amy Soloman, thank you for "adopting" me. Thank you, Devin Condren Bethel . . . for being Devin. And for always making me laugh. You are an amazing person and a great son and I love you even when I can't stand you (to quote you!). I'm incredibly proud of you and the person you've become. I cannot wait to see the brilliant, creative business ideas you will grace us with next. Always follow your dreams and be as ambitious as you really want to be. Make the contribution you were born to make.

Thank you, Jake Hertz, for bestowing upon me the honor of being your E.S.M. You are destined to do great things—I know this to be true. It meant a lot to me when you repeatedly asked me, those couple of years when I'd gone silent, "So Debra . . . how's the book coming?" I still think we should be the first stepson/stepmother duo to do *The Amazing Race*. They certainly wouldn't need a laugh track.

My deepest love and appreciation are reserved for S.R. and crossover redemption.

Notes

Chapter Two: What a Difference a Word Makes

22 **"importance of loving our work?"** Gail Evans, *Play Like a Man, Win Like a Woman* (New York: Broadway, 2001), pp. 15–16.

Chapter Three: Honorable Ambition?

32 **"The world would split open"**: Muriel Rukeyser, "KÄTHE KALL- WITZ" in *The Speed of Darkness* (New York: Library of America, 2004), p. 103.

Chapter Six

67 **Catalyst survey finding:** "Women 'Take Care,' Men 'Take Charge': Stereotyping of U.S. Business Leaders Exposed." Catalyst Report 2005. www.catalyst.org.

Chapter Nine: amBITCHous Rule 4

117 **"one percent of the world's property"**: Barber B. Conable Jr., at a joint meeting of the World Bank and the IMF, 1986.

121 **negotiations four times as often:** Linda Babcock and Sara Laschever, *Women Don't Ask: Negotiation and the Gender Divide* (Princeton: Princeton University Press, 2003), p. 3.

125 **"that few women can afford to miss":** Dr. Evelyn Murphy, *Getting Even: Why Women Don't Get Paid Like Men and What to Do About It* (New York: Touchstone, 2005). See also The Wage Project, http://www.wageproject.org/content/gap/costs.shtml/content/gap/costs.shtml.

126 **"32 percent more at their career peaks":** Babcock and Laschever, *Women Don't Ask,* pp. xi–16.

Chapter Twelve: amBITCHous Rule 7

188 **"dignified act of revenge":** Katy McLaughlin, "Uruguay Is Asking Why the Oscars Snubbed Jorge Dexler," *Wall Street Journal,* March 2, 2005, p. A1.

Chapter Thirteen: amBITCHous Rule 8

193 **"I am sufficient as I am":** Walt Whitman, "One Hour to Madness and Joy" in *Complete Poetry and Collected Prose of Walt Whitman* (New York: Library of America, 1982), p. 262–63.

195 **deserve their educational or career credentials:** Peggy McIntosh, Wellesley College, Wellesley Center for Women, The Stone Center, no. 18, "Feeling like a Fraud I," p.1.

199 **they would decline a public speaking opportunity:** R. Moulton, "Some Effects of the New Feminism," *American Journal of Psychiatry* 134, no. 1 (1977): 1–6, quoted in Irene Pierce Stiver, "Women's Struggles in the Workplace: A Relational Model," in *Women in Context: Toward a Feminist Reconstruction of Psychotherapy,* ed. Marsha Pravda Mirkin (New York: Guilford Press, 1994), p. 433.

205 **"women for their strengths":** Lois Wyse, *A Woman's Journal: A Blank Book with Quotes by Women* (Philadelphia: Running Press, 1986), p. 95.

Chapter Fourteen: Lifelong amBITCHous Maintenance

216 **"that gives me great fulfillment":** interview with Jewel in *Lilith Fair: A Celebration of Women in Music* (DVD), 2000.

Chapter Fifteen: Ambition Integration

240   **"us that life is being lived"**: Anne Lamott, *Bird by Bird: Some Instructions on Writing and Life* (New York: Anchor, 1995), p. 28.

249   **"have made myself happy"**: Whoopi Goldberg, interview with Rosanna Arquette in Ms. Arquette's film *Searching for Debra Winger,* 2002.

250   **"always had to make arrangements"**: Alfre Woodard, interview with Rosanna Arquette, ibid.

Chapter Sixteen: Dare to Be Great

264   **"one wild and precious life?"**: Mary Oliver, "The Summer Day" in *House of Light* (Boston: Beacon Press, 1992), p. 60.

Acknowledgments

267   **to invoke Adrienne Rich**: Adrienne Rich, "Women" in *Leaflets: Poems, 1965–1968* (London: Chatto and Windus, Hogarth Press, 1972), p. 41.

List of Contributors

Helen Abe is a certified investment management analyst, a first vice president, financial adviser, and senior consultant at Morgan Stanley. She has been in the financial services industry since 1985. Ms. Abe is a graduate of the University of Hawaii and the Executive M.B.A. program at Saint Mary's College in Moraga, California. She is a certified investment management analyst and has studied at the Wharton Business School in Pennsylvania. Ms. Abe frequently lectures for groups such as the Commonwealth Club, Board of Realtors, the Bureau of Alcohol, Tobacco & Firearms, the Golden Gate Senior Center, Sears Retired Employees Group, Pacific Bell, Kaiser Permanente, and United Airlines. She also provides educational investment classes that stress the importance of financial independence for women. Ms. Abe was an original contributor to the Women's Business Alliance.www .morganstanley.com/fa/helen.abe.

Lesley Alderman is a magazine editor and author in New York City.

Sherry Amanpour is a former diplomat from Iran. She was one of eleven women out of a total four hundred diplomats in the

Iranian Foreign Service during the Shah's regime in Iran. With the turn of political events, she started a new life in New York City, first as a banker, then as the founder of a search firm. Ms. Amanpour's numerous speaking engagements have included M.I.T. Alumni, New York University, Columbia University, and Drake Beam Morin. She is a graduate of Barnard College.

Jan Aronson's paintings have been exhibited in solo and group exhibitions in museums and galleries worldwide. In addition, her work is in numerous public, corporate, and private collections. www.janaronson.com.

Caroline Barnes founded Barnes & Associates, a full-service public accounting firm with the goal of demystifying what's behind an organization's numbers. Ms. Barnes spent over nine years with the accounting giant PriceWaterhouse before starting her own firm. She has an M.B.A. in accounting and finance. Ms. Barnes was an original contributor to the Women's Business Alliance.

Wayka Bartolacelli, Realtor with Pacific Union GMAC Real Estate in Central Marin, California, has lived in Venezuela, Germany, and Philadelphia. She speaks German and Spanish fluently. Ms. Bartolacelli has been a successful real estate agent since her first achievement as "Rookie of the Year" in 1986. She provides consistently award-winning service. Ms. Bartolacelli also shares her real estate expertise in a bimonthly column of a local newspaper and participates in Rotary and other local fund-raising events. Ms. Bartolacelli was an original contributor to the Women's Business Alliance. She lives in San Rafael, California, with her husband of twenty-four years and has two "children" in college. www.wayka.com.

Tanya Styblo Beder joined as CEO of Citigroup Alternative Investments' multi-strategy proprietary hedge fund Tribeca Global Management LLC in May 2004. Previously Ms. Beder was a head of the Strategic Quantitative Investment Division of Caxton Associates, LLC, a $10 billion investment management firm located in New York City; president of Capital Market Risk Advisors; and a vice president of the First Boston Corporation. Euromoney named Ms. Beder as one of the top fifty women in finance around the world. She has appeared as an invited expert before the U.S. Congressional Subcommittee on Telecommunications and Finance on derivatives, before the OECD on risk in the global financial landscape, and before the U.S. Senate Special Committee on the Year 2000 Technology Problem. From 1998 through 2003 Ms. Beder was chairman of the board of the International Association of Financial Engineers; currently she is on the board of directors and serves as the cochair of the Investor Risk Committee. She serves on the board of directors of OpHedge Investment Services and on the advisory board of Columbia University's financial engineering program, and is an appointed Fellow of the International Center for Finance at Yale and has served on the National Board of Mathematics and Their Applications. Ms. Beder has been on the adjunct faculty at Columbia and Yale universities and is widely published. She holds an M.B.A. in finance from Harvard University and a B.A. in mathematics from Yale University.

Suwen Bian is a senior financial analyst for Homestead Capital's Finance and Accounting Department. Prior to joining Homestead Capital, Suwen worked in a variety of positions for Wells Fargo in the Wire Transfer and Customer Service departments. Ms. Bian also taught middle school in Suzhou, in mainland China. Originally from mainland China, she came to the United States at age twenty-six. She received a B.A. in business and accounting from Portland State University and completed her M.B.A. in finance as one in the top 5 percent of students in her class in June 2002. She also worked as the official translator on the Chinese Classical Gardens project in Portland, Oregon, the first of its type in the United States.

Celeste Bishop is president of Bishop Market Resources, a competitive services agency that offers a range of projects and services for businesses, entrepreneurs, and professional service firms. Ms. Bishop provides expert advice about classic and Web-related competition at www.BishopMarketResources.com. She created AT&T's first Consumer Communication Competitive Analysis Organization. Her educational background includes a B.S. in marketing from Rutgers, as well as executive education at both Columbia University and Stanford University. Ms. Bishop was an original contributor to the Women's Business Alliance.

Franci J. Blassberg, J.D., is a partner at the New York law firm Debevoise & Plimpton LLP. Her areas of practice include mergers and acquisitions and private equity. She was named by the *National Law Journal* as one of the 100 Most Influential Lawyers in America and has been ranked as a leading practitioner in *Chambers Global* (2006), *Chambers USA* (2006), *PLC Which Lawyer? Yearbook 2006*, *Euromoney's* Best of the Best U.S. 2006, and the Best Lawyers in America 2005–2006. Ms. Blassberg has also been named a Dealmaker of the Year by *The American Lawyer* (2006). Ms. Blassberg has deep experience counseling private and public companies in domestic and international acquisitions and divestitures, securities offerings, and other transactions. www.Debevoise.com.

Anita L. Boss, Psy.D., ABPP, is a board-certified forensic psychologist who provides forensic psychological evaluations, consultation, and expert testimony. She previously worked at St. Elizabeth's Hospital, Maryland Department of Public Safety and Corrections, U.S. Department of Justice, Federal Bureau of Prisons, and Bellevue Hospital. Dr. Boss teaches doctoral-level personality assessment and master's level forensic psychology at Catholic University of America in Washington, D.C. She is a fellow of the American Academy of Forensic Psychology and a board member of the Society for Personality Assessment (SPA).

Jacqui Brandwynne is one of the first corporate turnaround executives. She is a noted business executive with more than twenty-five years' experience building successful brands and consumer strategies for Fortune 500 multinational corporations, including Citicorp, American Cyanamid, Bristol Myers/Clairol, Revlon, National Liberty Life, and Seagram & Sons. Currently founder and CEO of Brandwynne Corporation, she manages a successful venture-capital business that concentrates on communication, Internet infrastructure support, and fiber optics. During her tenure at Citicorp, Ms. Brandwynne managed an inside staff and an outside team of scientists and industry specialists, including academics from Harvard, MIT, Stanford, the Annenberg School of Communication, and Columbia University. Ms. Brandwynne served in Washington, D.C., under several presidential administrations in both advisory and negotiating capacities. She's also a consultant and women's health advocate. Today her column reaches more than six million newspaper readers, as well as a large radio and TV audience. She is a member of the Committee of 200, a global organization of top female entrepreneurs, as well as a member of the Los Angeles Trusteeship, whose members are top females in their professions.

Tiffany Bass Bukow is the CEO of MsMoney.com, the premier educational personal finance Web site. More than two million people have visited MsMoney.com. For five years, Ms. Bass Bukow has been on the board of advisers for Women's Technology Cluster, a preeminent business incubator with a socially responsible mission. Ms. Bass Bukow hosted a pilot for a money-makeover reality TV show in London called *Live Your Life at Half the Price.* She also appeared monthly as a money expert for the live TV show *Call for Help,* broadcast in forty million households in seventy countries. Her advice was featured in a TV segment on financial tips called "Prescription for Financial Health," broadcast in 250 local news markets and 80 million households. She also appeared on *ABC News* with Peter Jennings, the PBS *NewsHour with Jim Lehrer,* PBS's *Digital Think,* and *CBS News.*

Sheryl Menefee Cahill is the owner of the Station House Café in Point Reyes Station, California. She holds a B.A. in cultural anthropology from the University of California, Berkeley, from which she graduated with honors. She resides in Petaluma, California, with her husband and two teenage sons. www.StationHouseCafe.com.

Christine Comaford-Lynch is an author, an entrepreneur, and the CEO of Mighty Ventures, a start-up consultancy. She has built and sold five of her own businesses, served as a board director or in-the-trenches adviser to thirty-six start-ups, and invested in over two hundred start-ups. Christine has consulted to the White House, seven hundred of the Fortune 1000, and over a hundred small businesses. She has repeatedly identified and championed key trends and technologies years before their market acceptance. Christine has appeared on CNN, MSNBC, and PBS. She is frequently quoted in the business, technology, and general press at large. Stanford Graduate School of Business has done two case studies on her, and CNET has broadcast two specials covering her unconventional rise and success as a

woman with neither high school diploma nor college degree.
www.mightyventures.com.

Elizabeth Conn is president of ECONN design, a boutique
interior-design firm specializing in upscale family residences in
New York City. She holds a B.A. in English and political science
from Barnard College and a fine arts painting degree from the
School of Visual Arts. Ms. Conn paints and exhibits in New York.

Barbara Corcoran is the founder of the Corcoran Group, New
York City's premier real estate company, and one of the most
powerful brokers in the nation. Her credentials include straight
D's in high school and college and twenty jobs by the time she
turned twenty-three. She borrowed $1,000 from her boyfriend
and quit her job as a waitress to start a tiny real estate company in
New York City. Over the next twenty-five years, that company
became a five-billion-dollar real estate business. Barbara is the
author of *If You Don't Have Big Breasts, Put Ribbons on Your
Pigtails,* which has become a national bestseller. She is a regular
contributor to the Fox News Network and ABC's *Good Morning
America* and *The View.* www.BarbaraCorcoran.com.

Margaret ("Peggy") Andrews Davenport, cochair of Debevoise & Plimpton LLP's Private Equity Group, is widely recognized as a leader in the field of private equity M&A. Ms. Davenport has a broad-based transactional practice advising private
equity firms and other corporate clients in structuring and negotiating acquisition and finance transactions. Ms. Davenport is
ranked in the top tier of *Chambers USA* (2005) and *Chambers
Global* (2006) for private equity buyouts and investments. In addition, *PLC Which Lawyer? Yearbook 2005,* Legal Media Group's
Expert Guide to the World's Leading Private Equity Lawyers

(2005), and "The Best Lawyers 2005 NYC," the peer-review survey of the New York legal community conducted by Woodward/White, recognize Ms. Davenport as a leading private equity practitioner. Ms. Davenport has published articles in *Buyouts* and *The Deal* and is a regular contributor to the *Debevoise & Plimpton Private Equity Report*. Ms. Davenport joined Debevoise as an associate in 1987 and was made a partner in 1995. She received a B.A. magna cum laude from Amherst College in 1983 and her J.D. from the University of Chicago in 1987.

Jeanne Davis has a background working in corporate America and in small business. She started her own accounting firm in 1999. Her expertise is bookkeeping and helping people start up and organize businesses. She does public speaking and workshops on accounting and bookkeeping for start-ups. www.virtualjeannie.com.

Sherri Davis has built a twenty-five-year career in technical writing, courseware development, and Web design and development. A skilled executive, visionary entrepreneur, and adroit turnaround expert, she served as training development and marketing manager in charge of development of technical consulting services and courseware development at Symantec Corporation, managed a multimillion-dollar department, and served as creative partner and new media director for S. A. Bendheim, Inc. Ms. Davis has developed successful technical communications including Internet-based courseware for Autodesk, Inc., and salvaged floundering technical documentation projects from San Francisco to New York. Ms. Davis holds a B.A. from the University of California and STC's (Society for Technical Communicators) Merit Award for Technical Publications Excellence. She is a member of the Society for Technical Communications. She was an original contributor to the Women's Business Alliance.

Abbey Dehnert is the lead singer/dancer of BomberGirl, a New York City–based theatrical music group. Ms. Dehnert graduated from the Rhode Island School of Design. She is also a self-employed personal trainer specializing in women's fitness.

Ann Demarais, Ph.D., owns and operates First Impressions, Inc. The firm was founded in 1997, is based in New York City with an office in California, and provides a unique service to individuals interested in learning more about themselves and gaining insight as to how others see them. Dr. Demarais has more than fourteen years of experience in applied psychology, specializing in interpersonal communication, leadership, and executive coaching. She received her Ph.D. in psychology from New York University. With Valerie White, Ph.D., she coauthored *First Impressions: What You Don't Know About How Others See You*. www.FirstImpressionsConsulting.com.

Bonnie Digrius is vice president of The Deciding Factor, Inc. (TDF). TDF is an ROI/Business Case–dedicated provider of products and services for helping information technology buyers and sellers get top business value from IT investments. The company's software, Value-On-Demand, produces return on investment analysis and executive reports that can be used to justify IT projects. Ms. Digrius consults with senior executives on issues of vital importance to the enterprise, such as IT evaluation methods. She was the first female vice president at Garter Group, the top IT analysts. She has advised more than five thousand senior managers, including CEOs, CIOs, CFOs, and VPs of Fortune 1000 firms. Ms. Digrius is coauthor with Jack M. Keen of the book *Making Technology Investments Profitable: ROI Roadmap to Better Business Cases*. She has been frequently quoted in such publications as the *Wall Street Journal, Fortune, BusinessWeek*, and the *New York Times,* and has been interviewed on CNBC-TV. www.decidingfactor.com.

Susan Donegan is the director of AAA sales and marketing for Trafalgar Tours. Previously she was with sister company Insight Vacations as director of national accounts and a regional business development manager. Ms. Donegan has held several other account-management positions for wholesale tour companies since closing her retail travel agency in northern California in 1999. Her eighteen years in the travel industry follow a successful career in investment banking and financial analysis with such organizations as Morgan Stanley and VISA. She relocated to Orange County from the San Francisco Bay Area to work in Trafalgar's Anaheim, California, headquarters. Ms. Donegan was an original contributor to the Women's Business Alliance.

Lindsay Edgecombe is an assistant at the Levine Greenberg Literary Agency. Before starting there, Ms. Edgecombe graduated from Barnard College, where she edited the *Columbia Review.* She lives and writes poems in Brooklyn.

Tammy Brasuell Gattis, attorney at law, PA, has a solo practice in Little Rock, Arkansas, and practices mostly in the area of business law and family law. Ms. Gattis has also worked as a deputy prosecutor and as legal counsel for the Arkansas secretary of state. She served as special projects director for the Honorable John Paul Hammerschmidt, member of Congress, 1982–1986; and as law clerk for Arkansas Supreme Court justice Tom Glaze, 1989–1990. Ms. Gattis is married to Steven Owings, and they have a seven-year-old daughter, Adrianne.

Debbie Gisonni, a.k.a. The Goddess of Happiness, is a best-selling author, speaker, happiness expert, and columnist for iVillage.com. Ms. Gisonni is the author of the national bestseller *The Goddess of Happiness: A Down-to-Earth Guide for Heavenly Balance and Bliss* and *Vita's Will: Real Life Lessons about Life, Death & Moving On.* She has been a guest on numerous radio and TV shows across the country. www.goddessofhappiness.com

Chelsea Swett Hedquist is a publicist for the Sundance Film Festival. She earned a B.A. in international relations from Stanford and a master's from the Columbia School of Journalism. She has worked in the public affairs office of the U.S. Embassy in Copenhagen, on a 2002 congressional campaign, for Reuters during the 2004 Democratic National Convention in Boston, for the nonprofit Communities for Quality Education, and for Salt Lake City–based PR agency the Snapp Norris Group.

Andrea Henderson earned a bachelor of science degree from Georgetown University's School of Foreign Service, an M.A. in international relations from Clark Atlanta University, and an M.B.A. from Columbia Graduate School of Business. Ms. Henderson previously worked with the United Nations in New York; the Canadian Consulate General in Atlanta, Georgia; Operation Crossroads Africa in the Gambia, West Africa; and the U.S. Agency for International Development in Kandi, Sri Lanka. She later started her career in international human resources at a management consulting firm in New York and worked with Banker's Trust, Young & Rubicam, and Pfizer, Inc. She is the founder and executive director of the Basketball Academy in Newark, New Jersey, a youth basketball camp for boys and girls from six to sixteen, and is a managing director at Strategic Management Group, an executive search and diversity consulting firm in Manhattan. She writes a column on health and fitness for *Visions Metro Weekly,* a local Newark newspaper. Ms. Henderson resides in Harlem, New York, with her ten-year-old son.

Donna Maria Coles Johnson, Esq., is the founder and president of Lifestyle CEO Media Corporation, which is dedicated to helping women integrate home management and business ownership, with an annual conference, Internet radio and cable shows, books, newsletters, magazines, and one-on-one legal and business counseling. Ms. Johnson is the author of *The Lifestyle CEO: How to Break All the Rules, Build Your Own Corporate Ladder and Create the Life You Love*. Her Lifestyle CEO column appears weekly in *The District Chronicles,* a Washington, D.C., newspaper. Ms. Johnson is the founder and president of the Handmade Beauty Network, which provides business services to woman-owned cosmetics companies. She has been featured or quoted in *ABC World News This Morning, Time,* the *Washington Times,* the *Washington Business Journal,* the *Chicago Tribune,* the *Houston Chronicle, Parents* magazine, and *Ebony* magazine. She lives in suburban Washington, D.C., with her husband and their two children. www.LifestyleCEO.com.

Judy Johnson serves as regional director and executive vice president of GolinHarris, an international public relations firm, overseeing offices in Los Angeles, San Francisco, Orange County, and Seattle. With more than twenty-two years of experience, she has counseled while at GH clients ranging from Toyota, Amazon.com, the Walt Disney Company, Mead Johnson Nutritionals, Nestlé, Dole Food Company, Disneyland, the Venetian Hotel, the Ritz-Carlton Laguna Niguel, to name a few. Judy is a graduate of the UCLA School of Communications magna cum laude and lives in San Marino, California, with her husband and two children. www.GolinHarris.com.

Shirley Jump is an author and Booksellers' Best award winner. She sold her first book to Silhouette in 2001 and now writes books about love, family, and food. Her romantic comedies are profiled on her Web site, www.shirleyjump.com.

Aparna Umakant Katre leads global business innovation for Kanbay International, Inc. Ms. Katre has successfully managed organization change in the area of quality in software engineering. She has provided leadership in the areas of knowledge management and delivery management for global clients by leading program management for projects across multiple technologies. With a master's degree in statistics, she has specialized in the area of statistical quality control and operations research.

Patty McDonough Kennedy is founder of Kennedy Spencer. Her clients include emerging companies, economic development organizations, international nonprofits, and U.S. and foreign government leaders. She has lived and worked in the United States, Eastern and Western Europe, and Africa. She began her career at the Associated Press Broadcast News Center in Washington, D.C., holds a bachelor's degree from St. Bonaventure University, and is a dual American-Irish citizen.

Diana K. Kimbrell is founder and president of Kimbrell & Company, a marketing consultancy that creates partnerships between causes and business enterprises. Ms. Kimbrell has a sixteen-year background in media advertising sales, including radio sales in San Francisco for KCBS (CBS), KNBR (NBC), and KNEW/KSAN. In 1993 she moved to PBS and began working for San Francisco's KQED. Ms. Kimbrell has been recognized by the California Coalition on Donation with a Community Recognition Award for outstanding work on a public education campaign on the importance of organ and tissue donation. She was nominated for the National Association of

Women Business Owners' (NAWBO) Woman Entrepreneur of the Year award, and in 2005 she received the Muscular Dystrophy Association's honor at the Gateway to a Cure event for her unique work in cause marketing. Ms. Kimbrell is an original contributor to the Women's Business Alliance. www.kimbrell-co.com.

Deborah M. Kolb, Ph.D., is the Deloitte Ellen Gabriel Professor for Women and Leadership at the Simmons College School of Management. She is the former executive director of the Program on Negotiation at Harvard Law School. With Judith Williams, Ph.D., she coauthored *Everyday Negotiations: Navigating the Hidden Agendas of Bargaining.* www.negotiatingwomen.com.

Nancy Lafferty-Wellott is founder and CEO of Habits & Habitats, a strategy consulting firm focused on helping companies increase market value by aligning their brands to better resonate with today's female customers. Previously, Ms. Lafferty-Wellott was a vice president at Fitch Inc. in Boston, where she led the design research and strategy practice. Her clients included Reebok, Viacom, GE, Gerber, Fleet Bank, Symantec, and Compaq. She also served as director of brand strategy at Scient, where she delivered game plans in eBusiness brand strategy for clients such as Baxter Pharmaceutical and Chase Manhattan Bank. She also worked with DRI/McGraw-Hill, a business consulting arm of Standard & Poor's, aiding Fortune 500 companies like Procter & Gamble, Frigidaire, and Rubbermaid in their strategic planning and product-line forecasting efforts. www.habitsandhabitats.com.

Jane Curtis Land is a research consultant and licensed professional counselor associate. She has two master's degrees from the University of Louisville: a master's in business administration and a M.Ed. in the area of mental health counseling. Ms. Land has fifteen years of marketing experience from two major consumer packaged goods corporations. She is a licensed professional counselor associate. She resides in Louisville, Kentucky.

Jenai Lane is the president and CEO of Zealco. Ms. Lane has received myriad awards, including National Association of Women Business Owner's 1997 Woman Entrepreneur of the Year; NAWBO 1998 Young Entrepreneur of the Year; and SBA Young Entrepreneur of the Year. At twenty-four, Ms. Lane started her first award-winning company, Respect, Inc., and became an inventor of patented and trademarked products. She has appeared in national and international media, from the *New York Times* to *The Rosie O'Donnell Show.* Ms. Lane was an original contributor to the Women's Business Alliance.

Renee Lorton is the senior vice president and general manager of Performance Management Applications at Cognos Inc. Ms. Lorton is responsible for leadership of the company's performance management applications business. Previously, Ms. Lorton led PeopleSoft Financial Management and Enterprise Performance Management, two of PeopleSoft's most acclaimed product lines. Recently, Lorton was recognized as one of the 100 Most Influential People in Finance by *Treasury & Risk Management* magazine (2004 and 2006). She has also been quoted in major business magazines, including *BusinessWeek,* the *Wall Street Journal, Fortune,* and *CFO* magazine. Lorton joined PricewaterhouseCoopers as the company's CIO in 1997. Ms. Lorton, a CPA, earned a bachelor's degree in accounting and finance from Purdue University and a master's degree in taxation from Georgetown University.

Pat Lynch was the first woman to single-handedly begin an advertising agency in the South; it was 1969 and she was twenty-five years old. In 1996, she began Women's Online Media and

Education Network, which produces WomensRadio.com. In 2001, her company also began WomensCalendar, which today is the largest databank of women's events in the world. Ms. Lynch serves as the media chair for the California Women's Agenda. She is a member of the Women's Leadership Alliance of the Bay Area and is on the board of directors of the Afghan Coalition and Afghan Women's Association International.

Lea Ann Mabray is co-owner and vice president of Recovery Logistics, Inc. (RLI), in Fort Smith, Arkansas. RLI is a privately held company operated by its shareholders. Its management team has more than thirty years of experience in the successful implementation of pallet management programs for major clients throughout the United States. www.RecoveryLogistics.com.

Anna L. Marks is the owner, founder, publisher, and editor in chief of *Bay Area BusinessWoman News,* www.babwnews.com. Originally from New York City, she attended The New School in Manhattan and the University of Massachusetts, Amherst, before moving west. Ms. Marks is the recipient of the Women of Achievement Award from San Francisco Business and Professional Women and the Women and Industry Award from the Commission on the Status of Women. She is currently a member of the Alameda County Advisory Council for Women's Initiative, a member of A New America's Women's Business Center board of advisers, and media cochair for CAWA (California Women's Agenda). She served on the board of directors for the National Association of Women Business Owners, San Francisco, 1999–2000.

Sue Vest McKay is a second-career entrepreneur. She is a retired regional personnel manager, special division, of Wal-Mart Corporation in Bentonville, Arkansas.

Elizabeth Mizrahi is a tenure-track professor of history and a founding faculty member of the Middle East studies program at Santa Barbara City College. She received a B.A. from UC Berkeley and an M.A. from the University of Chicago, where she is a doctoral candidate. Ms. Mizrahi returned to academia after working for years in nonprofit management, highlighted by her role as national executive director of the American Sephardi Federation in New York City from 1999 to 2001. Ms. Mizrahi was selected in 2006 to receive the National Endowment for the Humanities Fellowship to study for a summer in Bolivia and Peru.

Anaezi Modu is founder and CEO of ReBrand, and director of ReBrand 100. ReBrand is the online source for case studies and programs focused on effective rebrands. ReBrand 100 is the first global awards competition recognizing the world's most effective rebrands: repositioning, revitalizing, or redesign of existing brand assets to meet strategic goals. Ms. Modu is a former SVP, brand experience and strategy, at Bank of America; and former SVP, information architecture and design, FleetBoston Financial Corporation Internet Strategy and Management Group. www .rebrand.com.

B. L. Ochman, a New York City native, ran an award-winning New York PR firm that grew into one of the hundred largest independent PR firms in the United States before she turned her talents to the Internet in 1995. Her Internet marketing strategy successes include consultation to Ford Motors, IBM, and Cendant. Ms. Ochman's internationally read blog covers Internet marketing strategies and trends.

Allison Karl O'Kelly, CPA, is CEO and founder of the Mom Corps, a professional staffing service that places highly educated professionals in contact with firms that require contracted professional services for outsourced projects, but do not have the capability to reach willing and able professionals. Ms. Karl O'Kelly also built an accounting practice, O'Kelly and Company Small Business Services. Prior to her entrepreneurial ventures, she was an executive at Toys "R" Us, where she had several roles, including launching the original Babiesrus.com Web site and running an $11 million Toys "R" Us store. She began her career in public accounting at KPMG Peat Marwick, where she ran various audits, including that of AFLAC. Ms. Karl O'Kelly received her M.B.A. from Harvard Business School and her B.B.A. in accounting from the University of Georgia, cum laude. As a CPA, she is licensed in Georgia and a member of the Georgia Society of CPAs. She is the mother of two little boys who appreciate their mom's flexible schedule. www.MomCorps.com.

Peggy Orenstein is an award-winning writer, editor, and speaker about issues affecting girls and women. She is the author of *Waiting for Daisy: A Tale of Two Continents, Three Religions, Five Infertility Doctors, an Oscar, an Atomic Bomb, and One Woman's Quest to Become a Mother; Flux: Women on Sex, Work, Kids, Love and Life in a Half-Changed World;* as well as the bestselling *SchoolGirls: Young Women, Self-Esteem and the Confidence Gap.* A contributing writer to the *New York Times Magazine,* Ms. Orenstein has also written for such publications as *Vogue, Glamour, Discover, Elle, Mother Jones, Salon,* and *The New Yorker.* She has been a guest lecturer and keynote speaker at numerous college campuses; at state, regional, and municipal conferences on gender equity and on juvenile justice; and at the National Education Association's National Conference on Women and Minorities. She has published editorials relating to her research in the *New York Times,* the *Los Angeles Times,* and *USA Today* and has appeared on, among other programs, *Nightline, Good Morn-*

ing America, the *Today* show, NPR's *Fresh Air,* and *Morning Edition.* Ms. Orenstein is a graduate of Oberlin College and lives in the San Francisco Bay Area with her husband, filmmaker Steven Okazaki, and their daughter.

Stefanie Polman-Tuin was born in Trail, British Columbia, Canada, in 1972. She obtained a B.A. in psychology and sociology from the University of Victoria and a B.Ed. from the University of British Columbia. Ms. Polman-Tuin is a customer sales and service coordinator in the power-generation equipment industry. She played Little League baseball on boys' teams and was recognized as the first girl to pitch and win games at both the Provincials and the Canadian Championships. She resides in a suburb of Vancouver, British Columbia, with her husband, Derek, and two cats.

Debra Pryor was named fire chief in Berkeley, California. Chief Pryor is one of twenty-four female fire chiefs nationally—one of three in California, and the second African American female chief in the United States. She received an athletic scholarship in track and field at Arizona State University. In 2001, she received a master's degree in public administration from California State University at Hayward. She served as president of Alameda County Training Officers Association, and is active in the northern California chapter of the Intergovernmental Management Training Program. Chief Pryor has been a student in the National Fire Academy's Executive Officer Development Program in Emmitsburg, Maryland, and is a graduate of the Carl Holmes Executive Development Institute at Dillard University.

Mary Lou Quinlan was called "the Oprah of Madison Avenue" by the *Wall Street Journal* because women tell her things that they wouldn't tell other people. Founder and CEO of Just Ask a Woman, Ms. Quinlan has twenty-five years' experience as a leading marketer, communicator, sales motivator, and senior executive. She also costarred on ABC's new product competition show, *American Inventor*. Her successes as director of advertising at Avon Products, EVP of ad agency DDBNeedham Worldwide, and CEO of New York agency N.W. Ayer won Ms. Quinlan her industry's highest awards, including Woman of the Year from Advertising Women of New York in 1995 and the 1997 Matrix Award from New York Women in Communications. She is the author of the bestselling marketing book *Just Ask a Woman: Cracking the Code of What Women Want and How They Buy* and of *Time Off for Good Behavior: How Hard-Working Women Can Take a Break and Change Their Lives*. Ms. Quinlan has spoken at more than three hundred major corporations, conferences, and universities across North America. She writes a monthly career advice column for *MORE* magazine, and has also been published in *O, the Oprah Magazine, Redbook, Good Housekeeping*, and *Marie Claire*. She has been featured as a woman's authority in the *New York Times, USA Today, BusinessWeek*, in city and local newspapers, and on the *Today* show, NPR, and city and local radio shows. Ms. Quinlan is a member of the board of directors of 1800Flowers.com and the Partnership for a Drug-Free America, as well as a trustee of her alma mater, Saint Joseph's University in Philadelphia, where she has taught consumer behavior. www.JustAskAWoman.com.

Betsy Rapoport is a writer, editor, and life coach. She is a twenty-two-year veteran of trade publishing, most recently as an executive editor at a division of Random House.

Rosalind Resnick is founder and CEO of Axxess Business Centers, Inc., which specializes in consulting, business-plan writing, and financing for start-ups and small businesses. Formerly one of the *Miami Herald*'s first women business journalists, she built her Internet marketing company, NetCreations, Inc., from a two-person home-based start-up to a public company that generated $58 million in sales during her tenure as CEO and president. She pioneered the concept of 100% Opt-In e-mail marketing in 1996 and spearheaded the company's successful IPO in 1999.

Elizabeth S. Roberts is the first vice president of wealth management at Smith Barney in San Rafael, California. Ms. Roberts was one of the original contributors to the Women's Business Alliance.

Amanita Rosenbush has been a successful editor and book doctor for twelve years. She specializes in helping authors make their manuscripts, fiction or nonfiction, publisher-ready. The services she offers include consulting on the book's organization, line editing, substance editing, and proposal writing. She lives in Oakland, California.

Virginia Beane Rutter is an analyst member and on the faculty of the C. G. Jung Institute in San Francisco. She has a private practice in Mill Valley, California. Her writing includes the books *Woman Changing Woman: Feminine Psychology Re-Conceived Through Myth and Experience; Celebrating Girls: Nurturing and Empowering Our Daughters*; and *Embracing Persephone: How to Be the Mother You Want for the Daughter You Cherish.*

Karen Salmansohn is a recovered senior vice president in advertising who's now a bestselling author/book packager with twenty-nine books, twenty-five of which have been created in the last six years. The *Philadelphia Inquirer* called her "a one-woman industry." Her titles include *Ballsy, How to Be Happy, Dammit,* and *Enough, Dammit.* Visit her at www.notsalmon.com.

Lisbeth Sanders founded LifeBio.com and released her book the *Memory Journal* in 2001 at age twenty-nine. LifeBio.com has thousands of members, investigates win-win partnerships, is embraced by the aging profession, and was featured in *Chicago Tribune/Associated Press* as one of six finalists in their "Baby Boomer Business Plan Challenge." Ms. Sanders has presented to the White House Council on Aging.

Deborah Saweuyer-Parks has been the president of Homestead Capital since July 1993 and chief executive officer since 1995. Ms. Saweuyer-Parks wanted to address the lack of affordable housing, and started a firm to provide it. The firm is a huge powerhouse now in ten western states. Ms. Saweuyer-Parks is a board member of Mercy Housing, Inc., the Oregon Public Broadcasting Board, and the American Leadership Forum of Oregon. Prior to joining Homestead Capital, Ms. Saweuyer-Parks was the Program Manager of the Low-Income Housing Tax Credit Program for the Oregon Housing and Community Services. www.HomesteadCap.com.

Janet Scarborough, Ph.D., is the founder of Bridgeway Career Development, based in Seattle and Colorado Springs. Dr. Scarborough attained a Ph.D. in counseling psychology at the University of Texas at Austin. She also completed a bachelor's degree in economics at the University of California at Los Angeles. Dr. Scarborough is a licensed psychologist and mental health counselor. When she is not working, Dr. Scarborough enjoys spending time with her husband, son, and baby daughter.

Anna K. Scheidegger, EPFL, earned a joint master of architecture degree in 1985 from the University of California, Berkeley, and the Swiss Federal Institute of Technology, Lausanne, Switzerland, and has been licensed to practice architecture in Switzerland since 1986. She worked for a variety of firms in the United States, Switzerland, and the Ivory Coast, West Africa. Ms. Scheidegger's diverse background provided opportunities for a variety of unique projects, from mountain cabins and small community museums to hotels and hospitals. While living in the Ivory Coast, Ms. Scheidegger designed and worked with local artisans to reproduce modern furniture pieces. She has collaborated with various firms on urban planning projects for Long Beach and Emeryville, California, as well as retail projects for The Gap, Gymboree, and Hèrmes Boutiques. Ms. Scheidegger has served on the Lucas Valley Homeowners Association board of directors and as chair of the Architectural Design Review Committee. Through her efforts to create a special design review zone in the Upper Lucas Valley community of San Rafael, she has been instrumental in protecting the unique design character of Eichler houses. Ms. Scheidegger was an original contributor to the Women's Business Alliance. www.st-architecture.com.

Karen Sermersheim has been with Union Bank of California's Private Bank as a vice president and relationship manager for the past six years. She works with a number of high net worth individuals; service industry companies such as attorney firms, CPA firms, and architectural companies; and large not-for-profit organizations. She is working toward a CFP and has an insurance license. Ms. Sermersheim graduated from Cannon Financial Management's Private Banking School in 2001. She was one of the original contributors to the Women's Business Alliance.

Beth Shaw is the founder of YogaFit Training Systems, a $4 million company that has been in business since 1994. Ms. Shaw employs fifteen full-time employees and thirty-five independent contractors and occupies six thousand square feet of office/warehouse space. YogaFit has trained more than fifty thousand instructors in the United States alone. Her company has done training on six continents. www.YogaFit.com.

Katrine Shelton works as a tax attorney in the San Francisco office of the Office of Chief Counsel at the Internal Revenue Service, focusing on litigation and financial products. She is a proud alumna of Douglass College, Rutgers University (B.A.); Washington College of Law; and Georgetown University (LL.M., Taxation). She lives in the Bay Area with her husband, Peter, and their two daughters.

Donna Shoemaker is a certified nutritional counselor in Marin County, California, and coauthor with Arlen Brownstein of the book *Rosacea: Your Self-Help Guide*. Ms. Shoemaker was an original contributor to the Women's Business Alliance.

Rebecca F. Silberstein is a corporate partner and member of the Investment Management Practice Group at Debevoise & Plimpton LLP. She focuses on advising financial institutions, investment banks, and boutique firms as sponsors of and investors in leveraged buyout, venture capital, international private equity, merchant banking, and other private investment funds. Ms. Silberstein recently represented Kelso & Company in the formation of Kelso Investment Associates VII, LP, a $2.1 billion private equity buyout fund, and assisted Stone Point Capital LLC (formerly MMC Capital) in the formation of Trident III, LP, a $1.1 billion private equity fund. In addition to Kelso and Stone

Point Capital, Ms. Silberstein represents Merrill Lynch, Morgan Stanley, Metalmark Capital, Ripplewood Holdings, AIG Healthcare Partners, Levine Leichtman Capital Partners, Solera Capital, and Fairview Capital in a variety of private equity matters. www.Debevoise.com.

Mindy Solkin is the owner and head coach of The Running Center LLC in New York City. She is certified by USA Track & Field (USATF) as a Level III Running Coach (the highest level) and by the American Council on Exercise (ACE) as a personal trainer. As a contributing writer and spokesperson on running and fitness, her articles and quotes have appeared in national publications. She is a frequent lecturer, presenting running clinics to runners, fitness centers, and corporations, and is the running adviser to many Web sites. Mindy has also appeared on the television shows *Today, Good Day New York,* and *Good Morning America.* www.TheRunningCenter.com.

Joan Stewart is a publicity expert. She worked as a newspaper editor and reporter for twenty-two years. Today, she is media consultant, speaker, and publisher of The Publicity Hound's Tips of the Week, a free online newsletter read by seventeen thousand people worldwide. www.PublicityHound.com. She blogs at www.PublicityHound.net.

Belinda Stronach has been elected a member of Parliament twice by her peers, and has been a senior Cabinet minister in government. She is now a leading member of the Liberal Party of Canada and chair of the national caucus of women Liberal MPs. She is a community, business, and public leader. In 2004, *Time* ranked Ms. Stronach one of the world's one hundred most influential people, and in 2005 the World Economic Forum named her a member of its network of global young leaders. Also in 2005, the Women's Executive acclaimed Ms. Stronach a "trailblazer" and one of Canada's top one hundred most powerful women. She is the former president and CEO of Magna International Inc., one of the largest global suppliers of automotive systems and components in the world, with eighty-two thousand employees in twenty-two countries. www.Belinda.ca.

Lisa Taylor joined Homestead Capital in July 2004 as investor relations manager, after spending three years at R.V. Kuhns & Associates, Inc., an institutional investment consulting firm based in Portland, Oregon, where she was an associate consultant. Among the special projects she completed were asset allocation analysis, market environment research, and investment manager due diligence. Ms. Taylor graduated with a B.A. from Linfield College in McMinnville, Oregon, and sits on the board of the Ford Scholar Alumni Association, an affiliation of The Ford Family Foundation. She also earned the designation of chartered financial analyst (CFA) by the CFA Institute.

Judith Thoyer is the first female partner of Paul, Weiss, Rifkind, Wharton & Garrison LLP in New York City. A partner in the corporate department and former cohead of the mergers and acquisitions group, she has extensive experience in the area of acquisitions and dispositions of both public and private companies, as well as in representing public company boards of directors and special committees. Her mergers and acquisitions experience covers negotiated transactions, contested takeovers and acquisitions, and dispositions of companies in connection with Chapter 11 proceedings. Ms. Thoyer was selected as one of the leading lawyers in the area of corporate law by the peer review organization *The Best Lawyers in America*. She received the 2003 Medal for Excellence Award from Columbia Law School, served as an editor of the *Columbia Law Review,* and was a Kent Scholar.

Wilma Wasco, Ph.D., is an associate professor of neurology at Harvard Medical School and Massachusetts General Hospital. She was born and raised in Fairfield, Connecticut, and graduated from the University of Connecticut at Storrs in 1981. She received her Ph.D. in molecular pharmacology in 1987 from the Albert Einstein College of Medicine and was a postdoctoral fellow at the Massachusetts Institute of Technology from 1987 to 1991. In 1996, Dr. Wasco's laboratory was part of an international group that discovered the genes that cause inherited Alzheimer's disease. Dr. Wasco is a member of the MassGeneral Institute for Neurodegenerative Disease and the Genetics and Aging Research Unit at Massachusetts General Hospital, and she is a Pew Biomedical Scholar. Dr. Wasco is by choice a single mother of two.

Nancy Webb is a graphic design consultant for Nancy Webb Graphic Design in Oakland, California. Nancy holds professional memberships with the American Institute of Graphic Arts and the Graphic Arts Guild. She was an original advisory board member for the Women's Business Alliance. www.NancyWebb.com.

Tanya Weiss, Ph.D., is the president and CEO of Marin Biologic Laboratories, Inc., a leading preclinical contract laboratory that provides collaborative and custom research, testing, and manufacturing services (GMP/GLP optional) for the biotechnology, pharmaceutical, cosmetic, diagnostic, and agricultural industries. Her company's client roster includes the largest pharmaceutical companies, midsize biotechs, and virtual companies. Dr. Weiss was an original contributor to the Women's Business Alliance. www.MarinBio.com.

Barbara Weldon, D.C., is a chiropractor practicing in San Rafael, California. Dr. Weldon was one of the original contributors to the Women's Business Alliance.

Joy Machelle Williams is the senior director of sponsorship development at ESPN, Inc., in Bristol, Connecticut. She was assistant vice president at JP Morgan Chase and has worked in television production at HBO, MTV, and Cablevision. She earned a bachelor of arts from Vassar College, a master of business administration from Columbia Business School, and a master of arts in media studies from the New School University.

May Tong Yang is the assistant controller for Homestead Capital. Ms. Yang has also held positions with Bank of America as a customer service representative and a case manager for the GIFT Program at the Asian Family Center. Ms. Yang graduated from Portland State University with a B.S. in business administration, accounting/finance in 2001. She is thirty-four years old and her oldest son is twenty years old. She is unique in her community in that she went to college after staying home with her four children, then obtained her degree.

Ellen Yohai began her career in marketing in the securities business. She then went to the California Culinary Academy and became a professionally trained chef. She owned and operated a San Francisco Bay Area catering company for fourteen years. Ms. Yohai developed and owns a gourmet sauce company, the Ultimate Sauce Company. She has been published in the *Marin Independent Journal* and the *Grass Valley Union*. Ms. Yohai is involved with the Palm Springs chapter of Les Dames d'Escoffier, most recently as chairman of an annual fund-raiser that raises scholarship funds for young local women to go to culinary school.

She serves as vice president of the Les Dames chapter. She is developing a program for elementary school children that will teach them how to grow produce and how to cook with the produce they grow. Ms. Yohai is an original contributor to the Women's Business Alliance.